[CHASTE MIMOSA]

THE PSYCHOLOGY
OF PLANTS

Terence McMullen

audiobooksradio

Publisher: Audiobooksradio
website: www.audiobooksradio.com.au

This edition published 2022
Copyright © Terence McMullen 2022
Cover design, typesetting: WorkingType (www.workingtype.com.au)

The right of Terence McMullen to be identified as the Author of the
Work has been asserted in accordance with the Copyright, Designs and
Patents Act 1988.

McMullen, Terence
Chaste Mimosa: The Psychology of Plants
ISBN: 978-0-6455996-1-9
pp346

CONTENTS

Images

(Images follow page 180)

The sensitive plant (*Mimosa pudica*)

Venus fly trap (*Dionaca muscipula*)

Sundew (*Drosera* family)

Aristotle, 384BC–322BC

Plato, 428BC–347BC

William Harvey, discovered the circulation of blood.

Gustav T. Fechner

Erasmus Darwin

Charles Darwin

Sir Francis Darwin

Maurice Maeterlinck

Samuel Butler, author of *Erewhon* and *The Way of all Flesh*.

John Broadus Watson

Richard L. Gregory

Preface

The inspiration for this book came when I was preparing a lecture on the stimulus —response (S —R) behaviourist movement in American psychology. I found myself asking why the behaviourists, given their particular conception of psychology as the study of external "behaviour", appeared to draw the line at the study of plant movements. This was followed by the question of whether in fact they had drawn such a line, and I began to ask just what the behaviourists had had to say, if anything, about plants. Inevitably this led to the larger question of what kind of interest psychology generally had had in the vegetable kingdom. I found that there was no history here to help me. I would have to write my own history. The topic turned out to be much larger than I thought it would be.

Chaste mimosa is intended primarily for those interested in the history and conceptual foundations of psychology —"history and systems" as many Americans call it. Some background knowledge of the history and philosophy of orthodox psychology is assumed: this is not another general history of psychology. Readers without such a background will find that there is available to them quite a store of good histories, dictionaries and encyclopaedias of psychology and philosophy. I hope that comparative psychologists will be interested, as will historians of biology and botany who have an interest in the heterodox fringe areas of their disciplines. I present no philosophical theses of my own in this monograph, but I think there is plenty of material here to provide entertaining and novel case illustrations for teachers of epistemology, the philosophy of mind, and the philosophy of science generally. It is not a botanical monograph: readers interested in the history of orthodox botany should consult appropriate histories (I found A.G. Morton's *History of Botanical Science*, 1981 to be most valuable), and there is no attempt here to encroach on the preserves of experts in the physiology of plant movements.

I am indebted to many people for their comments, questions and criticisms. Special thanks are due to the following heads of department who generously received me on study leave from Sydney: Professor A. Summerfield of the Department of Psychology, Birkbeck College, University of London, Professor the Reverend E. F. O'Doherty of the Department of Logic and Psychology, University College Dublin, and Mr R. F. Stalley of the Department of Philosophy, University of Glasgow. I thank also the staffs of the libraries at those universities, together with the staffs of the British Library, Bloomsbury, and of the Natural History Library, South Kensington, London. At home in Sydney, I acknowledge the support of these heads of the Department of Psychology who have supported my study leave applications: Professors J. P. Sutcliffe and P. Ley and Associate Professor H. C. Beh. I am grateful too to the staff of Fisher Library, University of Sydney, and especially grateful to a former student and academic colleague, Mrs Marie Clouston, for her translation of Fechner's *Nanna*. Other help in translation was given generously by two present colleagues, Olga Katchan and Agnes Petocz.

Dr Terence McMullen
Sydney, 2022

CHAPTER 1

Introduction

1.1   *Preliminary comments*

n this chapter the notion of plant psychology will be introduced
and the scope of this study indicated. The conceptual framework
of the history of plant psychology will be presented in an outline
which will be followed by a summary of the themes of the chapters
to follow.

The aim of this monograph is to present a systematic outline of the
history of plant psychology. The basic claim of plant psychologists is
that the species of the vegetable kingdom are legitimate subjects of
psychological enquiry. "Plant psychology" will be defined in the next
section. For the moment it will suffice to note that there are, and have
been, students of plant life who would claim that plant psychology is a
proper area of comparative psychology. Psychologists study man more
than they do other animals, but comparative psychologists, in their
concern to compare different species of animals in respect of their psychological capacities, study a host: rats, cats, pigeons, monkeys, goldfish
and cockroaches, to name a few. Plant psychologists see no good reason
to draw the line at the vegetable kingdom. To them it is reasonable that
some psychologists might spend their time with organisms which live
in garden beds or glass-houses rather than in compounds or cages.

Such a view is a controversial one. Some would find it defensible, others absurd. Psychologists are not agreed as to what the nature and scope of psychology are, even after more than a century of the existence of psychology as a discipline distinct from physiology and philosophy. There is, however, one excellent reason for taking up the topic of plant psychology and it is that the subject, defensible or absurd, has a history and that history has never been brought together. Most psychologists are unaware of it. Historians of psychology rarely allude to it. Most comparative psychologists mention plants only in passing, if they do so at all. But the topic *is* there: it is continuous with the history of mainstream psychology itself. If "psychology" is understood in its broader historical sense then plant psychology goes back to the ancient Greeks. If "psychology" is understood in a more restricted sense as an experimental science then plant psychology extends from the beginnings of modern comparative psychology in the nineteenth century. Indeed, as will be seen, for a few decades in this century plant psychology could be called a part of orthodox psychology, even, if, like an embarrassing family member who is not talked about, it was not acknowledged generally.

There is, then, a history to be written. Moreover, consideration of the history carries with it a salutary result. Regardless of one's verdict on the issue of the legitimacy of the concept it forces one to think about the fundamental conceptual structure of psychology. It poses questions about the theoretical underpinnings of psychology as an independent discipline. Because there is no agreement about the fundamentals of this subject it is important that students of psychology be confronted about such considerations. Over seventy years ago the philosopher John Laird said "psychologists are so radically and so acrimoniously divided upon the meaning, the scope and the methods of their science that anyone who explains his position in detail has to face the certainty of disagreeing with most of them" (Laird, 1920, p.150). If there is anything in Laird's comment which is not apposite to contemporary psychology it is perhaps the charge of acrimony. There may be less acrimony today, not because there is more agreement, but because there is less discussion; psychologists of differing theoretical persuasions tend to go their separate ways, trusting that ignoring central differences will make them disappear.

The study of plant psychology can be an entertaining and novel way of opening up basic questions and it could thus be argued that even if it is something from a cabinet of curiosities it is not to be condemned as a self-indulgent conceit in either antiquarianism in its remote aspect, or dilletantism in its modern aspect. In any case, man is not a rational animal, and there can be no study of any part of man's intellectual enterprises which does not have to come to grips somewhere with the irrational.

We should not be deterred by the observation of that sturdy advocate of Victorian Protestant morality in the plant world, the botanist J. E. Taylor: "to speak of *Vegetable Psychology* would cause a smile to ripple over the faces even of those who have granted the identity of the intelligence between man and the brute" (Taylor, 1884, p.5). Smile we may at the notion of vegetable psychology, but if we do should we not also smile at the notion of "machine psychology" which today engages the attention of many of our contemporary researchers? Propositions about machine intelligence are debated seriously, but machines, unlike plants, are not even living organisms: some say that mental states are the prerogative of humans (and maybe other higher animals) and that there is such a difference in kind between

3

the animate human and the inanimate machine that the latter could never have mental states in any serious sense; others urge that if no difference can be detected between the fruits of human intelligence and those of machine intelligence then there is no point in denying intelligence to computers if it is allowed to humans — structural differences between the two are irrelevant; yet others would claim that to pose the very question of intelligence or mind in machines is mistaken for it merely sets the same metaphysical trap to ensnare machine theorists as ensnares many psychologists and philosophers. Perhaps then one might take pause before dismissing suggestions of vegetable intelligence as being merely risible.

1.2   *The Scope of this Study*

The aim of this work is to bring together and organize the contentions of those serious students of plant life who argue that there are objective grounds for a plant psychology. Included in the ranks of the plant psychologists are those who would be designated variously according to their occupation and their era as psychologists, botanists, physiologists, biologists, scientists, naturalists (amateur or professional), natural philosophers, philosophers (metaphysical or mental) and men of letters.

Excluded in this work are these accounts of plant life:

(1)   *Folk-lore and ethnographic data.* These range from ordinary "folk-wisdom" about plants to ethnographic observations from other societies; they may embody animistic or personified conceptions of plant life. There is much material here which is of interest to students

of folk-lore and to social anthropologists, and it is well documented. Concerning plant folk-lore I mention on a personal note that I find Friend's *Flowers and Flower Lore* (1884) a most entertaining Victorian collection. I would also draw the attention of those modern occultists who exhort us to talk kindly and lovingly to plants in order that they might flourish, to the advice given Theophrastus centuries ago when he was collecting plant-lore: of cummin he wrote in his *Enquiry into Plants*, "they say that one must curse and abuse it, while sowing, if the crop is to be fair and abundant" (VII . 3 . 3: trans. Hort, 1916, p.77).

(2)   *Fiction.* The device in literature of personifying plants is a common one, but with the exceptions of Erasmus Darwin's verses *The Botanic Garden* and Samuel Butler's novel *Erewhon* no reference will be made to fiction here. The exceptions in Darwin's and Butler's cases are made because of their importance as plant psychologists, but the clear distinction between their literary efforts and their formal plant psychology is recognized.

(3)   *Mentalist and animist philosophical systems and outlooks.* Panpsychist and metaphysical mentalist systems of thought which either predicate mind of everything or regard the world as being ultimately mental are not in themselves of present interest. It is true that such approaches predicate mind of plants, but then they predicate it too of atoms, rocks, planets and solar systems — they might be said to have a psychology of plants but this is because they, in their most thoroughgoing versions, make psychology identical with ontology. Their "psychology" is of no real interest, for in predicating mind of everything they might just as well predicate it of nothing. If mind is

a pervasive uncharacterized metaphysical principle then the presence of mind can make not a jot or tittle of difference to anything we can observe or know. It is possible to know, to speak of mind, in a coherent way only if a distinction can be seen between the mental and the non-mental , i.e. if mind has some character(s) or property(ies) which is (are) to be found in some parts of the world (e.g. men), but not in others (e.g. rocks), and its presence or absence can make thereby a difference to what we can know or say. Thus the plant psychologists who are of interest in this survey are those for whom certain observations of plant activity count towards the presence of mind, and an absence of such observations counts against it.

Excluded also from this history are animists such as the hylozoists who see all matter to be living — e.g. those modern followers of Plato who maintain that the planet Earth (Gaia) is an animate organism. Hylozoists may be panpsychists, but they do not have to be — whether they are hinges on the interpretation they give to the concept of animation.

This does not mean that there will not be found adherents of panpsychism, hylozoism or various sorts of monistic ontological systems in these pages. Plato is one of the most important plant psychologists, historically speaking. Gustav Fechner, a panpsychist and hylozoist, is included here too as an historically important plant psychologist. Both Plato and Fechner earned their inclusion not because of their general metaphysical stances but because they had something specific to say about vegetable minds. Quite a few of the biologists of the second half of the nineteenth century and of the early twentieth century called themselves "monists", e.g. Ernst Haeckel. They saw their monism as opposing the dualist conception of mind and matter as occupying two different worlds, rather, mind and matter should be seen as different facets or aspects of the single reality. Some of these theorists allowed a mind of sorts to plants, and therefore are included here.

1.3   *The Concept of Plant Psychology*

Three different types of plant psychology can be distinguished. The first, which is the oldest and by far the largest, can be called "mentalist." The second, which had its beginnings in the Renaissance and its heyday in the nineteenth century, can be called "instinctivist." The third, the "behaviourist", is a twentieth century phenomenon.

The basis of the concept of plant psychology is the proposition that psychological categories can be predicated of plant life. This can be sharpened immediately by referring not to plant "life" but plant "movements", for it is on the basis of the movements of whole plants or of parts of them (e.g. leaves, flowers, individual structures within flowers) which claims of plant psychology rest. Thus the plant psychologist argues that in describing and explaining certain plant movements one must make reference to the descriptive and explanatory categories of psychology. What are these categories?

The answer to this question might be approached first by reference to the traditional version of Aristotle's doctrines concerning animate life which are summarized in the formula "plants live, brutes live and feel, men live, feel and think." In other words plants live (unlike inanimate objects) but they are otherwise relatively passive, devoid of a sensate nature, whereas brutes do have a sensate nature; some capacity for sensing the world is available to them.

Man, in addition to living and sensing, is rational, possessing a faculty which is capable of thinking and of self-awareness. Man can determine his own behaviour according to his reason. Brutes, lacking rationality, are prey to blind instinct, and plants, lacking passions as well as rationality, are as unaware of their surroundings, nature and destiny as are, say, mechanical toys. This is the framework of the traditional rationalist psychology which most people in the Western world acquire unquestioningly as a cultural inheritance, it is the vulgar psychology.

The most common kind of plant psychologist can be portrayed as one who maintains that the vulgar conception is wrong in that plants are sentient, at least, and perhaps in addition may be capable of some degree of rationality. Certainly there is no hard and fast distinction between plant life and brute life: both are capable of feeling. Some, in addition, maintain that there is no hard and fast distinction between plant life and human life: both are capable of thinking. This conception of plant psychology is by far the most common one, and it can be characterized by saying that it makes the claim that the category of *mind* is appropriate to the vegetable kingdom. A typical argument of plant psychologists here is that there are certain plant movements, such as the closing of a sundew's "tentacles" around an insect, which show evidence of *sentience*, of some kind of sensory knowledge of some aspect of the world. There are a number of different terms to denote such sentience, for example "sensibility," "sensation," "perception" and "discrimination." Plant movement showing the marks of sentience are to be distinguished from both mere passive displacements brought about by external forces, such as the movement of a leaf blown by the wind, and what in modern terms would be called mechanical movements not involving active sensory discrimination, such as the "popping open" of a ripe seed pod in a legume. The contemporary word "cognition," which arose in nineteenth century mental philosophy, could be used as a general term to cover "sentience" and its other synonyms. The mentalists, then, believe that there are certain plant responses which indicate cognition (and cognition is a mental process). The central notion is that any piece of cognition involves the active apprehension of some environmental event. A fisherman's net, which holds the larger fish but allows the smaller ones to swim free, is making no cognitive discrimination between larger and smaller fish, unlike the fisherman who does make such a cognitive judgement in order to determine which of his catch will be thrown back into the water as "too small." A game-poacher's snare, for all its sudden explosion of activity when set off by a hapless rabbit, is not cognizing "this is a rabbit," whereas the poacher does do this when he looks to see what he has snared. Neither the net nor the snare know anything. Thus to the plant psychologist of the mentalist persuasion some plants, some of the time, can know some things.

Two points of elaboration might be made now:

(i)   Most of the acts of vegetable cognition described in the literature are seen as rudimentary and basic. They do not involve consciousness, articulated self-awareness, abstract thinking and conceptualisation, which are prominent attributes in conventional psychology of the cognition of humans and perhaps some other advanced primates. Rather, they are acts of the most primitive discrimination (e.g. "light" vs. "dark", "warmth" vs. "cold", "nutritive" vs. "non-nutritive"), but, for all that, they are genuinely cognitive. If one grades cognitive acts on a continuum from elementary sensory discrimination at one end of the continuum to full-blown, self-reflective abstract thought at the other, then the plant psychologists tend to locate vegetable cognition at or near the first mentioned extreme. They see the plant mind as relatively primitive. As we shall find, however, there are glorious exceptions: some allow plants a relatively sophisticated mental life, capable of perceptions of the external world accompanying self-awareness, volition and emotion.

(ii)   To talk of cognition as the characteristic mental act is not to ignore will and feeling, because both of those necessarily have a cognitive component. Nineteenth century mental philosophy and psychology generally made a tri-partite division of mental states (and/or functions) into cognition (knowing), conation (willing) and affection (emoting or feeling). But, to speak in this traditional mentalist language, any act of willing, no matter how basic, must be directed on some object ("willing *that X occur*), and hence a cognitive act necessarily is bound up with the conative one; similarly any affective episode must involve the discrimination of one emotional state from some other or others (e.g. the distinguishing of "pain" from "non-pain" or even "pleasure") and hence cognition is involved necessarily in emotion.

It is out of place in this book to enquire further into the relations between cognition, volition and affect; all that is relevant here is to note that discussion of vegetable sentience or cognition *may* include volition and/or emotion. Perhaps in identifying the characteristic activity of mind as cognition we are using the term more broadly than some would permit. There should be no great problem in this, however, for it is generally clear in the particular context just what a particular thinker takes to be the distinctive nature of plant mentality.

There is another way of approaching the answer to the question of what are the psychological categories relevant to plants. It gives us another version of plant psychology, but not one which is necessarily incompatible with the first. Instead of referring immediately to the Aristotelian-based approach to animate life, we might refer first to the distinction between mechanist and teleological (or purposivist) accounts of activity. A common approach here says that inanimate systems behave according to linear cause-and-effect mechanical principles, their behaviour can be explained entirely in terms of antecedent causes. Complex animate systems (certainly man, maybe other higher animals too) exhibit behaviour which is designed to achieve a goal, a purpose: behaviour cannot be explained as the immutable consequence of mechanical cause, it must be explained in terms of the state of affairs which it aims to bring about. When we know, for example, what the mechanics of clock-work engines are we can explain the rat-tat-tatting of the toy drummer-boy, but no matter how complete our knowledge of a real drummer-boy's physiological structures are, we will never explain his rat-tat-tatting unless we refer to the object of his drum-beating ("he beats the drum in order to raise the soldiers' morale"). Now according to the wisdom of modern botanists the behaviour of plants can be explained mechanistically, e.g. there is in principle no difference between the behaviour of a mechanical computer and a plant, the plant's movements are fully determined by antecedent physicochemical principles.

The plant psychologist can be portrayed in this context as one who objects to the mechanistic analysis of plant behaviour, claiming that plant behaviour shows a purpose, a goal. The contention may not be that the plant itself knows or entertains any kind of goal or end in its behaviour, but simply that it exhibits in its behaviour *instincts* at work. No inanimate systems, the charge continues, show instinct. The thesis might be developed by appeal to those nineteenth century naturalists who revolted against Descartes' opinion that all animals except men were robots (to use a term not employed by Descartes), mere insensate machines. Against the seventeenth century Cartesian mechanism was urged a return to a teleological conception of brute behaviour as embodying design. Insects, for example, do not themselves foresee or plan their behaviour, or "know" in any rational way what they are doing; their behaviour appears to be designed to be rational, but this is just because it is unfolding according to the dictates of innate instinct. (Some nineteenth century naturalists revolted even further against mechanism by attributing insects with rational faculties, but that is another story.) Here the plant psychologist agrees with Aristotle that behaviour is goal-directed, that in addition to looking at causes coming before an item of behaviour occurs, one must look also at the *final cause*, the goal of the behaviour which shapes that behaviour.

The teleological conception of plant behaviour was relatively common in the eighteenth, nineteenth and early twentieth centuries, and in itself does not constitute what we would call plant *psychology*. What constitutes the psychology is the concept of instinct super-added to the teleology. "Instinct" in this usage (as contrasted with some later mechanistic usages, such as that of animal ethologists) is a psychological one, the psychology it belongs to being that of an ancient rationalism coming down through mediaeval renderings of Greek thought, even though the specific concept "instinct" as a motivating force was not used by the ancients. The flavour of this rationalist psychology would be illustrated in the claim that the growing towards a source of light by a plant could not be explained in mechanical physiological principles because it ignores the role of a light-seeking instinct inherited by the plant. The plant itself knows nothing of light nor the necessity to seek it, but it possesses, so to speak, an ancient, inchoate "wisdom" expressing itself through the plant's direction of growth. We can characterize this conception of plant psychology then by saying that it makes the category of *instinct* appropriate to the vegetable kingdom. The psychological basis of instinct is a metaphysical rationalist one.

So far two approaches to the concept of plant psychology have been outlined. The first sees plants as possessing mental states of some kind. Traditionally this approach has involved a teleological, anti-mechanistic conception of behaviour, although logically mentalism does not necessary entail teleology. The teleology is not necessarily explicit. (It is possible to find in human psychology a mechanist and a cognitive outlook combined, as in psycho-analysis.) The second approach is also teleological, and necessarily so, for it sees plants as possessing instincts, and these instincts are by definition teleological faculties.

There is a third version of the concept of plant psychology. It answers the question of psychological categories in the plant world by saying that the organisms which interest psychologists are those which "behave." The central phenomenon of psychology is behaviour, which may be innate or learned. Plants behave and are thereby of interest to psychology. The approach to organismic behaviour here is often in principle a thoroughgoing mechanistic one. All organisms — human, brute and plant, are mechanical systems, but some can learn and others cannot. This is the outlook of the twentieth century behaviourists in psychology, an outlook ushered in by J. B. Watson's *Psychology as the Behaviourist Views it* (1913). The plant psychologist here can be portrayed as one who sees as arbitrary and question-begging the exclusive concern of orthodox behaviourist psychology with the animal kingdom. Why take it for granted that only animal species can learn? The question of the meaning of "learning" arises, but discussion of that will be deferred to Chapter 10. This third, although small, approach to plant psychology — the behaviourist, includes also those who are not doctrinaire Watsonian-inspired behaviourists, but who nonetheless take "behaviour" as the sole datum of psychology, having no place for metaphysical notions such as mind and instinct. They may be teleologists, in contrast to the narrower Watsonian Behaviourists with a capital B, who traditionally purport to be mechanists.

The three approaches to plant psychology which emerge from its history are presented in summary form by the following table:

EXPLANATORY APPROACH TO PLANT ACTIVITY	APPROPRIATE PSYCHOLOGICAL CATEGORY
TELEOLOGICAL (I)	MIND
TELEOLOGICAL (II)	INSTINCT
MECHANIST OR TELEOLOGICAL	BEHAVIOUR

By far the most important approach is the first of the teleological ones, the mentalist. It could be referred to as the Platonic one because the tradition of predicating mind of plants can be traced back to Plato, although he was not the first philosopher to do so. As one might expect the majority of plant psychologists (with the exception of the mechanists as a class) are sympathetic to, if not adherents of, philosophical vitalism. In a broad philosophical context there is no necessary connection between teleology and vitalism, they are logically independent terms and thus to embrace one of them is not thereby to embrace the other. In the narrower biological context, however, the two are often found together. Theorists who see mental states as being non-material in nature (as the mentalist plant psychologists tend to do traditionally) and those who see instincts as rational principles supervening on the physiological determinants of plant growth could be identified as vitalists as easily as they could be identified as teleologists. The latter term has been chosen, however, as the generic descriptive one because the actual arguments for psychological processes in plants are characteristically analogical in nature, the analogies tending to be functional ones, i.e. ones concerned with identifying movements in plants which bring about the same end or goal, such as fertilization or nutrition, as certain movements in animals achieve. Most of plant psychology is based upon a combination of analogical and teleological reasoning. Even the tiny class of behaviourists whose advocacy of plant psychology is not based upon argument by analogy, have been charged by critics of behaviourist psychology with the smuggling in of teleology in their concept of behaviour.

Proponents of the second of the teleological approaches to plant behaviour, the instinctivists, have a direct Aristotelian view that the purpose of any piece of behaviour must be invoked in understanding it, but their conception of plant "instincts" goes sufficiently beyond the mere Aristotelian notion of the "plant soul" as a material vital principle to permit them to be distinguished from the mainstream Aristotelians. For example amongst nineteenth century botanists one can readily find vitalists/teleologists, but only a few of these suppose that instincts need be postulated and named; and, as those instincts are innate capacities and not biological structures we can separate out members of this small Aristotelian species as being plant psychologists.

In some theorists both the Platonic and the instinctivist versions are combined, it being believed that plants are possessed of cognitive capacities and also grow according to the unfolding of instinctive capacities. Thus it should be stated that the conceptual distinction in the summary table will not serve to allocate individual theorists necessarily to mutually exclusive classes. It should be pointed out also that the table is a taxonomy of approaches to plant psychology only, it is not applicable to psychology in general. For example, as has been stated, it is logically possible to find within general psychology mentalists who are also mechanists, but in plant psychology this combination tends not to occur.

To conclude this theoretical section it must be emphasized that in the pages of the historical narrative itself there is little attempt to stop to take up basic conceptual issues such as the nature of mind and the mind-matter problem, vitalism and teleology vs. mechanism, the epistemological status of mentalist terms such as "sensation", "feeling", "perception", "consciousness", "knowledge" and "volition", the adequacy of functional criteria of the mental, and so on. This is not because they are unimportant, on the contrary they are, as has been stated already, of the utmost importance to the serious study of psychology. But the primary aim of this work is to present an historical narrative, and although the secondary aim is to introduce basic conceptual issues in psychology in a novel way, to pause to work them out in detail is to run the risk of getting bogged down and losing the sense of historical continuity.

Perhaps at this point I should state my own position on the

conceptual states of plant psychology. I do not believe that there can be a plant psychology because I believe that cognition is the basic psychological category, and I know of no evidence that plants are capable of sentience, or cognition generally. I do not think that there is a necessity here to spell out what is wrong with argument by analogy, with violation of the principle of parsimony in scientific explanation and with anthropomorphism in particular, all of which will be found readily in the ranks of plant psychologists. My concern is primarily historical.

1.4 *The structure and theses of this history*

The concept of plant psychology is treated as an historical narrative, whose themes are presented broadly in temporal order. The themes are not necessarily classed according to temporal sequence, however, and therefore the order of the narrative does not always correspond to the temporal order of events. After beginning with the ancient bases of plant psychology, the establishment of the mentalist tradition in the Renaissance is discussed. Then follow chapters on the concept of plant "irritability", the gathering momentum of the mentalist tradition, the great days of plant psychology, the impact of evolutionary theories, the wilder shores of mentalism, the behaviourists, and the moderns. An appendix is devoted to plant parapsychology.

Here in outline are the arguments presented in those chapters:
(1)   The concept of plant psychology is found in the ancient world, but not in the form of any well articulated continuing tradition there. Plato is the principal source of a long tradition beginning in Renaissance Europe.

(2)   Renaissance Europe saw the revival of systematic botany, with importations of new plant species from Africa, Asia and the Americas. It saw also technological advances, especially the invention of the microscope. In the seventeenth century the sensitive plant (*Mimosa pudica*) and close relatives began to attract European curiosity. Suggestions were made that their movements, together with certain other plant and physiological phenomena, indicated the existence of a certain order of cognition or sentience, "natural perception". At the end of the seventeenth century and in the eighteenth century the doctrine of physiological "irritability" became formulated and progressively accepted, its source being in the Platonic doctrine of the plant soul.

(3)   By the end of the eighteenth century the doctrines of physiological irritability and of animal-vegetable analogy (associated with the Aristotelian conception of the chain-of-being) had been drawn together to provide clear statements of the existence of plant mental activities. The main exponent of this, the culmination of the early history of plant psychology, was Erasmus Darwin.

(4)   The mentalist tradition continued on throughout the nineteenth century and into the twentieth. A few teleologists had made claims of the existence of plant instincts and these claims were maintained also throughout the nineteenth century and into the twentieth. Charles Darwin's evolutionary theory and his experimental researches on plants boosted both orthodox botany and plant psychology. Neo-Lamarckian evolutionary theory prompted claims of memory in plants. The development of microbiology gave rise to speculations about the mental life of micro-organisms. Psychology had begun to

emerge as an independent discipline; some comparative psychologists were faced with the problem of deciding whether plant psychology was a legitimate part of comparative psychology.

(5)   Watson's behaviourist revolution in the early twentieth century brought with it claims that plant behaviour, *qua* behaviour, was a legitimate psychological datum in its own right. For a while the promise of plant psychology, albeit of a non-cognitive kind, became a part of orthodox psychology. By the 1940's it had been forgotten, but in the 1960's there was a revival of interest in plant conditioning.

(6)   In the past two decades there has been an interest in plant behaviour on the part of some orthodox psychologists who appear to be unaware of its history.

(7)   Parapsychological activity has caught the fancy of the vulgar occult whose partisans claim that there are objective data for supporting the notion that plants have paranormal faculties such as extra-sensory perception and psychokinesis. These "phenomena" do not appear to be sustained under properly controlled experimental conditions.

1.5   *A Note on Plants and What They Can Do*

As is stated in the there is no attempt in this book to present outlines or details of plant physiology, but it is appropriate as an end to this introductory chapter to glance at orthodox botany's approach to plant movement and behaviour.

Plants and animals may have had a common origin, but they have taken separate evolutionary lines. According to the botanist N. G. Ball this evolutionary divergence was inevitable

"after certain kinds of organisms had acquired a definite cell wall, accompanied in many cases by the ability of the organism to carry on photosynthesis.

Broadly speaking, the animal habit of taking in solid food through a mouth had favoured the development of a compact type of body capable of being easily moved as a whole in search of nutriment. On the other hand, the special requirements of photosynthetic organisms have led to the evolution of plants with relatively large surfaces. Large areas are needed for absorbing light rays in sufficient quantity and for taking in carbon dioxide and other inorganic substances which enter the plant by passing in solutions through the cell walls. In most plants the extension of surface area has been assisted by profuse branching. As a result, a structure had developed which is totally unsuited to any form of active locomotion. It is not surprising therefore that, in plants, active movement of the body as a whole is confined to some of the smaller aquatic types, in addition to being retained by certain detached reproductive cells" (Ball, 1963, p.228).

It is clear that the vegetable world is not an inert passive one. Plants live, and in living, *do* things. Most, but not all, autonomous plant movements are so relatively slow that they are not perceived when viewed with the naked eye, but now their occurrence can be seen easily with the aid of time-lapse photography. By "autonomous" movements are meant those which occur as a result of internal plant processes (which themselves may be stimulated by sources external to the plant), as opposed to those forced by direct action of external agents, such as the rustling of the leaves of a tree when it is blown by the wind. Of autonomous movements a broad distinction is made between *growth* and *turgor* ones.

As tissues grow, limited movement is possible. A conventional classification of growth movements is in terms of tropism, nastic movements and nutations. *Tropisms* are produced by stimuli which are more intense in one direction from the plant than in other directions, such as a single small source of light in an otherwise darkened room. Many species will grow towards that light source. Tropistic responses are mostly toward the stimulus but many are away from it. Stimuli eliciting tropistic responses include light ("phototropism" is the name given to responses here), gravity (geotropism), chemical substances (chemotropism), water (hydrotropism) and mechanical stimulation (thigmotropism). Some lists include galvanotropisms (response to electricity) and traumatotropisms (response to wound lesions). *Nastic movements*, which occur primarily in leaves, are brought about by a diffuse, non-directional change in stimulation, such as an overall change in the amount of surrounding light, or in the amount of surrounding temperature. For example in the young leaves of some plants a change from light to darkness produces an unequal growth rate between the upper and lower sides of the leaves resulting in their drooping at night, or "sleeping". In closed crocus flowers an increase in temperature accelerates the growth of the inner petal surface, causing them to open. *Nutations* are the rotational curvature movements of the growing tips of young organs. They are seen best in the spiralling of the tendrils of climbers, but time lapse photography shows that they occur in other plant organs, such as stems, roots and flower stalks.

More obvious to the naked eye than growth movements are the turgor (or variation) movements, effected by changes in the turgidity (the stiffness or degree of inflation) of certain cells. This is controlled mainly by their water content. They may be induced by diverse stimuli such as sudden physical contact, changes from light to dark or the reverse, exposure to gases or electricity, and injury. The "sleep" movements of some leaves are turgor movements. The best examples of turgor movements are the dramatic quick changes observable in the sensitive plant and the Venus fly trap. The movements of the sundew's "tentacles" around its prey are noticeable, too. Indeed, the responses of the sensitive plants and of some of the insectivorous plants, showing remarkable turgor movements, are more than any other source responsible for claims of mentality in plants.

The botanist H. J. Fuller pleaded in the pages of an orthodox journal of psychology some sixty years ago for a behavioural plant psychology, and here are some of his examples of plant behaviour (most of which had been known by the end of the nineteenth century).

"Plants", writes Fuller, "are dynamic sensitive organisms capable of many responses to environmental changes. The stimuli which initiate their behaviour are nearly as numerous as those which affect animals and in many cases are much the same. Moisture, temperature, light, gravity, acidity and alkalinity, gases, contact, pressure, poisons, anaesthetics and nutrients are the principal stimuli to which plants respond. The degree of sensitivity of plants to some of these stimuli is much greater than that of many higher animals. For example, the tendril of a wild cucumber responds to the small pressure of .00025 milligrams, a pressure which probably lies below the threshold of stimulation in higher animals. A young lupin root of 1 millimeter in diameter responds to a difference on opposite sides of .04 per cent of the moisture content of the substratum ....

Inherent in the numerous responses of plants to the above-mentioned stimuli is survival value. Roots react positively to the stimulus of gravitation and grow down into the soil, the natural substratum from which they absorb salts and water. Stems react negatively to the same stimulus; they grow upward above the soil into regions penetrated by light ....

In many of these cases, the direction of response is relative and varies usually with reference to optimum conditions. A plant organ bends normally from cold to warm temperatures but should the heat become too great the bending may occur in the direction of a lower temperature. The flower stalks of Kenilworth ivy in the early stages of their growth are positively phototropic, but when the seeds have matured the reaction becomes a negative one and the fruits are thus pushed into crevices where the seeds are able to germinate" (Fuller, 1934, pp. 379-381).

Fuller's detailed account of plant behaviour draws attention to some aspects which might interest experimental psychologists. For example Weber's Law, well known to psychophysics, holds in a wide variety of plant responses:

"chemotaxy of bacteria, swimming spores, sperms of ferns and mosses, chemotropism of pollen tubes and fungus typhae, geotropism in higher plants, and in at least some cases phototropism", as in the case of young shoots of some higher plants "grown in the light for phototropic study the intensity of light used in the phototropic stimulus must be greater in a definite degree than that of the light in which the plants have been grown" (Fuller, 1934, p.391).

It is unnecessary to elaborate further here. It is clear that whilst plants "typically have few, simple and poorly differentiated receptors, conductors and effectors" (Simpson and Beck, 1965, p.388) they are capable of a wide range of reactions to a wide range of stimuli, and at least sometimes are extremely sensitive organisms.

It will be seen, however, that "sensitive" means different things to different people. Indeed this is a crucial issue in this history, for most of it is concerned with those who believe that there is a cognitive *core* to the notion of "sensitivity", and insofar as plants are sensitive, they have some degree of cognition. Clearly, plants are sensitive in a way which rocks and gases, for example, are not: but does *sensitivity* connote *sentience?*

CHAPTER 2

Plant pleasure and pain:
the Ancients

2.1   *The Pre-Socratics*

So influential on modern thought has been Descartes' psychology that words such as "soul", "mind" and "consciousness" always connote dualism. Of course, opinions differ as to what to make of dualism. However, we have been warned (e.g. by Kathleen Wilkes, 1988) that in approaching Ancient Greek thought we must not wear Cartesian spectacles: there are no synonyms of "mind", or "consciousness" as we might now understand them.

This warning should not be taken to be saying that the Greeks had no conception of psychology: on the contrary, there is a great deal of psychological discussion in the ancient literature, and questions of the nature of thinking, feeling, sensing, perceiving and imagining were vigorously pursued. Standard histories of philosophy and psychology give testimony to this point.

According to repute three philosophers of the early Pre-Socratic period of hellenistic thought believed that plants were capable of mentation. They are Anaxagoras (c. 500 — c. 428 B.C.), who is credited with the discovery of the cause of eclipses but is better remembered for his system embracing the notion of a developing cosmos, formed by *Nous* (Mind) out of an infinite number of physical ingredients;

Empedocles (c. 493 — c. 433 B.C.), a father of evolutionary thought, who conceived the universe as being composed of the four fundamental elements water, air, earth and fire, which mingled and separated under the contrary impulses of love and strife; and Democritus (b. 460 — 457 B.C. — ?), to whom the universe, made out of atoms, was infinite and perishable, and in which causes were efficient and mechanical, not teleological (goal-directed). Democritus may have been an exception to the rule that the mentalists favour teleology.

None of Democritus's writings come directly to us, and the fragments remaining of the works of Anaxagoras and Empedocles do not mention the mental life of plants. The source of the claim of their beliefs here is *On Plants (De Plantis)*, formerly taken to be one of Aristotle's minor works, but now thought (e.g. Owen, 1970) to be by the historian Nicolaus of Damascus (b. c. 64 B.C.) who was born some three centuries after Aristotle. Book I of *On Plants* begins with the nature of plant life and takes up questions of the "plant soul" and plant sentience.

"The question of issue", says Nicolaus, "is whether plants have or have not a soul, and a capacity for desire, pain, pleasure and discrimination. Anaxagoras and Empedocles maintain that plants are moved by desire, and they assert emphatically that they can feel and experience both pain and pleasure. Anaxagoras says that plants are animals, and feel both pleasure and pain, concluding this from the fall of their leaves and from their growth. Democritus supposed that the two classes (plant and animals — T. McM.) were mixed in plants" (Nicolaus of Damascus, trans. Hett 1936, p. 143). A little later comes the statement "But Anaxagoras, Democritus and Empedocles said that plants have intelligence and can acquire knowledge " (p. 145).

It is not clear how much reliance can be placed on *On Plants*. In his history of Greek philosophy W.K.C. Guthrie states that "The *De Plantis* as we have it is a poor Latin translation of a lost Arabic version of the lost Greek original of a work once attributed to Aristotle" (Guthrie, 1965, p. 469). He calls it a "dubious authority" (p. 469). Unfortunately we are not told in *On Plants* what the bases of the three philosophers' claims were, except for the passing reference to Anaxagoras's belief that leaf-shedding and growth indicated the presence of hedonistic faculties. An early thirteenth century translation of *On Plants* from Arabic to Latin by the Englishman Alfred of Sareshel (Long, 1985) gives a little more detail here. Alfred provided a commentary on the text. "The opinion of Anaxagoras, explains Alfred, was that trees were much saddened both by the loss of "solar time" (that is, the shortening of daylight hours) and by the loss of their flora, fruit and sap. The fact that trees lose their leaves in the fall of the year is evidence of this sadness" (Long, 1985, p. 131). If Alfred's report was correct, then Anaxagoras's anthropomorphism is apparent. As far as the logic of the matter is concerned there is always analogical reasoning at the heart of anthropomorphism. This is not to deny that there will be individual psychological and/or social determinents of the anthropomorphic outlook, but what these are would have to be considered case by case. Presumably analogical reasoning on Anaxagoras's part lies behind Brett's charge in his history of psychology that Anaxagoras, in treating psychology from a "biological point of view", was led to "a confusion between vital function and consciousness" : because an action is intelligible it is not necessarily intelligent (Brett, 1912, p. 39). It could be suggested here that a more accurate formulation is that Anaxagoras treated biology from a psychological point of view.

In Anaxagoras's cosmology Mind had become localized in living things after they came into existence. "All living things, of course from plants at the bottom of the scale to man at the top have a portion of Mind" (Kirk, Raven and Schofield, 1983, p. 383). Thus it could be that Nicolaus did report views actually held by Anaxagoras.

It might be noted too that Nicolaus's mention of Empedocles is consistent with a declaration coming directly from him that in a previous incarnation he was a plant: "For before this I was born once a boy, and a maiden, and a plant, and a bird, and a darting fish in the sea" (Empedocles, *Fragments*, Book I, 383; trans. Fairbanks, 1898, p. 207).

If Anaxagoras and Empedocles saw plants as wholly or partly animal, and if, with Democritus, they saw plants as possessing not only the more primitive capacity to experience pain and pleasure, but also the more developed one of having intelligence and acquiring knowledge, then they did indeed have an elevated conception of the plant mind. Whether or not *On Plants* was an accurate report of the three philosophers' opinions, it, as a supposed minor work of Aristotle, was to exert an historical influence.

2.2 *Plato*

On Plants also contains references to Plato (c. 429 — 347 B.C.), the first of which reports, after noting that Anaxagoras and Empedocles asserted that plants can feel pleasure and pain that "similarly Plato averred that plants must know desire, because of the extreme demands of their nutritive capacity" (Nicolaus of Damascus, trans. Hett, 1936, p. 143).

With Plato we are not dependent solely on what an author had to say about his opinions some hundreds of years after he lived (if Nicolaus is taken to be the author of *On Plants*) for we have Plato's own account, given in the dialogue *Timaeus*. The *Timaeus* comes from Plato's last period of dialogues, and it is concerned with natural science. The material on plants is only a tiny and unimportant part of the dialogue, but it illustrates well the charge that is often made against Plato as a natural scientist, viz., that he makes little or no appeal to observational data. This is what Plato says about plants: the gods created after man

"another kind of animal. These are the trees and plants and seeds which have been improved by cultivation and are now domesticated among us; anciently there were only the wild kinds, which are older than the cultivated. For everything that partakes of life may be truly called a living being, and the animal of which we are now speaking partakes of the third kind of soul, which is said to be seated between the midriff and the navel, having no part in opinion or reason or mind, but only in feelings of pleasure or pain and the desires which accompany them. For this nature is in a passive state, and is not endowed by nature with the power of revolving in and about itself, repelling the motion from without and using its own, in such a way as to observe and reflect upon any of its own concerns. Wherefore it lives and does not differ from a living being, but is fixed and rooted in the same spot, having no power of self-motion"

(Plato, trans. Jowett, 1953 pp. 764-5).

Plato's mention of the midriff and the navel refers to his construction of the soul on the model of the body (see Jowett, p. 685). There is a three-fold division of the soul into the rational, passionate and appetitive, corresponding respectively to the head, heart and belly. Plants, then, are animals which have only the base appetitive soul, that of the belly. They live, but are rooted in passivity, having no volitional powers, being capable of no sophisticated cognitions, nor any developed emotional life beyond that of sensations of pleasure and pain and the accompanying "desires".

The Plato scholar F. M. Conford had this commentary on the plant passage in the *Timaeus*:

"Plants are regarded as sensitive to the group of qualities discussed .... as 'common affections of the whole body' and attended by pleasure and pain .... They feel heat and cold, and some at least shrink from contact with hard or heavy or rough objects. The pleasurable or painful character of such contacts is supposed to be accompanied with some faint degree of desire to seek or shun. Galen observes that plants have the power of distinguishing and drawing to themselves congenial substances on which they feed, while rejecting those which are harmful. But plants have no perceptions such as we receive through the special organs of sense .... with the corresponding qualities .... Nor have they anything corresponding to the rational revolutions of the immortal soul seated in the brain of man. It may be for this reason that they are excluded from Plato's scheme of transmigration, though they were admitted to that of Empedocles" (Cornford, 1937, p. 303).

Cornford adds that the denial of self-motion in plants means only motion from place to place. It does not mean denial of any motion because plants do have a soul which by definition is the self-moving thing.

Cornford's commentary is written with the hindsight of the psychology of the platonist Galen, who will be discussed later. For the present let us concern ourselves with Plato's contention that we find elementary hedonistic states and desires in plants. Now Plato's account of plant mentality is a much more parsimonious one that that attributed to Anaxagoras, Empedocles and Democritus. Prompted by Plato, however, we can pause in the narrative to ask whether on Plato's relatively impoverished description of plant mentality, we can say that plants are capable of cognition. As has been stated in the previous chapter there can be no question of cognition-less mentality, because the category of the mental is cognition. In Plato's case it is clear that there is cognition involved in the description of the appetitive plant soul, for to speak of the "desires" accompanying pleasures and pains of necessity requires cognition. Normally there would be a cognized object, no matter how vague, of a desire (e.g. desire "that this pain cease"); even to deny a cognized object and to say "there is something I want but I do not know what it is" is itself an act of knowing, of cognizing.

Plato rules out any self-awareness in the appetitive soul, presumably plant "desires" are of the form "feeling good" or "feeling bad", or even "this feeling should commence" (or "continue", or "cease"). The latter desires, "this feeling should commence", etc., clearly are fully structured cognitions, but we could ask whether generally these are basic hedonistic states of the form "feeling good" (or "bad") which carry with them no cognitions, i.e. whether forgetting for the moment problems of anthropomorphism and the like, there could be either in humans, brutes or plants mental occurrences of "pleasure!" or "pain!", which are otherwise inchoate, and are unlocalized, unfocused on any sources or objects. The notion here is of some rudimentary hedonistic *tone* state which is prior to cognition, which is proto-cognitive, so to speak. There is a great deal of contemporary discussion about the role of intentionality in emotional ascription, but it will not be taken up here. All that will be said here is that it seems doubtful whether the concept of rudimentary proto-cognitive hedonistic states can be sustained. To begin with there is a distinction in quality between "pleasure" and "pain", the two must be discriminable from each other, otherwise there would be no difference between them, and to discriminate is to cognize. Next, any occurrence of pleasure and pain is contoured in time and space: the occurrence can be distinguished from a background of the absence of pain or pleasure (the distinguishing itself being a cognitive act) temporally as having duration ("the pain comes in bursts", "the onset of pleasure") and spatially as having magnitude ("a tiny bit of pain", "an ocean of pleasure"). Further, it could be argued that pleasures and pains are in themselves complex (in addition to their temporal and spatial extension) in that each occurs in qualitatively different tones or "colours" ("a sharp, stabbing pain" vs. "a dull steady one", "the pleasure of lustful arousal" vs. "the pleasure of the relaxation of exhausted muscles"), and the appreciation of these different kinds of pleasures or pains is cognitive. The yet further issue of the conceptual status of pleasure and pain, e.g. whether they are real mental states, or are merely dispositions or even reifications will not be pursued here. It is, however, a question which should be pursued by serious proponents of psychological hedonism, whether their psychological organisms are philosopher-kings or lowly cabbages. As will be seen, there were many advocates of vegetable hedonism after Plato. The general point now is that no matter how rudimentary, how primitive, a mental act might be taken to be (in any organism), it cannot be less than cognitive.

2.3   *The Aristotelian Verdict*

The position of Aristotle and his followers on vegetable sentience is worthy of note because of its explicit opposition to the concept.

Having been acquainted with Nicolaus's descriptions of the views of the three Pre-Socratics and of Plato, we can consider his evaluation of them.

After outlining Anaxagoras' and Empedocles' accounts *On Plants* mentions Plato's thesis of "the extreme demands of their nutritive capacity" on plants, which indicates that they must experience desire. Nicolaus concedes that "if this were established, it would be in accord with it that they should really know pleasure and pain, and that they should feel. And once this is established, it will be in accord with it that plants should know desire, if they ever have sleep and are aroused by awakening" (Nicolaus of Damascus, trans. Hett, 1936, p. 143). A little later attention is drawn again to Plato's belief that "if anything receives food, it also desires and has pleasure in satiety, and suffers pain when it is hungry; moreover these conditions do not occur except in combination with sensation" (p. 145). Then comes the verdict:

> "Plato's theory is marvellous, though its errors are not slight, I mean the theory in which he supposed that plants could feel and desire. But Anaxagoras, Democritus and Empedocles said that plants have intelligence and can acquire knowledge. Let us dismiss those theories as trivial and abide by sound reasoning. We maintain, then, that plants

know neither desire or sensation. For desire cannot exist apart from sensation, and the accomplishment of our will depends upon sensation. Now in plants we find no sensation, nor any organ which can feel nor anything in the least like it, nor any differentiated form, nor anything issuing from it, nor any local movement, nor any method of approach to sense apprehension, nor any sign by which we could judge that plants have sensation, corresponding to the signs by which we know that they are nourished and grow"

(p. 145).

The claim is then made that plants, as living things, do have "some part" of a soul in them (the nutritive soul), but they are not living *creatures*, because "sensation …. is the only test by which the term living *animals* is assigned" (p. 147).

Nicolaus presents here an orthodox Aristotelian line. He has the advantage of access to the corpus of material on the natural history of animals and plants which Aristotle and Theophrastus had begun to assemble systematically a long time before, and he can appeal therefore to observational data such as the one that plants have no organ "which can feel nor anything in the least like it, nor any differentiated form ….". Of course to talk of the "findings" of Aristotle and Theophrastus is to realize that there is much in them which is erroneous, confused and fabulous, but they were attempting to order and describe observations drawn from nature. Plato's argument for sensation and appetite in plants makes no reference to a single plant species.

What Aristotle (384 — 322 B.C.) himself had to say about the mental life of plants can be found in his *On the Soul (De Anima)*.

Plants, he states, live and thus may be said to have a "nutritive soul", it is what is meant by their "living".

"Living .... may mean thinking or perception or local movement and rest, or movement in the sense of nutrition, decay and growth. Hence we think of plants also as living, for they are observed to possess in themselves an originative power through which they increase or decrease in all spatial directions; they grow up *and* down, and everything that grows increases its bulk alike in both directions or indeed in all, and continues to live so long as it can absorb nutriment.

This power of self-nutrition can be isolated from the other powers mentioned, but not they from it — in mortal beings at least. The fact is obvious in plants; for it is the only psychic power they possess"

(Aristotle, II.2., trans. Smith, 1931, p. 413a).

Plants have a single "psychic" power: the nutritive one. Brutes possess it too, but have in addition appetitive and sensory faculties and, in some animals, a locomotive one. Men possess all of those faculties, and beyond them, that of thinking. Plants embody a nutritive soul, brutes a nutritive and sensitive one, and humans a nutritive, sensitive and rational one, as in the familiar formula previously stated: plants live, animals live and feel, men live and feel and think. Aristotle agrees with Plato that there is a nutritive soul in plants but denies that they have any kind of cognition: "plants cannot perceive, in spite of their having a portion of soul in them and obviously being affected by tangible objects themselves" (II. 12, p. 424 a); "plants .... have no sensation" (II. 12, p. 435 a). For Aristotle the sense of touch is the primary sense — without it no other sense is possible and plants can have no sense of touch.

At this point some general observations might be made about the "plant soul", not only in relation to the Greeks, but in anticipation of references to it in later writers. Aristotle's notion of the plant soul was used by his Greek followers, by the mediaeval Aristotelians, and by botanists after the revival of botany following its two thousand year stagnation during which the founding work of Theophrastus was largely forgotten. Echoes of the plant soul reverberated down to the nineteenth and early twentieth centuries. To Aristotle the soul was a material principle, all life contains it, but plants are less fully "ensouled" than are animals. Cuttings or slips taken from a plant can themselves live as complete plants. According to Morton soul is used here in "a simple materialist sense to describe either the total organized unity of a living thing or some aspect of that organization" (Morton, 1981, p.28). This is the conception of the plant soul to be found in later botanists, for example Cesalpino (1519-1603) who worked in the early Renaissance.

This materialist conception of the plant soul is all very well as long as it remains strictly that, and as long as it is understood that it is conceptually only a make-shift device awaiting the unravelling of the actual mechanics of plant growth and behaviour. Theophrastus, as will be mentioned, attempted to explain "the causes of plants" in terms of the non-teleological operation of physiological plant structures in relation to conditions external to the plants, and, as more became known about the details of plant physiology so there was less room to appeal to a "plant soul". The plant soul was, so to speak, an explanatory promissory note which had become cashed in.

If we call this doctrine of the plant soul a "vitalist" one then the Aristotelian vitalism should be seen to be a materialist one, i.e. the vital principle is potentially expressible or translatable in terms of material principles.

The materialist conception of the plant soul can be a dangerous one to flirt with, however, because all too easily it becomes an explanatory principle in its own right, sufficient in itself. The presence of the plant soul to "explain" plant growth and behaviour then can stifle search for the real material causes, i.e. the physiological processes in the plant. The plant soul can thus become a metaphysical principle, hallowing a dualistic conception of nature according to which it is believed that material (i.e. physico-chemical) causes of plant activities will never be sufficient, in principle, to explain them. Physiological processes are sustained and shaped by the continuing necessary presence of a non-material principle of activation. This metaphysical end of vitalism should be borne in mind in consideration of some of the vitalist accounts to follow.

2.4 *The Question of Theophrastus*

The late nineteenth century historian of Greek thought, Theodor Gomperz, drew attention to a passage in which Theophrastus, the great Greek founding-father of botany (371-286 B.C.), seeks to explain why the stalk of the Euphrates lily rises above the water by day but dips below it by night, moving down from sunset to midnight. Gomperz says that "while dealing with this subject he even once let slip the word "sensation", and so unconsciously connects himself with those researchers of the most recent times who treat or have treated "the irritability or sensitivity of plants" " (Gomperz, 1909, p. 478).

Now many of those to whom Gomperz refers did believe that plant irritability and sensitivity indicated some degree of awareness. It would be a mistake, however, to make too much of Gomperz's remark and to include Theophrastus, at least in the moment of this "lapse", as a believer in plant cognition. There are good reasons for this claim: (1)   The word "sensation" appears presumably in Gomperz's translation of the Greek, but it is not a necessary rendition. In that of Einarson and Link we find the adjective "sensitive", but not the noun "sensation" as follows:

(Theophrastus has noted that the lilies open by day and shut by night, as well as their daily stalk-rising and falling).

"The closing and opening of the flowers is a less difficult matter and easier to solve, since it is brought about by cold and heat, the flowers being cold and weak. Thus they close up when their fluid condenses and (as it were) freezes (since at this time their heat leaves them too), and open when the fluid dissolves again and thaws, this being done by the sun.

The plants that sink under water and emerge above it to a greater extent are evidently colder and weaker than the flowers, and for this reason are affected by the changes. That a flower under water should be so keenly sensitive is not unreasonable, especially in a torrid region of fiery heat. Indeed even in temperate regions the transmission to water of all effects arising from the position of the sun and the heavenly bodies is rapid. At any rate not only surface water but also waters under ground appear to be influenced by the solstices and the risings of the stars and with some stars land itself and sea are changed"

(Theophrastus, *Causes of Plants*, II. 19. 3 and 4; trans. Einarson and Link, 1976, pp. 357-359).

The term "sensitive" here does not necessarily connote "sentience", or cognition generally, a point which will be taken up below. We see in the above passage the characteristic mechanistic approach of Theophrastus, in his attempt to give a fully deterministic physiological explanation of the lily's movements in terms of the dispositions of its "fluid" in relation to the peculiar internal "strength" and "temperature" of the plant structures as affected by external environmental conditions. Theophrastus goes on (II. 19. 5) to sketch a physiological explanation of plant heliotropisms without any reference to sensitivity, whereas a number of other writers were to be tempted to account for heliotropisms by reference to plant awareness.

(2)   There are other occasions where Theophrastus, were he unconsciously attracted to the idea of plant sentience, could have betrayed himself, but he does not do so. for example, he describes the shrinking behaviour of the *mimosa asperata* from North Africa without appealing to psychological causal factors, (*Enquiry into Plants*, II. 2. 11). Again, in *On the Senses (De Sensibus)* he attacks the eclectic philosopher Diogenes of Apollonia, a contemporary of Anaxagoras, for arguing that thinking is due to the presence of pure dry air. (Diogenes had concluded that plants therefore cannot think, because they are not hollow). Diogenes' criterion of thought, says Theophrastus, is unworkable, but he in no way suggests that plants might think (Theophrastus, *On the Senses*, I. 39-49 in Stratton, 1917, pp. 101-109).

(3)   Theophrastus was a co-worker with Aristotle, often regarded as his mentor, but not so in the foundation of systematic botany, as has been pointed out by historians of botany such as Morton (1981).

39

Aristotle explicitly denied that plants sense anything, and, had Theophrastus differed with Aristotle on this point, it is likely that he would have so indicated, even though he might not have mentioned Aristotle by name. Theophrastus otherwise corrected or modified Aristotle's botanical opinions when he believed this to be necessary — e.g. he warned that Aristotle's practice of drawing analogies between plants and animals could be dangerous (see Morton, 1981, pp. 32-33). Nowhere, however, does Theophrastus call into question the doctrine of the insensate vegetable world. It is true that in both of his botanical works, *Enquiry into Plants* and *Causes of Plants* he often talks of plants "seeking", "liking" and so on. He mentions the sensitivity to smell of the grape vine, which is "injured" by the odours of bay and cabbage (*Causes of Plants*, II. 18. 4), and even refers to plants as "collaborating with" and "being fond of" other plants of the same species. It is obvious in the context that these are everyday figures of speech, and nothing more — the same figures of speech that we use when, for example, we talk of a plant "not liking lime", or of a climber "seeking the light". Theophrastus's observations on the Euphrates lily should no be taken as cognitive lapses on his part.

In the opening chapter it was stated that attributions of "soul", "spirit" or some other vital principle to plants is not of great interest here unless such attribution carries with it the claim that the presence of the vital principle endows plants with a degree of percipient or sentient ability. Plato clearly emerges as an originator of plant psychology, as do Anaxagoras, Empedocles and Democritus if later commentators are correct. Aristotle, though a vitalist, clearly could not be called a plant psychologist. There is no real case for the inclusion of Theophrastus in that class.

CHAPTER 3

The beginnings of a mentalist tradition: from the ancients to the arrival of mimosa.

3.1 *Later Classical writers.*

At least three writers later in the Classical world are known to have noted the claims relevant to plant sentience made by the Pre-Socratics and/or Plato.

The Greek historian, biographer and philosopher Plutarch (c. 50 A.D. — c. 120 A.D.) recorded under the heading of "causes of natural phenomena" in his *Moralia* that "...Plato, Anaxagoras and Democritus think that a plant is an animal fixed in the earth" (Plutarch, trans. Pearson and Sandbach, 1965, p. 149).

Sextus Empiricus, Greek doctor of medicine and sceptical philosopher (c. 200 A.D.) stated that "but Empedocles .... held that all things are rational, and not animals only but plants as well, as he writes expressly -

Wisdom and power of thought, know thou, are shared in by all things"

(Sextus Empiricus, *Against the Logicians*, Book II. 286, trans.

Bury, 1935, p. 389).

The great Galen who counted Plato as one of his heroes, advanced in Plato's name a theory of a sentient vegetative or nutritive soul. This fact was to be of sufficient importance in a later historical period, the European Renaissance, that discussion of Galen's theory will be deferred now.

3.2 *The Middle Ages*

There is a continuity of plant psychology from Ancient Greece to the Renaissance. If we take the conventional dating of the "Middle Ages" as the period between the fall of the Western Roman Empire and the Renaissance (approximately from the fifth to the fifteenth centuries), then it is clear that the doctrine of vegetable cognition was known in the Middle Ages. This is not to say, of course, that it was necessarily advanced by anyone then. Indeed, given the influence of Aristotelian thought (through Latin translations) in the Middle Ages, metaphysicians and natural philosophers would be expected to subscribe to the Aristotelian view of an insensate plant world.

The only writing of Plato known in the West before the end of the twelfth century was the *Timaeus*. Apart from a fragment translated by Cicero the version to which the scholars had access was a Latin translation by Chalcidius, which, although substantial, was incomplete (see e.g., Barrett (1940), Lee (1969)). Inspection of Chalcidius's translation shows that the passage on plant life and the plant soul is one of the missing passages, hence we can say that the Middle Ages had no direct knowledge of Plato's plant views. However, they did have access to an indirect account. viz., Nicolaus's *On Plants*, which was widely circulated and copied. Of course, they believed it to be by Aristotle, so were reading in it what they took to be Aristotle's attack on vegetable cognition.

The earliest Mediaeval commentary on *On Plants* was that of Alfred of Sareshel, (Long, 1985), mentioned in connection with Anaxagoras in Chapter 2. Alfred staunchly upheld Aristotle against Plato, declaring that it is impossible to assert that plants could have desire, because there can be no desire without sensation, and we know plants have no sensation. Morton's history of botany (Morton, 1981) mentions four mediaeval scholars who knew and disseminated *On Plants*: Bartholomew the Englishman, Thomas of Cantimpré, Roger Bacon and Albert the Great.

Bartholomew the Englishman (Bartholomaeus Anglicus, fl. 1230-1240) wrote the encyclopaedia *De Proprietatibus Rerum (On the Properties of Things)* which included in its book on plants many scarcely altered passages from Nicolaus. An English translation by John Trevisa of Bartholomew's work was completed in 1398/9. In the book on herbs and plants there is a passage in which Bartholomew cites "Aristotil" (p. 882) as saying that plants cannot move from place to place as do beasts. They do not have feelings, although some philosophers such as Anaxagoras say otherwise. Such philosophers are reproved by Aristotle: "in trees is soule of lif .... but therinne is no soule of feelynge" (Bartholomew, in Seymour, 1975, p. 883).

Roughly contemporary with Bartholomew's encyclopaedia was *De Natura Rerum (On the Nature of Things)* by the theologian, natural historian and onetime pupil of Albert, Thomas of Cantimpré (also known as Thomas Brabantinus, c. 1201 — c. 1270/72). Thomas's work contains an uncritical rendition of parts of Nicolaus's treatise. One of the famous figures of mediaeval science, Roger Bacon (c. 1219 — c. 1292), a pioneer of natural history, optics and calendar reform, showed Nicolaus's influence in lectures he gave at the University of Paris sometime between 1236 and 1247.

Especially important in the history of botany is Albert the Great (1200-1280, known also as Albertus Magnus, and canonized by the Roman Catholic Church). Nicknamed "The Universal Doctor" for his proficiency in all branches of science, Albert, in his *De Vegetabilibus et Plantis* (c. 1250), provided the only botanical work in the Middle Ages which could be regarded as having significant theoretical content. He went beyond the herbals of other writers, a "herbal" is a catalogue of names and descriptions of plants, and a list of their properties with an eye mainly to their medicinal application. The first five books of *De Vegetabilibus* consist of Albert's paraphrase of, and comments upon, Nicolaus. As Arber says in her history of herbals, Nicolaus's treatise is "of importance in the annals of western science, because it formed the starting-point for the botanical work of Albertus Magnus" (Arber, 1986, p. 4).

In his study of Anaxagoras, F.M. Cleve (Cleve, 1973) claims in effect that Albert should be included amongst the ranks of the plant psychologists, because Albert, together with Thomas Campanella and Gustav Theodor Fechner, considered plants to have "individual consciousness" (Cleve, 1973, p. 117). Campanella and Fechner will be discussed in due course in this work. Cleve's claim is made in the context of citing Nicolaus on the opinion of Anaxagoras, Democritus and Empedocles on plant mentality, but this is of no help in enabling us to know why Albert is mentioned here, and Cleve offers no evidence from Albert. It is puzzling why Cleve attributes to Albert the belief that plants have individual consciousness. Cleve would appear to be alone here.

Albert's treatise has yet to be translated into English, but the

44

nineteenth century expert on Albert, and historian of botany, E.H.F. Meyer, explicitly states in the section on Albert in his history that Albert rejected the Platonic conception of the plant soul, and endorsed the Aristotelian one (Meyer, 1857, p.42).

Recent studies by authorities on Albert's natural philosophy give no support to the claim — e.g. Cadden (on the place of nutrition in Albert's physiology, (Cadden 1980)) and Reeds (on Albert's philosophy of plant life, (Reeds 1980)) both indicate that Albert was an orthodox Aristotelian in that he allowed that plants possessed a vegetative or nutritive soul and that there was no question of such a soul being sentient. On some other issues concerning the soul Albert appealed to Plato rather than Aristotle, but those issues are not relevant here.

The general point so far is that the doctrine of plant mentality was known in the Middle Ages through the wide dissemination of the pseudo-Aristotle Nicolaus's treatise. There is no evidence that his opinions were questioned.

3.3 *The Renaissance*

With the "revival" of learning in the fifteenth century came the ability to read the classical Greek texts in the original language. In itself this had no important direct influence on plant psychology.

The specific comments on the cognitive nature of the vegetable soul in the *Timaeus* were to have an important influence on plant psychology, but that influence was indirect, a "sleeper" effect as it were, and was not a direct consequence of the revival of Greek scholarship.

The increased influence of Neoplatonic thinking in Renaissance philosophy, which sought to find in the natural world marks indicative of an underlying principle of unity, a unity which was evidence of authorship by a transcendent mind, generally had no direct influence on plant psychology. Although the Neoplatonists challenged the place of Aristotle as the prime authority on the explanation of natural phenomena many of them sought to reconcile Plato and Aristotle, and it was Aristotle's account of the vegetable mind which was accepted. There appears to be at least one Neoplatonist, however, who did subscribe to the doctrine of vegetable sentience: the Dominican philosopher Tomasso Campanella (1568 -1639). Campanella spent much of his time in prison, mainly on charges of heresy, and is today best remembered for his political utopian work *City of the Sun (Civitas Solis,* 1623). Campanella embraced an empiricist outlook which argued that direct observation of the world was a valid source of knowledge. It complemented God's revelations in the Bible, and the blessing of Aristotle was not necessary. He was an animist: " .... every creature is animate in some sense, and nothing is without some degree of perception and feeling" (Copleston, 1953, p. 257). According to other commentators, he specifically talked about feelings in plants. J.H. Randall says that despite his "sturdy devotion to observation, Campanella finds soul everywhere, mysterious forces, the sympathies and antipathies of the prevailing Platonism. Space abhors a vacuum and yearns to be filled; plants grieve when they wilt, and rejoice after a rain" (Randall, 1962, p. 215). Ritterbush says of Campanella that he wrote that "No one should doubt the senses of plants — they are born, nourished, grow, produce seeds and young even as animals do" (from Campanella's *De Sensus Rerum et Magia* .... (1620), cited by Ritterbush, 1964, p.145). He drew attention to the movements of the heliotrope and the Euphrates lily — just as Theophrastus had done centuries earlier, but Theophrastus had sought a mechanical explanation of their movements.

There was, however, one plant which Campanella did not mention, because he did not know about it. It was this plant which was to have a central place in the history of plant psychology: the sensitive plant. It was the arrival of this plant in Western Europe which was responsible for the emergence of a small but identifiable tradition of plant psychology in the Renaissance. The sensitive plant was to awaken the sleeping doctrine of the sentient plant soul, as well as, in orthodox botany, to stimulate the study of plant movements.

3.3.1. *The sensitive plant.*

Two events associated with the revival of botany in the seventeenth century were technological innovation, especially the invention of the microscope, and the introduction of new plant species from Africa, the East and the Americas. Amongst these new species were the sensitive mimosas, which, more than any other kind of plant, were to provide the observational basis of the claims of plant psychologists. Of the sensitive mimosas, *Mimosa pudica* was to attract most attention and today the term "the" sensitive plant usually denotes *m. pudica*. It is not always clear in earlier discussions whether "sensitive plant" refers to *m. pudica* or to a close relative, such as *m. sensitiva*. "Mimosa" had been brought to European notice late in the sixteenth century. In his *Tractado de las Drogas, y Medicinas de las Indias Orientalas* (1578), the Cape Verde born but Spanish speaking physician and collector, Cristoval Acosta, published the results of his first-hand observations

47

of medicinal and other useful plants of the East. In the *Tractado* were descriptions and wood-cut illustrations of what Acosta called the "yerve biua" ("herb viva") and the "yerve mimosa" ("herb mimosa"). An important historical paper on the recognition of plant sensitivity in the seventeenth century was written by Charles Webster (Webster 1966), and the use of it to be made in this chapter should be apparent. It should be noted, however, that Webster nowhere addresses the status of "sensitivity" as a physiological category, in particular he does not raise the issue of whether sensitivity connotes "cognition" ("sentience", "percipience"), and, if not, whether it is to be distinguished from mere reactivity to stimuli. This issue has been addressed in the opening chapter, and will be passed over here.

Webster doubts that Acosta actually described *m. pudica*. Early writings sometimes called what is now *m. pudica* the "herb viva", and Acosta's crude wood-block illustration of "herb mimosa" (Acosta, 1578, p. 243) could be taken to be *m. pudica*, but he certainly was describing sensitive mimosas. Most of the sensitive mimosas are natives of central and south America (*m. pudica* comes from Brazil). Acosta's "mimosa" was recorded as having been seen in gardens in the East Indies. M. *pudica* and some of its close relations had been grown in the East by the time of Acosta's visit — presumably arriving there either as items collected by Iberian plant-hunters to be displayed as garden curiosities in their Eastern colonies, or as themselves "accidental" plant colonists.

Webster (1966) credits the French botanist, Charles de l'Ecluse (Clusius) with the first European description of *m. pudica*. This he introduced into the third edition of his translation of Acosta's book into Latin (1605), the first edition having appeared in 1578. French translations of Acosta by Antoine Colin of Lyons came out in 1662 and 1619 (e.g. see Colin, 1619, pp. 163-165 for the "Herba Mimosa de Acosta"). The great Swiss Renaissance botanist Gaspard (or Casper) Bauhin incorporated the "Herb mimosa" in his *Pinax Theatrici Botanici* (Bauhin, 1623, p.360).

Webster believes that the first English description of *m. pudica* was by John Layfield (d. 1619), who, as chaplain to George Clifford, Earl of Cumberland, went with Clifford in 1596 to the English enclave in Puerto Rico. Layfield's account was written in 1598 and published in 1625. He wrote of the "Yerva viva" that

"this hearbe is a little contemptible weed to looke upon, with a long woodden stalke creeping upon the ground, and seldome lifting it selfe above a handfull high from the ground. But it hath a propertie, which confoundeth my understanding, and perhaps will seem strange in the way of Philosophers, who have denyed ever part of sense to any plant; yet this certainly seemeth to have feeling. For if you lay your finger or a sticke upon the leaves of it, not onely that very piece which you touched, but that that is neare to it, will contract it selfe, and run together, as if it were presently dead and withered, nor onely the leaves but the very sprigs, being touched, will so disdainfully withdraw themselves, as if they would slip themselves rather then be touched, in which state both leafe and sprig will continue a good while, before it returne to the former greene and flourishing forme. And they say, that so long as the partie which touched it standeth by it, it will not open, but after his departure it will, this last I did not my selfe observe: and if it be so, it must be more then sense, whence such a sullennesse can proceed; but for the former, I have my selfe been often an eye-witnesse to my great wonder, for it groweth in very many places in the little Iland" (Layfield, in Purchas 1625/1906, pp. 98-99).

Layfield was wise to be cautious about the claim that the plant will not revive until the person who touched it has left. The claim is not true, of course, and that piece of folk-lore did not gain currency in England.

Another early English account of the *m. pudica* (or the *m. sensitiva* if a later editor is to be believed (Harris, 1928)) was given by the sea-captain Robert Harcourt, in his story of a voyage to Guiana in 1608.

Of "certaine Plants" he says

"These Plants or little trees had assuredly the sence of feeling, as plainly appeared by touching them: for if you did but touch a leafe of the tree with your finger, that leafe would presently shrinke, and close up it selfe, and hang downe as if it were dead …. which evidently shew a restriction of the Spirits, invincibly arguing a Sense" (Harcourt, in Purchas, 1625/1906, pp. 394-395).

A more widely read English account of the plant, based on Acosta's and Clusius' descriptions was given in 1633 in Johnson's *Gerard's Herbal*. This was a much enlarged, amended and improved budget of plant descriptions by Thomas Johnson, based on the famous herbal of John Gerard. Johnson, apothecary and soldier as well as botanist (he inspired Joseph Banks to an interest in botany) writes "that which I here call the sensitive herb, is that which *Christopher a Costa* sets forth by the name of *Herba mimosa*, or the Mocking herbe, because when one puts his hand thereto it forthwith seems to wither and hang downe the leaves; but when you take it away againe it recovers the pristine greenesse and vigor (Johnson, 1633, p. 1599). Johnson adds that one James Garret in 1599 had a mimosa which "he had of the right Honourable the Earle of Cumberland, who returning from

Saint *John de Puertorico* in the West Indies, brought it put in a pot with some earth, but could not preserve it alive" (p. 1599). Johnson himself saw a dried specimen in 1632, and in 1638 the first living plant was introduced to England (Grigson, 1974).

The *mimosa pudica* to give it its contemporary botanical name, is a small shrub, the delicate appearance of which is often described as "fern-like", but it is not a fern. The leaf or petiole is divided into 2 to 4 feathery leaflets or pinnae ("pinna" means "feather" in Latin), each pinna being itself divided into 10 to 20 pinnules or sub-leaflets, which are oppositely arranged. If the plant is stroked briskly the sub-leaflets fold up along the stem of the pinna, and, if the plant is touched or jolted sufficiently vigorously, each leaflet and stem droops downward. The plant reacts immediately, and to a number of stimuli besides touching or shaking, e.g. cutting, burning, electric shocks and air puffs. The plant will recover in about 15 minutes. The plant movements take place at the pulvinus, the swollen base of the petiole, in the cells of which a movement-producing change in turgidity, or fluid content, occurs. The release of a hormonal substance may be involved in the wave of movement which occurs down the stems of the plant if it is vigorously jostled, and the movement is accompanied by a wave of electrical depolarization like a slow motion nerve action potential. The onset of darkness also will cause the subleaflets to fold (the "nictitropic response"), and during this phase the plant is much less sensitive. After the onset of prolonged light (e.g. daylight) the plant will open up and in about an hour will be fully sensitive again.

"Mimosa" derives from the Latin "mime" and alludes to the ready movements of the plant appearing to make it "mimic" conscious life, and "pudica" refers to its chastity or virtue, manifest in its shrinking from those who would profane it with their embrace. The term "sensitive" did not connote refined moral sensibility or delicacy of temperament, but referred to, at least the appearance of, what we might now call the existence of a sensory capacity. Its movements prompted some of the seventeenth and eighteenth century writers to call it the "sensitive and humble plant". They distinguished between mimosas which were merely "sensitive", i.e. whose reactive movements were confined to the folding of the sub-leaflets along the pinnae, and those which were "sensitive and humble", i.e. whose reactive movements showed additionally the downward drop of leaflets and stems, as in the *m. pudica* and the *m. sensitiva*.

Mimosa pudica is a species of the some 500 strong *Mimosa*, a genus of the family *Leguminosae* and the subfamily *Mimosoideae*. (The golden-balled "mimosa" sold by European florists is an Australian acacia, the acacias being another subfamily of *Mimosoideae*.) Other sensitive mimosa species include the extremely similar (to *m. pudica*) *m. sensitiva*, (also often called the "sensitive plant"), *m. casta*, *m. dormiens, m. humilis, m. viva* and the *m. asperata* (or *pigra*). Other sensitive species include *smithia sensitiva, cassia nictitans* ("wild sensitive plant"), *aeschynomene indica, a. americana* ("bastard sensitive plant"), *a. lispida* ("false sensitive plant") and *oxalis sensitiva. Mimosa pudica* is much more reactive than most of the other sensitive species, and has received much more attention than they have, thus, unless indicated otherwise "sensitive plant" will mean the *m. pudica*.

After its introduction to England the sensitive plant soon attracted the interest of those who had the knowledge and means to attend to new botanical curiosities. The diarist and gardener John Evelyn went on a trip to Oxford University on 12 July, 1654, "hence we went to the *Physick* Garden, where the Sensitive (and humble) plant was show'd us for a greate wonder" (Evelyn, in de Beer, 1955, pp. 109-110). In 1661 on 9 August Evelyn was able to experiment on it: "I tried severall experiments on the *Sensitive plant* and *humilis*, which contracted with the least touch of the Sunn, thro a burning Glasse, though it rises and opens onely, when it shines on it: also with *aqua fortis*; but it did not with its fume, nor touch'd with Spirit of *Sulphur*" (Evelyn, in de Beer, 1955, p. 293). Evelyn and his friends were conducting the experiments on behalf of the Royal Society at the request of Charles II. A Welsh schoolmaster, John Jones, who was moved to translate Ovid's *Invective or Curse against Ibis* into English, remarks with some hyperbole in his commentary "Thus the sensitive tree, if ye touch on leaf the whole tree will quake" (Jones, 1657, p. 45). Samuel Pepys' diary entry for 7 March 1660 records that at the house of Mr Crew "among many that were here I met with Mr Lynes, the surgeon, who promised me some seeds of the sensitive plant" (Pepys, in Wheatley, 1904, p. 83).

To the writers mentioned so far the sensitive plant was a curiosity, but one which did not impel them to attribute any animal-like sensory capacity to it. As far as we can tell this was also the case with those ancient writers who had heard of the strange movements of some of the mimosas. Most of the mimosa species are native to the tropical American regions, but not all. One exception is the *m. asperata* (or *pigra*) which occurs in parts of North Africa, including Egypt, and which is sensitive. After Alexander's conquests the Greeks had access to many previously unknown flora. Theophrastus, who was very interested in foreign plants, wrote in the *Enquiry into Plants* that

"There is a peculiar bush which grows about Memphis, whose

peculiarity does not lie in its leaves shoots and general form, but in the strange property which belongs to it. Its appearance is spinous and the leaf is like ferns, but, when one touches the twigs, they say that the leaves as it were wither up and collapse and then after a time come to life again and flourish"(II.2.11; trans. Hort, 1916,p.303).

Pliny the Elder, who lived some 300 years after Theophrastus, mentioned in his *Natural History* (77 A.D.) a plant which to him may have been fabulous:

"Apollodorus, a follower of Democritus, added to those plants one that he called aeschynomene (the "shy" plant, T. McM) because on the approach of a hand it contracts its leaves" (Pliny, Book XXIV, ch. 167; trans. Jones, 1956, p. 119).

Authority for the assertion that Theophrastus and Pliny were writing of the *mimosa asperata* is in each case the commentary of the translator. Thus the phenomenon of mimosa sensitivity was not first recorded in the Renaissance — unless we dismiss the statements of Theophrastus and Pliny because their accounts were not first hand — but Western acquaintance with that paragon of sensitivity, *m. pudica*, was first recorded then, and so were claims that its dramatic movements evinced a faculty of sentience or perception, i.e. the plant was not "sensitive" merely in that it possessed a specific reactive disposition, but that it possessed some capacity for cognition.

CHAPTER 4

Sentience, irritability and natural perception

4.1 Seventeenth century controversy about sentience

t is hard to tell what quantity of controversy was generated by the arrival of the sensitive plant in England, but we know that by the end of the seventeenth century there certainly was controversy.

In this section we shall look at the pro-cognition views of a small but distinguished group, and at a sample of opposition views from "mainstream" natural philosophy.

By the mid-century it had been claimed in print that the sensitive plant was capable of some degree of cognition. William Harvey, the discoverer of the circulation of the blood, proposed in a late work *On Animal Generation* (1651) the theory that organisms possess two orders of sensation. The first is the everyday sensory awareness mediated by the five classical senses and their seat, the brain ("sensorium"). The second is a form of perception which is not conscious, does not depend on the brain and, in animals, belongs to the physiological structures and systems which today we would describe as being under autonomic nervous system control. This Harvey called "natural". Natural perception occurs not only in animals with brains (e.g. man) but also in organisms without central nervous systems, with rudimentary "brains" or no brains at all. "Now such a sense", said Harvey, "do we observe in zoophytes or plant-animals, in sponges, the sensitive plant, etc." (Harvey, 1651, p. 433). The zoophytes ("plant animals") included lower sessile organisms such as sea-anemones and corals, which superficially seemed to be intermediate between plants and animals. That they were in fact animals had yet to be established clearly.

Harvey has nothing more to say about the sensitive plant, his reference to it being a passing one but the distinction he makes between the two orders of perception is a most important one for us and the next section will come back to it. It is interesting that Harvey saw no need to argue for the inclusion of the sensitive plant in those systems manifesting natural perception.

Harvey's account of perception was repeated a few years later by his follower Henry Power in his *Experimental Philosophy*, published in 1663.

Power (1623-1668), a physician and naturalist, and one of the first two elected members of the Royal Society, believed that the telescope and microscope would result in the rapid acquisition of knowledge. He himself was a pioneer in microscopic research, and was one of the first Englishmen to support Harvey's discovery of the circulation of the blood. He followed the Aristotelian inspired physiology of Harvey and of Francis Glisson, who was one of his teachers, but his general biological outlook showed too the Neoplatonic influence of Thomas Browne and the Cambridge Platonist philosophers generally (Webster, 1967).

In Book 1 of *Experimental Philosophy* ("Microscopical Observations") the distinction between "Animal sensations", for which a brain is necessary, and "Natural sensations," which can be found in organisms without brains (as well as those with brains) is discussed:

> For certainly such Animals as have distinction of Senses, as Seeing,
> Feeling, etc. must needs have an Animal-Sensation; an Animal, I
> say, for I hold also a natural Sensation, which is performed without
> a Brain, and such a one is discoverable even in Animals, and in our
> own Selves; for besides the Animal-Sensation (whose original is
> in the Brain) the Stomach, Guts and the *Parenchymata* (e.g. other
> internal bodily organs as opposed to connective tissue and muscular
> tissue — T. McM.) of the Body, yea and the Bloud too has a natural
> Sensation of what is good, and what is bad for them, As Doctour
> *Harvey* has excellently proved .... and so some of the lowest rank of
> Animals (as the Zoophyta and plant-Animals) may perchance be
> utterly devoid of Animal, and have onely a Natural Sensation; but
> this belongeth to some Anatomical Observations I have by me, where
> I may perchance prove that all Vegetables (as well as the Sensitive and
> humble plants) have this latter kind of sensation, as well as Animals"
> (Power, 1663, pp. 79-80).

Whereas Harvey mentioned only the sensitive plant, amongst plants, as having natural perception, Power allowed it to all the vegetable kingdom. It was his hope that the microscope would reveal the marks of natural perception in all plants, but he never realized that hope.

Four years earlier Power had written to his mentor, Thomas Browne (Cowles (1933) described Power as a "disciple" of Browne), prompted by some botanical reports of Browne's: "In another Paragraph you doe not only take notice but handsomely prove, a continuall transpiracion in plantes like to that in Animals: wch continually renews their lopt off flowers, & where it is large & excessive perchance doubles their flowers; now I am soe much yr convert in this point, that I can easyly stretch my beliefe a little farther, & that is to conceive that all plants may not only have a transpiration of particles, but a sensation also like Animals. This is eminently enough discoverable in those 2 exotick Hearbs (the sensitive and humble plants, vid. my letter to Dr Robinson, 2d August, 1656)" (Power, 1659, in Keynes, 1931, p. 291).

Browne replied "That there is a naturall sensation in plants as Dr Harvey hath discoursed seemes verie allowable & besides some other reasons, from the experiment of the sensible plant, wch is also to bee found in minor degree in some others as Jacea, Scabious, Thistles & such as Borellus observed & published some yeares agoe, & might be observed in others. Such a sense may bee in plant animals & in the parts of perfect animals even when the head is cutt of" (Browne, 1659, in Keynes, 1931, p. 294).

"Jacea" was the name then for centaurea species, e.g. the knapweed. "Borellus" was Pierre Borel (c. 1620 — 1671), a French physician, historian and chemist, and a pioneer of telescopy and microscopy. Power's letter to "Dr Robinson" (his friend Dr. Reuben Robinson of Maldon, Sussex) referred not only to the "sensitive and humble" plants, which Power took to be respectively male and female plants of the same species, the female (the humble plant) being the more sensitive, but also to knapweeds, thistles, sunflowers and saffron-yielding crocuses. It is in this letter that the passage already quoted from *Experimental Philosophy* occurs. Power suggested to Robinson "that possiblely all plants whatever may have a kind of sense in them", even though it may be "obscure" in some. He hoped that Robinson might be able to look into these "extravagant phancys" and "experimentally condemn or avouch them" (Power, 1656). There is no evidence of Robinson taking up the problem.

Sir Thomas Browne (1605-1682), writer and physician, was celebrated for his "vast and curious learning, set in language of rich and gorgeous eloquence" (Thorne and Collocott 1983, p. 183). His best known works are *Religio Medici* (c. 1635) and *Pseudodoxia Epidemica, or Enquiries into .... Vulgar and Common Errors* (1646). He was an early champion of Harvey, and, which is not well known, was a pioneer student of plant movements (see Webster, 1966). In his biology, i.e. in his conception of digestion, respiration, circulation, sensation and generation, Browne was an eclectic and synthesizer, influenced by both Aristotle and Plato, and showing "an animistic view of matter and a vitalistic view of life" (Merton, 1949, p. 60).

"A vitalistic view of life" in itself can be seen as an Aristotelian heritage. As Pagel puts it, Aristotle's vitalism was *monistic* in that the individual (person, brute or plant) is "viewed as being alive by virtue of a disposal of matter according to a specific plan; it takes place through an inseparable union with a *form*, that is to say, a schedule that leads the individual to perfection in development, growth, function — arrival at a destined end" (Pagel, 1969, p. 21). "An animistic view of matter", however, bespeaks a Platonic *dualist* heritage, "dualistic" in that lying *behind* creation is Mind. This was a familiar notion to the Neoplatonists of the Renaissance, and to natural philosophers such as Harvey, Power and Browne who had been brought up in a Neoplatonist outlook. It was exemplified in Browne's *Religio Medici* in the theme that there " "is a common spirit to the whole World", which increased in activity with the ascent of the "Scale of creatures". Plants had certain vital activities, but they lacked the sensitive behaviour of higher creatures" (Webster, 1966, p.11).

Webster makes the point that Neoplatonism was congenial to the idea of plant *sensitivity*, because it believed that "the whole of nature was activated by an immaterial animistic force" (p. 21). This does not mean that all nature is *percipient*. The Mind or Spirit had an hierarchical nature: a non-percipient function in plants, a vegetative and sentient one in brutes and a vegetative, sentient and rational one in man. Webster can find only one of the English Neoplatonists who talks about the vegetable soul as being cognitive, and even he elsewhere denies the general sensitivity of plants. This is Thomas Vaughan (1622-1666), alchemist and poet, twin brother of the better known poet Henry Vaughan. In his *Anthroposophia Theomagica* (1650) Vaughan stated:

"Not withstanding in the Flowers of severall *vegetables* (which in some sort represent the *Eyes*) there is a more subtile, acute perception of heat and cold, and other *Coelestiall* Influences then in any other part. This is manifest in those *Herbs* which open at the Rising, and shut towards the *Sunset*; which motion is caused by the spirit being sensible of the Approach and departure of the *Sun*. For indeed the Flowers are (as it were) the spring of the Spirit, where it breaks forth and streames, as it appears by the Odours that are more *Coelestiall* and Comfortable there. Again, this is more evident in the *Plant animals*, as the Vegetable Lamb, the *Arbor Casta*, and severall others" (p. 40).

The "arbor casta" refers to a sensitive mimosa species. The "Vegetable Lamb", sometimes referred to as the "Tartary lamb," was a fabulous plant which was supposed not only to resemble and taste like a lamb, hence providing a source of food, but to be sensitive over the surface of the body. It was still being mentioned at the end of the eighteenth century (see Excell, 1932).

It would be a mistake to argue that the theory of vegetable sentience advanced by Vaughan and the trio of pioneers of Renaissance science, Harvey, Power and Browne, was directly attributable to a Neoplatonic outlook. Whilst one could speculate that Neoplatonism might have been a *necessary* condition of holding that doctrine, it was certainly not a *sufficient* one, otherwise all Renaissance Neoplatonists would have subscribed to the thesis, rather than just the handful who did. The influence of the sensitive plant would seem crucial here: its dramatic movements provided such a forceful analogy with the behaviour of sentient organisms, that some who were clearly sympathetic to the idea of a pervasive sensitivity in creation were persuaded that, at least in some plants, there was sentience.

An example of a natural scientist of the day who took a rather more cautious position on plant percipience is Martin Lister (1639 — 1712). Lister, a frequent contributor to the Royal Society and friend of the great botanist John Ray is best remembered today as a pioneer in invertebrate zoology and paleo-zoology. A decade after Power's *Experimental Philosophy* was published Lister had this to say in a contribution to the Royal Society:

"There seem to be in Plants manifest Acts of *Sense*. We instance in the suddain shrinking of some Plants; the frequent closing and opening of flowers; the critical erecting of the heads of Poppies from a pendulous posture, and particularly the *Vermicular* motion of the veins when exposed to the air .... Further there are natural and spontaneous excretions of venting of superflous moisture in plants, visible and constant, in the *Crown Imperial, Rorella, Pinguicula,* etc»

(Lister, 1673, p. 5137).

Lister does not commit himself. Whereas Harvey and Power could appeal to what they took to be established principles of perception in animals to support a strong claim of plant sentience, Lister makes no reference to any such basis. He merely wants to say "there *seem* to be in plants .... " and, in the title of his paper, "acts in plants *resembling* those of sense" (my italics — T. McM). But Lister does bring some new observations to bear on the possibility of plant sentience. Some new plant species are mentioned: poppies, a large majestic frittilary (the "Crown Imperial"), the sundew ("rorella") and the butterwort ("pinguicula"). In addition to the shrinking of the sensitive plant new plant movements are mentioned. Theophrastus, as we have seen, wrote about the opening and closing of the flowers of the Euphrates lily, but did not see manifest in this a psychological process. Plant excretions, e.g. the sticky drops of "dew" on the insectivorous sundew, are introduced as evidence pointing to some active sensitive principle in the plant.

If has been mentioned that the interpretation of the shrinking movements of the sensitive plant was a matter of controversy in the seventeenth century, and we may turn to three instances of opposition to the contention that the plant has feeling. (Webster, 1966, gives an earlier instance: Francis Bacon (1561-1626)). These three exemplify the new scientific attitude of the age, the belief that in principle it is possible to interpret all nature as a gigantic mechanism, that natural phenomena can be explained according to the categories of that branch of physics known as mechanics.

The first comes from that famous early work in microscopy, Robert Hooke's *Micrographia*, 1665. In his speculations on the fine internal structures of plants Hooke suggests that they might have something analogous to *"valves*, in the heart, veins, and other passages of Animals, that open and give passage to the contain'd fluid juices one way, and shut themselves, and impede the passage of such liquours back again" (Hooke, 1665, p. 116). Hooke thinks this is likely in the sensitive plant, and then reports the experiments of Evelyn and his party on it (the ones of 9 August 1661). One member of Evelyn's party was a "Dr. Clark" (Dr. Timothy Clarke, physician and original Fellow of the Royal Society) who argued that the key to the plant's behaviour will be found in the details of the circulation of its "liquor".

"The motion of this Plant upon touching, might be from this, there being a constant *intercourse* betwixt every part of this Plant and its root, either by a *circulation* of this liquor, or a constant pressing of the subtiler parts of it to every extremity of the Plant .... " (p. 120).

If one knew more about the internal canals "through which this fine liquor circulateth...such a one would easily from the motion of this liquor, solve all the *Phaenomena*, and would not fear to affirm, that it is no obscure sensation this Plant hath" (Clarke, cited by Hooke,

1665, p. 120).

The spirit rather than the letter of Clarke's theory is of interest here. We recognize that by seventeenth (and eighteenth) century botanists "the mechanical processes in plants were described much in the way in which a person with very indefinite ideas as to the nature of steam and the construction of the inside of a steam-engine might speak of its movements" (Sachs, 1890, p. 540). The important point here is that we have a Theophrastian mechanical explanation of the plant's movements proposed.

In 1686 John Ray, the first of the English botanists to attempt a systematic incorporation of physiology to botany, realized that it was difficult to present a mechanical interpretation of the sensitive plant's vivid movements, but believed nonetheless that there had to be one. As Sachs puts it in his history, Ray, in his *Historia Plantarum*, denies that the mimosa is endowed with sensitivity, its shrinking is due to

"Known physical causes; the movement of the leaf when it is touched is caused by a contraction, which again is due to a withering or relaxation of its parts. He endeavours to apply the knowledge of his time to the explanation of the mechanical process: leaves, he says, remain tense only because the loss by evaporation is kept constantly supplied by the water that flows to them from the stems; if then in consequence of a touch the sap-passages of the leaves are pressed together, the supply of water is not sufficient to prevent their becoming relaxed"

(Sachs, 1890, p. 536).

Ray was an admirer of the philosopher John Locke. To modern psychology Locke is one of its more important historical figures because he was the main founder of the "British empiricist" tradition of epistemology, a tradition upon which experimental psychology was based when it became an independent discipline in the nineteenth century, and upon which a great deal of contemporary experimental psychology is still based. Locke's view on the sensitive plant might be taken as the paradigm expression of that of orthodox psychology (and orthodox botany, insofar as it may be said that orthodox botany has any interest in cognition).

In his discussion of perception in *An Essay Concerning Human Understanding* (1690) Locke's point is clear and simple. What is distinctive of the animal kingdom is its ability to perceive. Some vegetable behaviour may resemble that which is indicative of cognition in animals, but it is just that: a resemblance. Vegetables do not perceive anything. Accordingly their movements must be mechanical.

"This faculty of *Perception*, seems to me to be that, which *puts the distinction betwixt the animal kingdom, and the* inferior *parts of nature*. For however Vegetables have, many of them, some degrees of Motion, and upon the application of other Bodies to them, do very briskly alter their Figures and Motions, and so have obtained the name of sensitive Plants, from a motion, which has some resemblance to that, which in Animals follows upon Sensation: Yet, I suppose, it is all bare Mechanism; and no otherwise produced, than the turning of a wild Oat-beard, by the insinuation of the Particles of Moisture; or the short'ning of a rope, by the affusion of Water. All which is done without any Sensation in the Subject, or the having or receiving any *Ideas*" (Locke, 1690,

pp. 147-8).

We see then that seventeenth century mechanists were forced by the excitement generated by the arrival of the mimosa to consider seriously the claim that it manifested some degree of perceptual capacity. The mechanistic approach to botany was still at too early a stage of development to win over opponents by a show of scientific triumphs: just as the eighteenth century was to see the consolidation of mechanism in mainstream botany, it was also to see the zenith of the mentalist tradition in plant psychology.

4.2. *Into the eighteenth century*

Controversy continued in the eighteenth century concerning the theoretical framework appropriate to the understanding of plant movements.

In 1739 *The Gentleman's Magazine* reported that the sensitive plant "is now grown pretty common amongst us, and may be found in most of our *Physick Gardens* "(p. 477). Richard Bradley, F.R.S. (d. 1732) was a prolific writer on botany, best remembered to-day for his observations on the movement of sap and on sexual reproduction in plants. In his *A Philosophical Account of the Works of Nature* he took to task "some unskilful people" who believed that some plants had "a Share of Sensation, as the *humble and sensitive Plants,* the *Wild or Spurting Cucumber,* the Seed-Pods of *Female Balsoms.....* but this is far from Reason, when we consider that the fruit of the *Wild Cucumber* never flies from its *Vine* till its Vessels are over-repleat with Juices, which is the same case with the *Seed-Pods* of *Balsoms,* whose parts are so full when they are quite ripe, that the *Pod* bursts upon the least Touch .... " etc. (Bradley, 1721, p. 47). On the other hand the German botanist Casper Bose argued in 1728 that, as the historian Ritterbush puts it, "the movements of plants in following the sun or chasing their leaves when touched, and the existence of zoophytes .... indicated that plants enjoyed sensation" (Ritterbush, 1964, p. 145).

The "sun-following" (heliotropic) behaviour in some plants

distinguished by Bose as a basis of the claim of their capacity to enjoy sensation, was to be invoked repeatedly in later years by others. Theophrastus mentioned the movements of the flower "heliotrope". (The statement of Sachs that Varro (116-27 B.C.) was the first to mention heliotropic movements (Sachs, 1890, pp. 535-6) is wrong. It is wrong on at least two counts, for we can add to Theophrastus the poet Nicander of Colophon (? second century B.C.), who wrote in his *Theriaka* in recommending herbal remedies for snakebite

"Administer .... the plant whose name is that of the sun's turnings, and which, like the glaucous leaves of the olive, marks the path of the retreating scion of Hyperion" (Lines 678-682; trans. Gow and Scholfield, 1953, p. 73).

The plant is identified by Gow and Scholfield as a heliotrope.

Another class of plant movements which was of great interest is the "sleep" movements of plants. Very commonly these are seen when flowers and/or leaves of plants "fold up" or "droop" at sunset and "open up" or "stand up" at sunrise. There are species whose flowers open at night and close by day, and others whose flowers open or close at various hours, according to the species. It is possible in theory to gather a series of flowers whose "opening" and "shutting" times are so staggered that a floral "clock" could result, as Linnaeus stated. The sensitive plant shows "sleeping" behaviour in addition to its shrinking upon contact movements. We have seen that Theophrastus drew attention to these movements in the Euphrates lily. In 1757 another blow for mechanism was dealt by John Hill (or "Sir" John, as he became known to those of his British countrymen who were prepared to recognize his Swedish knighthood) in his *The Sleep of Plants*, bravely subtitled *Cause of Motion in the Sensitive Plant Explain'd*. Hill objected to the use of the term "sleep", derived as it was from analogy with animals, calling it "affected" and "improper". He explained sleep movements as being occasioned by the "motions" in plant fibres caused by the impact of rays of light. Obviously this could not explain the shrinking movements occasioned by touch, and it was not until nearly a century later that another avowed mechanist, R.-J.-H. Dutrochet, published the first systematic experiments on the physiology of the mimosa's shrinking movements. (The Royal Society had been presented in 1789 and 1791 with reports, probably both by John Lindsay the elder, of Jamaica, of systematic experiments on the *m. pudica*, but these were not published (Ritterbush, 1962)).

Hill's work could be regarded perhaps as a rebuke to Linnaeus (1707-1778) who had argued a few years previously that the "sleep" of plants was analogous to that of animals, and he had tried to justify his use of the term "sleep". This was no concession on Linnaeus's part to play psychology, however. He was in this respect, as he was in some others, a staunch Aristotelian, agreeing with the seventeenth century German botanist Jung that "planta est corpus vivens, non sentiens" (Green, 1914, p. 138), and he refused to attribute any psychological characters to the movements of mimosa or a sensitive oxalis.

The weight of learned botanical opinion was against that of those "unskilful people", referred to by Bradley, who believed that plants had a share of sensation. But the orthodox botanists had to come to grips with the job of explaining the "reactivity", the dramatic, animal-like "responses" of the sensitive plants (not to mention other classes of movements such as the "sleep" ones), without referring to animal sentience being involved. To their help came the doctrine of irritability. The doctrine of irritability they saw as a sword to wield against the plant mentalists, but they did not know it was to be a double-edged sword.

4.3 *Irritability and Natural Perception*

Why was the doctrine of "irritability" to be a double-edged sword for the mechanists? With it they hoped to slay vitalism, but they did not appreciate that vitalism historically had the first claim to "irritability", and, at its core historically, irritability was a manifestation of "natural perception": a cognitive concept. We have seen that Harvey, and following him, Power and Browne, had invoked natural perception as an explanatory principle. We shall see now that "natural perception" was derived directly from Plato's description of the sentient vegetative soul. Hence to appeal to irritability to explain certain plant movements is to run the grave risk of reviving that ancient metaphysical cognitive concept.

In 1755, the year that Linnaeus published his work on the sleep of plants, there appeared the first English translation of a most influential treatise by Albrecht von Haller: *A Dissertation on the Sensible and Irritable Parts of Animals*, which had been written in Latin one year earlier. Haller (1708-1777) was Swiss born, became a professor at the University of Gottingen and is famous for his work in anatomy, physiology and botany. Although by no means the originator of the concept or "irritability", as Haller himself points out, he was the first to try and "clean it up" as a concept and it was he who gave it to the biological world at large. In the outline of the nature and development of the irritability concept that follows I am indebted especially to the writings to Owsei Temkin (Temkin 1936, 1964, 1972).

Haller's aim was to draw a clear distinction between sensibility and irritability in animals. Some parts of the body are *sensible*, i.e. their stimulation by a foreign agent is either consciously noticed (in human beings) or causes unrest (in brutes). Some parts of the body are *irritable*, i.e. their stimulation results in an observable contraction. Haller adduces experimental considerations to argue that sensibility is possessed only by those bodily parts supplied with nerves, whereas irritability is a property of muscular fibres. Haller said

"I call that part of the human body irritable, which becomes shorter upon being touched; very irritable if it contracts upon a slight touch, and the contrary if by a violent touch it contracts but little.

I call that a sensible part of the human body, which upon being touched transmits the impression of it to the soul; and in brutes, in whom the existence of a soul is not so clear, I call those parts sensible, the Irritation of which occasions evident signs of pain and disquiet in the animal" (Haller, 1755, pp. 8-9).

For Haller, then, irritability is a mechanical notion and is to be distinguished from vitalistic notions, including sensitivity. Only animals have muscles, therefore only animals may evince irritability: " .... all animal fibres when they were irritated contracted themselves .... this character distinguished them from those of vegetables" (Haller, 1755, p. 44). We might note that on Haller's own account the sensitive plant would seem to show irritability, and this point was not overlooked in Haller's own day.

Haller's attempt to "clear up" the notion of irritability was an attempt to rid it of any vitalistic overtones. Muscles contract, not because there are "souls" at work or because they perceive pain at being aroused, but for thoroughly mechanical reasons. Here we come to a central problem of irritability conceived purely mechanically: if it is just the *fact* of muscle contraction which is the content of the term irritability (an "operational" definition, as Temkin puts it) then we still have to say what it is that *causes* the muscles to contract. We cannot say that they contract *because* of irritability: to do this would be to offer a verbal pseudo-solution, to indulge in crude circularity ("Why do muscles contract? Because they are irritable. How do we know they are irritable? Because they contract"). If left at this then irritability has no better conceptual status than Aristotle's "souls" — to declare them to be material in nature is just to offer (to use the metaphor again) a promissory note, and the task of discovering the actual physiological processes involved in muscular activities is still to be done.

That particular issue need not detain us now, however. Haller's purified and narrowed account of irritability did not gain acceptance in his terms. To begin with it was in its historical basis a cognitive notion, and Haller was not able to exorcise the mentalistic ghost in it; further, irritability became such a general term that not only did it cover plants as well as animals, but it provided a respectable explanatory refuge for mentalists and mechanists alike. For the botanical mentalists plant irritability could be seen to *point to* (to be in modern parlance an "operational definition of") vegetable sentience and feeling. If any kind of general responsiveness or reactivity to stimulation constituted irritability in animals, and, if in brutes it was evidence of their sentient faculties, then, by analogy, similar responsiveness or reactivity was evidence of plant sentience. Thus plant irritability could be taken as the primary datum of plant cognition.

However we are getting ahead of the story here. Let us go back to look at the claim that the physiological concept of irritability has a psychological heritage, for this story turns out to be of particular interest to us.

According to Haller credit for the introduction of "irritability" should go to the anatomist Francis Glisson (1597?-1677), an early member of The Royal Society and Regius professor of *physic* at Cambridge from 1635. (Temkin (1964) traces the word "(irritibilitas)" back to Apuleius in the second century A.D. who used it to denote the emotion of anger, which Plato localized in the heart.) Temkin summarizes Glisson's account thus:

> " .... irritation is the experience by some part of the body of a molesting sensation with ensuing attempts to remove the offending agent. In the *Anatomia hepatis*, Glisson believes this sensation (or perception) to be mediated by nerves which also mediate the movements towards removal of the agent. In the *Tractatus de Ventriculo* (1677 — T. McM), a "natural perception", independent of nerves, is assumed. Consequently, the parts of the organism, especially fibers, by themselves are assigned the capacity of being irritated, and this capacity is called "irritability" (Temkin, 1964, p. 306).

Temkin notes that Glisson's concept of irritation, although it concerns physiological events, is frankly psychological, even anthropomorphic. The diverse parts act like irritated people: they react because they have been "burdened" or "provoked".

The term "natural perception" has been encountered already in reference to William Harvey, and Glisson followed Harvey in making it a central concept in his physiology: natural perception was necessary for irritability, body organs and systems could not respond to stimulation unless they could perceive it, but the perception is not of the same order as that in "normal" conscious perception when it occurs in organs without nerves.

Pagel makes explicit that Harvey and Glisson were talking about the same concept:

"It is true that what Harvey had called *sensus* as intrinsic to vital substance was elaborated by Glisson into *naturalis perceptio* with a much wider application in Nature including its inorganic realm. *Sensus* is normally associated with sensual *organs* — but Harvey had made it quite clear that the response which had been ascribed to *sensus* took place in the absence of organs and was therefore true *naturalis perceptio*, i.e. the true phenomenon of Glissonian irritability" (Pagel, 1969, p. 12).

Temkin says:

"By 1677 .... natural irritability was a property attributed to almost all living parts of the body including the blood (an idea implicit in Harvey's theory), a property independent of the nerves Irritability presupposed perception of the irritating object, appetite to attain it (if pleasant) or to flee it (if unpleasant) and motion to realize the appetite" (Temkin, 1972, p. 426).

Glisson knew Harvey's work and mentions him prominently, as Pagel has pointed out (Pagel, 1967), and thus we come to Harvey's account of natural perception. By the way, there is nothing "implicit" about Harvey's idea that the blood is irritable and thereby perceptive,

Harvey is quite explicit about it in a paen of praise of the physiological and philosophical primacy of the blood ("Exercise the seventy-first" in *On Animal Generation*). It includes these statements:

"No one can ever sufficiently extol its admirable, its divine faculties. In the first place, and especially, it is possessed by a soul which is not only vegetative, but sensitive and motive also .... " (Harvey, 1651, p. 432).

In "Exercise the fifty-seventh" in *On Animal Generation* Harvey's doctrine of natural perception is set out.

"The motions and actions", he writes, "which physicians style *natural*, because they take place involuntarily, and we can neither prevent nor moderate, accelerate nor retard them by our will, and they therefore do not depend on the brain, still do not occur entirely without causing sensation, but proclaim themselves subject to sense, inasmuch as they are aroused, called forth, and changed thereby. When the heart, for example, is affected with palpitation, tremor, lipothymia, syncope, and with great variety in the extent, rapidity, and order or rhythm of its pulsations, we do not hesitate to ascribe these to morbific causes implicating, deranging its sensation. For whatever by its divers movements strives against irritations and troubles must necessarily be endowed with sensation" (Harvey, 1651, pp. 430-431).

Then follow examples of such changes involving no "sensation dependent upon the brain" in cases of disturbances in stomach, bowels, skin and uterus. Even though the brain is not involved

"yet neither are these to be presumed as happening without all consciousness. For that which is wholly without sense is not seen to be

74

irritated by any means, neither can it be stimulated to motion or action of any kind. Nor have we any other means of distinguishing between an animate and sentient thing and one that is dead and senseless than the motion excited by some other irritating cause or thing which as it incessantly follows, so does it also argue sensation" (p. 432).

The brain is conceived of as another sense, or "sensitive organ", i.e. the "sensorium" which examines the incoming representations of the external world mediated by the sensory systems:

"And this brain is like a sensitive root to which a variety of fibres tend, one of which sees, another hears, a third touches, and a fourth and a fifth smell and taste" (p. 432).

In addition to the order of sensation dependent on the brain is that of natural perception, which Harvey tries to describe:

"But as there are some actions and motion the government or direction of which is not dependent on the brain, and which are therefore called *natural*, so also is it to be concluded that there is a certain sense or form of touch which is not referred to the common sensorium, nor in any way communicated to the brain, so that we do not perceive by this sense that we feel; but as happens to those who are deranged in mind, or who are agitated to such a degree by violent passion that they feel no pain, and pay no regard to the impressions made on their senses, so must we believe it to be with this sense, which we therefore distinguish from the proper animal sense" (pp. 432-3).

Then comes the sentence quoted at the beginning of this chapter allowing the possession of this sense to lowly marine creatures and the sensitive plant. This "certain sense or form of touch" is "a genus of sensation different from sight, hearing, smell, taste and touch" (Temkin, 1964, p. 316). It is hard to see what more Harvey could do to describe the nature of this order of perception: whilst it is going on we cannot *enjoy* it, i.e. cannot *know* that we are perceiving in the way we know we are seeing or smelling or tasting because such enjoyment is a manifestation of the sensorium at work. This is not so say, of course, that we might not become consciously aware of the after-effects of some bodily changes consequent upon irritation (such as ingestion of a nauseating compound), that we cannot become aware that an act of natural perception has taken place, but that we cannot be aware of it *as such* taking place. We could strive with the hindsight provided by various doctrines of unconscious, co-conscious, "multi-channel" etc. mental functioning of the twentieth century to gloss Harvey's account, but it is difficult to see how such an attempt would illuminate it. Anyway in Harvey's own day a better answer to the question "what is natural perceiving *like?*" could be given than by saying "it's like seeing (or hearing or touching) something under such abnormal conditions (e.g. of emotional upheaval) that you don't know you are seeing (hearing, touching, etc.)". Maybe no better answer is possible today if one attempts to make the notion intelligible.

We have seen so far the doctrine of irritability, formulated by Haller as a physiological concept, is in its genesis a psychological one because it devolves upon the notion of natural perception. We are now in a position to see more precisely how it is important for plant psychology. It is important because behind Glisson and Harvey hovers the ghost of Plato, Plato the author of *Timaeus*.

Harvey knew his Galen, Glisson knew his Harvey and his Galen, and it was Galen who first proposed that there are bodily organs lacking nerves which are nonetheless capable of some kind of perception.

Hippocrates was the "founding father" of medicine, but it was Galen (A.D. 129 — ?199) who determined the nature of medical science (and physiology generally) in the Middle Ages and into the Renaissance. He respected Aristotle and venerated Plato, but accepted fully neither Plato's nor Aristotle's account of souls (Siegel, 1968). He did accept, however, Plato's theory of plant life.

On Galen's view there was a discharging faculty, named variously "propellant", "excretory" and "secretive" in every organism and in its parts. The parts attract the food they need, keeping it and altering or assimilating it and propelling that leftover. Natural organs (belonging mainly to the abdomen) were to be distinguished from psychic organs (endowed with sense perception and will). All organs, including the psychic, are natural in that they are alive and need veins and arteries. But the functions of the natural organs, being innate, can be lost only if those organs themselves are damaged. In contrast the psychic organs can lose their functions without being themselves damaged but having their communication with the brain intercepted, because they require nerves to furnish them with the means of sensation and movement. According to Galen "the stomach, uterus, and bladders possess certain inborn faculties which are retentive of their own proper qualities and eliminative of those that are foreign" (in Temkin, 1964, p. 315).

The questions arise as to how the natural organs function when they do not have the kind of sensation conveyed by nerves, and how is it that they can recognize their "own proper qualities". Galen's answer was to turn to Plato: the *Timaeus* tells us that plants possess a level of sensation which can distinguish between what is nourishing and what is not.

Galen, quoted by Temkin, writes of his hero Plato that

> "Hence Plato seems to me to speak rightly when he says that plants have sensation, namely of what is familiar and what is foreign, and thus may be suitably called living beings, since, at the same time, they are not without autonomous movement .... I am content .... to praise Plato, who calls his plants living things and says that they partake only of a discriminating perception of things familiar and foreign. If considered accurately, this seems to be of the category of what is pleasant and unpleasant. For on no other account can one say that they attract the familiar or assimilate it to themselves, except for the sake of enjoyment and the pleasure engendered in them. But .... for medicine it suffices to know this alone, that they attract the familiar, whereby they are also nourished, but reject the foreign. For ethical philosophy the exact inquiry into such things is even more useless, wherefore Plato did not have it in mind either" (Galen, in Temkin, 1964, p. 316).

Elsewhere Galen wrote

> "...we have shown that they (i.e. plants) possess a cognitive faculty for familiar substances, which nourish them, and for foreign substances which harm them. Hence they attract the familiar substances but turn away and reject the foreign. Therefore Plato said that the plants participate in a special genus of sensation, for it makes known what is familiar and what is foreign" (Galen, in Temkin, 1964, p. 316).

Thus for Galen in addition to the conscious perception of irritation, for which nerves are necessary, there is the irritation of the organ (e.g. stomach, uterus), i.e. its attempt to eliminate material it perceives to be harmful. The justification for this latter kind of perception comes from Plato's theory of the sentient plant soul.

Given the fact that the doctrine of irritability is originally a cognitive concept, moreover that its historical core is the Platonic vegetable soul, it is understandable that the later plant psychologists who were to use "irritability" for their own purposes might have claimed an historical right to do so, had they known their history. Although no longer invoked as a concept in its own right in the eighteenth century, natural perception had done its damage — irritability was for some not merely a vital principle but a cognitive one as well. For Haller they had no right to the concept, standing for him as it did in opposition to sensation, and limited to animal muscles. But Haller's efforts to purify the concept were in vain. To begin with, he had to contend with opposition to his views. For example Robert Whytt (1714-1766) argued that the basic distinction between irritability and sensibility left no room for phenomena such as reflex actions: Haller saw Whytt as an animist but was himself discountenanced by the arch-mechanist De La Mettrie (1709-1751) who used irritability as a concept to argue against the existence of a spiritual soul. Next, his views were modified by later workers. By the end of the eighteenth century irritability had become so broadened in meaning that it was seen as a general principle extending over all tissues, and not restricted to animal muscular fibre contractility. Vitalists claimed it as their own: for them irritability was a phenomenon which in principle was inexplicable by mechanical principles; botanists took it up, seeing irritability manifest in certain types of plant movements. As we shall see so did some of the plant psychologists, who argued from vegetable irritability to cognition. For them it might be said that irritability was the doctrine of the percipient vegetable soul "gone underground". The concept became a basic one in physiology, but one which was to continue to be difficult. There is nothing wrong with "irritability" if it is used to refer to certain unambiguously specified observable physiological phenomena, it being understood that it is only *naming* them and not *explaining* them. Botanists were not always able or willing to understand irritability in this way and as botany in the twentieth century progressed, there was a gradual abandonment of the term in plant physiology (see Morton, 1981, footnote 19, pp. 443-444).

Two natural philosophers who were quick to seize on the concept for the interests of botany were Charles Bonnet in Switzerland and Giovambatista Dal Covolo in Italy.

Bonnet's *The Contemplation of Nature* was published in Amsterdam in 1764 and appeared in English in 1766. A chapter on irritability in the second volume asks whether that phenomenon might be the particular character which will distinguish between vegetables and animals, Bonnet having so far failed to find such a distinguishing character. He says that irritability must not be confounded with sentience, they have nothing in common, nor must it be confounded with elasticity. A dry fibre may be very elastic but it is not irritable. Irritability constitutes the vital power in the animal. It has not yet been found in plants but we cannot be certain they do not have it, thus it is not clear that it is the elusive distinguishing character between animal and plants. Bonnet's logic here is faulty ("we cannot prove plants do *not* possess irritability"), but there is something else to be noted about his discussion. It is that he makes no reference to the sensitive plant as possibly being irritable, although he has mentioned it earlier in the book, nor does he permit an inference from plant irritability to plant cognition, having earlier in the book taken the possibility of vegetable cognition seriously.

Dal Covolo's *A Discourse Concerning the Irritability of Some Flowers* was also first published in 1764. The English translation was published in 1767. It was known by the middle of the century that the stamens and anthers of some flowers were capable of explosive movements. It was decided, following the work of Camerarius (1665-1721) which had demonstrated the sexual and reproductive function of pollen, that these movements helped in pollination. Dal Covolo's concern is to reveal the reactivity of filaments supporting the anthers of the small flowers ("floscules") of a relative of the star-thistle (a *centaurea*). When the "floscules" are touched they show their sensitivity to touch by bending or moving, and Dal Covolo discovered the mechanism of this to be the shortening of the filaments.

He concludes his description of the event by stating

"Thus have i represented this extraordinary motion of the floscules; but certainly none of the parts described have any intrinsic motive faculty; nor are they sensible of this motion" (Dal Covolo, 1767, p.27).

He can name the phenomenon but not explain it:

"Let me call this contracting power the irritability of flowers .... a very fit name, provided it is used to signify only a power which the mechanical writers themselves do not pretend to understand" (pp. 40-41).

Dal Covolo is clear that irritability does not involve sensation and that it is a name for the phenomenon described, but not an explanation of it. The phrase "a power which the mechanical writers themselves do not pretend to understand" does not rule out the possibility that in time they will be able to understand it.

From Bonnet and Dal Covolo on, the word "irritability" is to be found often in discussion of plant and flower movements, but it must be examined closely whenever it occurs.

Thus it can be concluded that Plato's doctrine of the cognitive vegetable soul was revived in the seventeenth century. The revival was not a self-conscious one — that part of the *Timaeus* dealing with the concept was unknown at first hand in the Middle Ages and was irrelevant to the burgeoning Neoplatonism of the Renaissance. In Chapter 3 the "sleeper" metaphor was used: the concept named in the old metaphysical term as a certain sort of "soul" disappeared, but was reawakened under new names: "natural perception" and "irritability". There is a direct line of influence from Plato to Galen to Harvey to Glisson. Haller's lack of success in purifying "irritability" by getting rid of its vitalist connotations saw the flourishing of the mentalist tradition in plant psychology.

CHAPTER 5

Analogy and new plant wonders: Mentalism gathers momentum, the emergence of instinctivism

5.1 *The Argument from Analogy*

We are now approaching the stage where it will be necessary to examine a little more critically the formal bases of the arguments of the plant psychologists because they themselves begin to pay more attention to formal defence of their claims. Discussion of the concept of irritability has helped prepare the way for this, and now we may take up the central argument of the mentalist tradition: the argument from analogy between animals and plants. The basic line is that there is a continuous chain or scale being from the highest of the creatures (e.g. man) through to the lowest (e.g. single-celled organisms); if we find in some organisms that certain behaviour and/or structures are sufficient to indicate mentality then organisms elsewhere in the hierarchy of being showing analogous behaviour/structure could be presumed to possess mentality.

This theme is dealt with in two useful historical sources: Francois Delaporte's *Nature's Second Kingdom: Explorations of Vegetality in the Eighteenth Century* (Delaporte 1982, original French 1979) and Philip

C. Ritterbush's *Overtures to Biology: The Speculations of Eighteenth-Century Naturalists* (Ritterbush, 1964).

Delaporte's fourth chapter ("Movement") is of relevance for us because it mentions Charles Bonnet, Thomas Percival, James Tupper and Erasmus Darwin, giving also an account of some of their critics. Amongst Delaporte's points is a concern to disarm any critics who might say that we find in the seventeenth century an interest in plant/animal analogies: he says that such an interest then applies "only to the motions of the sensitive plant, a curiosity" (Delaporte, 1982, Note 2, p.223), and cites Webster (1966) on the history of plant sensitivity in the seventeenth century. This is unfair to Webster, because Webster does not claim that the sensitive plant was the *only* one of interest then. Webster mentions *inter alia* Henry Power, Thomas Browne and Martin Lister. We have seen that they were all interested in plants which had highly irritable structures in their flowers, and that Pierre Borel had begun investigation of these. It is not true that, apart from the curious aberration of the sensitive plant, that the seventeenth century had no interest in plant/animal analogies.

Ritterbush's *Overtures to Biology* is very useful for discussion of the eighteenth century, especially its fourth chapter ("The triumph of botanical analogy"). It contains a section on the "super-life of plants" (pp. 141-157) which overlaps considerably, but not exactly, with the late eighteenth century and early nineteenth century material in this monograph. Ritterbush's interests here are broader, being concerned generally with those botanists and natural philosophers who were so ensnared by the web of analogy to make extravagant claims for plant life; we are more interested in those amongst the extravagant set who specifically make psychological claims for plants. For example Ritterbush is interested in a writer who might make a great deal of plant irritability, using analogies between plants and certain animals, but that writer is of interest here only if he goes on to argue from irritability to sentience.

No attempt will be made to paraphrase Ritterbush, but his general theses warrant mention. There are, he says, two recurring themes in eighteenth century natural history: (1) the nature and power of electricity, (2) the problem of the explanation of the life of plants. On the latter theme he writes

"Fluids circulated within them as in animals. The discovery that plants were differentiated into sexes invited other analogies with animals. Plants were seen to move their leaves and flowers, and some varieties even to react suddenly to the touch. Might not plants then feel and perhaps even think, feel emotions of love, and change into animals and back again?" (Ritterbush, 1964, pp. vii-viii).

Ritterbush defines "the idea of botanical analogy" as the notion that "plants were analogous to animals because of their close proximity in the scheme of nature" (p. 1).

"Many eighteenth century writers chose to dwell upon the similarities between plants and animals until the recital of analogies became an end in itself. Drawing analogies throughout nature gave rise to the satisfaction of creating comprehensive explanations, rewarding those who overlooked the differences between plants and animals in order to dwell upon their similarities" (p. 57).

The doctrines that natural beings can be ranked on a continuous scale from "highest" to "lowest" in respect of some basic property or set of properties, and that there can be found in plants structures analogous to those in animals (e.g. nerves, a blood system, heart, etc.) are both ancient doctrines, and they have been expressed in a variety of forms. The scale or chain of being to the Greeks was not then an *evolutionary* ranking. Although Anaximander and Empedocles both had conceptions of evolution Aristotle and Theophrastus did not; Morton's history notes that "however deep and fluctuating the class conflicts in fourth-century Greece, the main classes were now firmly established, and this relative stabilisation of social structure was projected by Aristotle and Theophrastus into biology, where evolution was replaced by the conception of a scale of nature, a hierarchy of natural classes or kingdoms" (Morton, 1981, p.42). Some of the more elaborate rankings of the Christian era began with the inanimate world, passing through classes such as the mineral kingdom, progressing to the animate world of creation (plants and animals) and finishing in the supernatural kingdom of the angels and the deity. The fact of continuity rather discrete gaps between classes at different levels (at least in beings in the kingdom of animate creation) was emphasised by the existence of forms which seemed to be intermediate, or at any rate posed a problem in allocation to one level rather than the next. This was especially the case with the animal/plant distinction which puzzled many writers from Aristotle onwards. The job of deciding whether certain marine organisms (corals, sponges, diverse minute swimming and sessile creatures, "polyps", etc.) were animals, plants, both animal and plant, or sometime animal and sometime plant, was one which had no quick ending, and the fact of this difficulty made it all the more plausible to draw plant-animal analogies. The term "polyp" was coined in the eighteenth century, and became a source of zoological confusion because it covered a variety of different water-dwelling (mostly marine) invertebrates (Schiller,

1974). It included the hydra, whose ability to regenerate complete new organisms from the several parts of a single organism, fuelled the mechanism vs. vitalism debate in eighteenth century zoology.

The general problem of how to draw the line between animals and plants in the scale of being is well illustrated in its eighteenth century context in Buffon's *Natural History*. Georges-Louis Leclerc, Count de Buffon (1707-1788), famed as the first man of his era to write a natural history which was not only encyclopaedic in scope but also popular in style (he was the most widely read author on science of his day), brought out his first volumes in 1749. Buffon could find no absolute or necessary differences between plants and animals, the links of the chain of being were "imperceptible". Of particular interest to us is his discussion of whether the presence of sensation could be used as a differential criterion between plants and animals. This quotation comes from the first English translation of 1775:

" A more essential difference might be drawn from the faculty of sensation which belongs to animals, and which vegetables seems to be deprived of; but this faculty includes such a number of ideas, that we ought not to mention the word before we analyse it: for if by sensation we understand only a motion, occasioned by a check or resistance, we shall find the *sensitive* plant is capable of this kind of sensation, as well as animals: if, on the contrary, we would have it signify to apprehend and compare preceptions, we are sure the animals possess this faculty; and if we allow it to dogs, elephants, *etc.* whose actions seems to result from the same causes as ours, we shall refuse it to an infinite number of other animals, and especially to those which seem to be motionless. If we could give to oysters, for example, the same faculty of sensation as to dogs, but in an inferior degree, why should we not allow it to vegetables in a still lesser degree: this difference between animals and vegetables is not only not general but even not well decided"(Buffon, 1775, vol. 4, pp. 109-110).

The above passage was written before Bonnet's *Contemplation of Nature*, although the latter was made available to English readers before the former was. Whereas Buffon was content to let his puzzle remain as it was, his contemporary, Bonnet, as the previous chapter stated, felt that he had to give a verdict on plant sensation.

Because Charles Bonnet (1720-1793) was considered to be one of the great natural philosophers of his day, it is therefore meet, especially because Ritterbush provides a detailed general account of the relevant biological background, to proceed by looking a little closely at how Bonnet handled the plant-animal analogy.

We have seen already how Bonnet in *The Contemplation of Nature* uses the misapplied logic of "one cannot prove a negative" to argue that it cannot be demonstrated that plants do *not* possess irritability. He also argues that it cannot be demonstrated that they are *not* "endowed with a soul capable of *feeling*" (Bonnet, 1766, vol. II, p.47).

"Feeling" is defined as a hedonistic construct, it is either agreeable or disagreeable. It is impossible to give a definite dividing line between animals and plants and

"We judge the existence of feeling in an organized body, either by the conformity or analogy of its organs with ours, or by the conformity or analogy we observe between the motions it affords in certain circumstances, and those we should exhibit were we placed in the same circumstances. The first method of judging is pretty certain; it is very probable that an organized body which has eyes, ears and a nose, is endued with the same sensations which these senses excite in us.

The second method of judging seems less certain, or less free from ambiguity; we are often apt to transfer to other beings those sensations which are peculiar to ourselves" (Vol. II, p. 50).

He expresses his sympathy with Plato when he asks of plants "did not that philosopher who defined them rooted animals, discourse in a very rational manner?" (Vol. II. p. 51).

Bonnet's reference to our readiness to admit that other beings who are constituted corporeally as we ourselves are (possessing eyes, ears, etc.) possess the same kind of mental life as we do calls to mind the limiting case of the philosophical "problem of other minds". Without worrying whether other animals such as horses, dogs and parrots (let alone plants) have minds how can we be sure that other human beings have minds? How can I be sure that *I* am not the only person in the world possessed of a mental life and that other people are not merely unconscious automata, simulacra of sensate humans? If all I can do is to observe their behaviour systematically to see whether they act as do I, a sensate being, then, to follow Bonnet, I will be less certain than I might want that they are my fellows psychologically. But Bonnet's concern here is with plants, not people. What if we conclude from observing plants that they show no sign of feeling, that their behaviour is purely mechanical?

Bonnet does not like this conclusion. Doubts arise, especially after we observe the behaviour of inferior animals, for example creatures which regenerate themselves into new wholes from divided parts, creatures to which we scarcely hesitate to attribute sensation.

"We have already remarked, that the expression of feeling is relative to the organs which manifest it. Plants are utterly unable to make us acquainted with their feeling; this sensation is perhaps extremely weak, without will and without desire, since their inability to manifest it to us proceeds from their organization, and that there is room to think the degree of spiritual perfection corresponds to the degree of corporeal perfection.

Be this as it may, by depriving plants of feeling, we can cause nature to take a leap, without assigning the cause; we see feeling gradually decrease from the man to the sea-nettle or muscle; and we persuade ourselves that it stops there, on considering these least animals as the least perfect. But perhaps there may be many degrees between the feeling of the muscle and that of the plant. There may possibly be still more between the most sensible plant and that which is less so. The gradations we observe everywhere should convince us of this philosophy; the new degree of beauty it seems to add to the system of the world, and the pleasure there is in multiplying sensible beings, ought to contribute still farther to induce us to admit it" (Vol. II, p. 51).

Perhaps then if we do attribute minds to other persons (assuming that in the first place we attribute mind to ourselves) then we are drawn inexorably to attributing minds to other animal species and to plants. Further, if we follow Bonnet, we can justify this not only in terms of our own pleasure but on aesthetic grounds as well. Bonnet's speculation that plant sensation might be extremely weak, without will or desire, is reminiscent of Plato's account of the plant soul, but there is in these accounts at least a conative core, a hedonistic one: elemental pleasurable sensations entailing striving for (say food) and striving against (say organic irritation). Bonnet's reference to the "most sensible plant" should be seen in the context of his placing mimosa in the next class above ordinary plants in his elaborate scheme of the chain of being.

Bonnet urges a fresh outlook on the question:

"Plants present us with some circumstances which seem to indicate that they have feeling; but I don't know whether we are in a proper situation to observe them, or whether the strong persuasion we have so long entertained of their being insensible, will permit us to judge rightly of them. In order to do this, we must be a *carte blanche* on the question, and bring plants to a new trial, both more important and more exempt from prejudices. An inhabitant of the moon, who has the same senses and the same share of understanding with ourselves, but who is not prepossessed conceiving the insensibility of plants is the philosopher we are seeking for" (Vol. II, p. 52).

If such a lunar philosopher were to come there would be a range of plant observations he could make. He would note that if a seedling were planted upside-down the roots and leaves would reverse their direction of growth so that the roots now went into the earth and the leaves would be appropriately re-orientated. He would note by dint of experiment that the roots gravitate towards sources of nourishment and moisture, and that leaves and flowers orient or open themselves, as the case may be, in various ways according to species. Some, shut in the philosopher's closet or cellar would direct their angle of growth towards a window or air-holes, a phenomenon which had been demonstrated experimentally originally by Sir Thomas Browne and repeated by Robert Sharrock in the preceding century ("All plants have a peculiar delight in the air" (Sharrock, 1660, p. 41)). But the observation which would make him terminate his researches is "the *phaenomena* of the *sensitive,* its various motions, the quickness with which it contracts itself on the approach of the hand" (Vol. II, p. 56).

Having already investigated the behaviour of the lowest animals, especially those such as the pond hydra which reproduce from "slips" (in the gardener's sense of the word) will he now find in favour of feeling in plants or will he suspend his judgement? Bonnet inclines to the former, but

> "it will be said, your philosopher might know that it is easy to explain mechanically all these facts, which seem to prove him the sensibility of plants .... This is true, and our philosopher knows it very well; but he likewise knows that some have undertaken to explain mechanically all the actions of animals, not only those which demonstrate they have feeling, but also those that seem to prove they are endued with a certain degree of understanding. Extraordinary procedure this of the human mind! Whilst some philosophers attempt to ennoble plants by raising them to the rank of sensible beings, others endeavour to debase animals by reducing them to the rank of mere machines" (Vol. II, pp. 56-57).

Thus the lunar philosopher has a choice of siding with Plato or Descartes: if he is offended by the contention that the brutes are mere machines then his sympathies may be with the author of *Timaeus.*

Bonnet himself does not actually grasp the nettle, however (perhaps the expression here should be "does not actualy ennoble the nettle"). His conclusion is uncertain: "I have not pretended to prove that plants are *sensible*; but I would shew that it has not hitherto been proved that they are not so" (Vol. II, p. 57).

Bonnet is quoted here at some length in order to convey the

method and atmosphere of the way that analogical reasoning was used to argue for vegetable sentience. After Bonnet a long list of successors followed, and, to anticipate nineteenth century events, we find considerable debate about the strengths and weaknesses of the analogical method. By the way, there is no claim that Bonnet was the first to use the analogical argument for plant sensibility (note, e.g. Lister's use of it in the long title of his 1673 paper) but Bonnet was one of the first of the prominent eighteenth century thinkers who employed it in more than a sketchy fashion.

There are three points concerning argument from analogy generally about which there should be no disagreement. Analogy may be suggestive, but it is not compelling:

(1)   It is formally (logically) invalid. Analogy is not a matter of mere direct resemblance. The argument arises when two things which are alike in some respect(s) are taken thereby to be alike in some other respect(s). For example a brain and a root are not in themselves alike, but respectively they bear the same relation to the animal and its obtaining nourishment on the one hand, and to the plant and its obtaining nourishment on the other. Therefore it is claimed that the brain and the root are in some sense identical.

This can be expressed thus: if it is said that "all roots are enablers of some organisms to obtain nourishment" and "all brains are enablers of some organisms to obtain nourishment" then obviously it would be fallacious to conclude "therefore all roots are brains". The middle term, "enablers of some organisms to obtain nourishment" is undistributed.

(2)   It is psychologically tempting to argue analogically, especially where there is considerable emotional investment in the case being argued. William Smellie's expression, "the alluring seductions of analogical reasoning" is a good one (Smellie, 1790, Vol.I, p. 245).

(3)   Although the logical argument from analogy is invalid and analogical observations can be misleading, they can also at times be useful, suggesting fruitful new lines of enquiry or hypotheses. The philosophy of science literature contains some well known examples, but an example of present interest comes from Morton's text. Nehemiah Grew's *Anatomy of Plants* (1682) was the first publication to suggest that stamens and pollen in flowers correspond to the male reproductive organ and semen in animals. Morton notes that "some of Grew's reasons were rather obscure .... but one was the analogy between hermaphrodite plants and snails. Hermaphroditism had recently been established in snails by J.J. Harder of Basle, and this argument from zoology had a big effect on botanists" (Morton, 1981, p. 213).

5.2 *Two New Plants*

In the second half of the eighteenth century two new plants arrived in Western Europe, plants which, as the mimosa had, were to attract the analogical propensities of those disposed to plant psychology.

The first is probably the most striking of all the generally sensitive plants, not only because of its marked movements but because it is insectivorous as well. This is the Venus fly-trap, (*Dionaea muscipula*). It appears that news of it first reached the Old World in a letter from

Arthur Dobbs, former Governor of North Carolina, to the British botanist Peter Collinson in 1759 (Harper, 1958, p. 494).

John Ellis of London was described by Linnaeus as "a bright star of natural history" (Desmond, 1977, p. 208). Amongst his achievements was the demonstration that corals and corallines are animals, not plants. In 1768 William Young of Philadelphia sent him some live specimens of the plant which grew in a restricted range in North Carolina. Ellis sent Linnaeus a detailed description of it and published the letter in 1770. The publication gives a beautifully engraved plate of the plant; accompanying the drawing is the description "Each leaf is a miniature figure of a Rat-trap with teeth". Part of Ellis's account to Linnaeus consists of a somewhat Gothic passage:

"You have seen the Mimosa; or Sensitive Plants, close their leaves, and bend their joints, upon the least touch: and this has astonished you; but no end or design of nature has yet appeared to you from these surprising motions; they soon recover themselves again, and their leaves are expanded as before.

But the plant, of which I now inclose you an exact figure, with a specimen of its leaves and blossoms, shews, that nature may have some view towards its *nourishment*, in forming the upper joint of its leaf like a *machine* to catch food: upon the middle of this lies the bait for the unhappy insect that becomes its prey. Many minute red glands, that cover its inner surface, and which perhaps discharge sweet liquor, tempt the poor animal to taste them: and the instant these tender parts are irritated by its feet, the two lobes rise up, grasp it fast, lock the rows of spines together, and squeeze it to death. And, further, lest the strong efforts for life, in the creature thus taken, should serve to disengage it; three small erect spines are fixed near the middle of each lobe, among the glands, that effectually put an end to all its struggles. Nor do the lobes ever open again, while the dead animal continues there. But it is nevertheless certain, that the plant cannot distinguish an animal, from a vegetable or mineral substance; for if we introduce a straw or a pin between the lobes, it will grasp it full as fast as if it was an insect" (Ellis, 1770, p. 37).

The first insectivorous plant to appear in the plant psychology literature was the common English sundew, a *drosera*. The droseras are virtually world wide in range, unlike their notorious relative, *dionaea*. Ellis's speculation that the Venus fly-trap's prey was a source of nourishment turned out to be correct, but this was not proven until many years later, and was a contentious issue until then.

The second new plant to provide a weapon in the plant psychologists' armamentarium came from India and was described by George Bell in 1777. It is a legume (*Desmodium gyrans*) which was known earlier mainly as the *Hedysarum*, sometimes by its native name, *burrhum chundalli*. Its popular name now is the "telegraph plant", after the semaphore-type signalling telegraph: by day, if the temperature is not below 72° F the two small lateral leaflets of each leaf describe steady elliptical orbits. By night the plant "sleeps". Smellie, in 1790, was astonished by it: the

"moving plant, or hedysarum movens, furnished the most astonishing example of vegetable motion .... Its movements are not excited by the contact of external bodies, but solely by the influence of the sun's rays. The motions of this plant are confined to the leaves, which are supported by long flexible footstalks. When the sun shines, the leaves move briskly in every direction. Their general motion, however, is upward and downward: But they not infrequently turn almost round; and then their footstalks are evidently twisted. These motions go on incessantly as long as the heat of the sun continues: But they cease during the night, and when the weather is cold and cloudy. Out wonder is excited by the rapidity and constancy of the movements peculiar to this plant.

The frequency, however, of similar movements in other plants, renders it probable that the leaves of all vegetables move, or are agitated by the rays of the sun, though many of these movements are too slow for our perception" (Smellie, 1790, p. 5).

The telegraph plant has attracted less attention than have the mimosa and dionaea (to the modern dynamic psychologist, the *Venus fly-trap* would neatly "lock into" unconscious archaic phantasies), but its own special attraction is its apparent spontaneity. To the plant psychologist its movements suggest a faculty of volition: if the day is warm enough it will decide to rotate its leaflets.

5.3 *The Varying Limits of Analogy*

Two well known Scots physicians, both M.D.'s of the University of Edinburgh, provide an interesting contrast in the extent to which the plant-animal analogy was taken. One baulked at the notion of vegetable mind, the other accepted it.

Alexander Hunter (1729-1809) declared his method in the title of his fourth essay in the collection *Georgical Essays* published in London in 1770. The title of the essay is *"On Vegetation, and the analogy between plants and animals"*. He draws common analogies between plant and animal parts, for example referring to the body or "placenta" of a bean, and shows his Aristotelian heritage in passages such as:

"Vegetables are placed in a middle degree between animals and minerals. They are superior to minerals, in having organized parts; but inferior to animals, in being destitute of sensation" (Hunter, 1770, p. 79).

"From the moment that the seed is lodged in its parent earth, the vegetative soul begins its operations, and, in one continued miracle, proves the wisdom and bounty of an almighty providence" (p. 95).

At one point Hunter makes a reference to "instinct" in connection with plants. Of the plant root he writes:

"By a kind of principle, which seems to carry with it some appearance of instinct, it seeks a passage downwards, and fixes itself into the soul. .... These leaves take a contrary direction to the root. Influenced by the same miraculous instinct, if I may be allowed the expression, they seek a passage upward .... " (pp. 89-90).

The purposivistic language ("they seek" etc.) should be taken as everyday figures of speech. It is not to be taken literally, but should be read as nothing more than the expression of Aristotelian teleology in action.

Whereas Hunter was enticed by the blandishments of analogy George Bell (1755-1784) was indeed seduced. His *De Physiologia Plantarum* (his inaugural dissertation for the M.D. degree) was published in Latin in 1777, in Edinburgh. He died in Manchester in 1785, and as part of the local Literary and Philosophical Society's tribute to him it was published in that year in English translation by James Currie.

After listing many similarities and differences between animals and plants the *Physiologia* declares

"The chain (of being — T. McM.) is continued between vegetables and animals. Both have the power of propagating their species, and their modes of procreation are similar. In the lower classes of animals, the powers of sense and motion are very indistinct. The coral and the water polypus adhere to rocks, as plants to the earth; and, like these, die on being severed from the place where they grew. There are likewise plants, which in many things resemble animals. The Burrham Chundalli, lately brought from the *East Indies*, possesses a living principle, which discovers itself in the spontaneous, and almost constant motion of its leaves. The *Sensitiva Mimosa*, and *Muscipula Dionaea*, show wonderful activity on the slightest impressions, and take the flies and other insects prisoners, by the contraction of their leaves. That these plants *live*, will be granted, but I suspect that they likewise *feel*. I doubt whether we are right, in confining the capacity of pleasure and pain to the animal kingdom. This I may affirm, that some circumstances, common to the generation of plants and animals, and many similarities in their functions and structure, would lead us to the opinion, that sensation likewise is bestowed on both. It is vain to attempt to establish absolute rules, by which plants may be distinguished from animals, in every case whatsoever. There are animals, which grow to a spot, and , like plants, are nourished by the pores of the skin. And there are plants, which surpass some animals in vital power, and, perhaps, in sensation" (Bell, 1785, pp. 417-8).

A footnote by Currie points out that Bell's botany professor at Edinburgh, Dr. Hope, spoke of his student with esteem but disapproved of his view that plants "possess feeling, or perception". Bell evidently believed that the mimosa was insectivorous, but perhaps the

Latin or the translation is loose in expression here. John Hope's botanical interests included the study of plant movements. As well as the
sleep movements of *oxalis* and *trifolium* (clover), the leaf movements
of *mimosa,* he noted the sudden movement of stamens in *berberis*
(barberry), *parietaria* (pellitory) and *urtica* (nettles). He showed his
students experiments on the interaction of gravity and light in the
induction of growth curvature in plants. He did not publish these
and it was not until nearly a century later that similar studies were
published (Morton, 1986, p.22).

5.4   *The Doctrine of Plant Instincts*

With Alexander Hunter's observation that the downward movements of plant roots might seem to suggest the appearance of
instinct we might pause to look directly at the instinct concept.
From a contemporary standpoint one can see that "instinct" is
such a loose term in biology and psychology, having been used in
a number of quite different senses, that the frequent calls for its
abolition from the scientific vocabulary are understandable. The
term persists, however, and thus the context of its usage must be
examined before a meaning of it is read. In the plant psychology
literature "instinct" tends to be used unambiguously; even for post
eighteenth-century writers it has the same broad meaning as it did
for those in that century.

Hunter's usage of the term conforms to the notion of "instinct" as
a tendency or propensity, mainly but not exclusively in lower species,
to perform actions which would appear to be rational, consciously

purposive, but which in fact are quite "blind". This conception of instinct as an explanatory category began to gain currency in the eighteenth century and became more widely used in the nineteenth. It was defined pithily by the philosopher Sir William Hamilton: "An Instinct is an agent which performs blindly and ignorantly a work of intelligence and knowledge" (Hamilton, 1849, p. 761).

Hunter allows only the "appearance" of an instinct in plants, but the suggestion of plant instinct was not new then. It occurred a century earlier in the treatise, not by a naturalist, but by a lawyer, Sir Matthew Hale, a one time Chief Justice of England who had presided at trials of witches. In *The Primitive Origin of Mankind, Considered and Examined According to the Light of Nature* (1677) Hale argues that there are naturalistic grounds for holding the Book of Genesis story of the origin of mankind to be true. In the course of his exposition of the nature of creation there is a lucubration on the advantages that animals enjoy over plants:

"The third superadded advantage of Animals is their instincts. It is true, Vegetables have their instincts radicated in their nature .... yea even things Inanimate have certain simple Instincts, as in the motions of ascent of light bodies, and descent of heavy bodies: But the instincts of animals are sensible instincts of a more noble kind and nature than those of vegetables, and such as seem to favour more of an active principle; as sagacity of Brutes in taking their prey, defending themselves .... " etc. (Hale, 1677, pp. 47-48).

Hale allows even inanimate objects to have instincts, and his general conception of instinct is in line with Hunter's. Plants, for Hale, have no "real and true sense", but they do have instincts. Plant instincts have no cognitive component, whereas animal ones are "sensible", i.e. involve sensory processes in the animals.

Hale was not the first writer in English to use the word "instinct", or even to predicate it of plants. Half a century earlier Edward Herbert (Lord Herbert of Cherbury, 1583-1648) published his treatise *De Veritate* (*On Truth*), which is claimed to be the first purely metaphysical work by an Englishman. In it is presented a rationalist faculty psychology of man (later to be challenged by Locke with his empiricist epistemology). To Herbert, man's reason and senses are secondary sources of knowledge, secondary to the primary faculty of Natural Instinct. Natural Instinct is not merely the prerogative of man, it is pervasive in Nature, permeating humans, brutes, plants, "elements" and "minerals". The goal of Natural Instinct is self-preservation of the individual or species, in whatever form is appropriate to the vehicle of its expression — it "promotes similar functions" throughout the elements, minerals, plants and animals in an identical form according to the variety of species" (Herbert, 1624, p. 119). Plants (and inanimate things) have only the faculty Natural Instinct. In human psychology it is the source of innate pre-rational intuitive knowledge, it is prior to the knowledge of the senses and the intellect: " .... it must be remembered that it is the nature of "natural" instinct to fulfil itself irrationally, that is to say without foresight. For the elements, minerals and vegetables, which give no evidence of foresight or reason, possess knowledge peculiarly suited to their own preservation" (Herbert, 1624, p. 120). Natural processes, then, under the prime faculty of Natural Instinct, are manifestations of an unfolding plan, a "whole future design" (p. 146).

Hamilton names Cicero and two of Herbert's contemporaries,

Scaliger and Francis Bacon, as authors who used "instinct", and provides a list of other seventeenth and eighteenth century philosophers who did so (Hamilton, 1849, Note A, section v.3, pp. 760-761).

There is a continuity between Herbert's conception of instinct and later eighteenth and nineteenth century ones in that they are teleological, the goal of self-preservation of the vehicle (man, animal, plant) being central to them. They denote innate, species-universal, non-rational activities "designed" to a goal. By the nineteenth century, however, "instinct" had come to be narrowed in its focus, no longer was "instinct" a cosmic metaphysical principle, as it was for Herbert, but a generic name for a plurality of particular explanatory principles peculiar to the *animate world*, very often exclusively to the animal kingdom, i.e. animals (and, in some accounts plants) possess *instincts*, rather than being the carriers of an extrinsic single Instinct. Hale's notion of a number of instincts predicable of both the animate and inanimate world stands between Herbert's monism and biological pluralism. It should be noted here, however, that in Herbert's account of human psychology, there is a plurality of faculties, in fact an infinite number, at work in us individually, but that aspect of his thinking is beyond the present scope.

It is clear then, to anticipate some future instinct theorists as well as to draw a conclusion from those already mentioned, that the conception of instinct we have been outlining is Aristotelian even though the Greeks had no word "instinct". The notion of the immanence of design in natural processes, of the full description of any natural phenomenon necessarily involving the description of some "unfolding" to an end, is the Aristotelian world-outlook. "Instinct" as a biological category in the eighteenth century, has become the new name for the monistic vital principle, which, to re-quote Pagel's neatly expressed summary, saw the individual unit as "being alive by virtue of a disposal of matter according to a specific plan; it takes place through the inseparable union with a *form*, that is to say, a schedule that leads the individual to perfection in development, growth, function or arrival of a destined end" (Pagel, 1969, p. 21). Herbert's cosmic "Natural Instinct", is as the philosopher Sorley stated a century ago "Natural Instinct is .... simply the Aristotelian *nous* or intellect" (Sorley, 1894, p. 501).

I think it is fair to suggest that the specific "instincts", the teleological principles performing "blindly and ignorantly a work of intelligence and knowledge", as Hamilton put it, which have been claimed to be explanatory biological categories since the eighteenth century, are really Aristotle's vegetable souls transformed. As talk of "souls" in natural philosophy declined, so did talk of "instincts" increase, and one cannot help but see the instincts doing the job in post-eighteenth century biology that the vegetable soul did in earlier eras. Here an earlier injunction should be repeated: there are in modern comparative psychology and ethology a variety of accounts of "instincts" and they are not all covered necessarily by the preceding comments.

Often the teleological conception of instinct has with its conceptual luggage not just the Aristotelian heritage, but a Platonic one as well. This is seen in those writers who say not merely that nature is suffused (immanent) with design as self-contained, but that, rather, it is the *creation* of a Designer of Planner who transcends it. We have a dualism of the kind expressed by Plato in the *Timaeus* when he talked of the "demi-urge" creating the world. The Neoplatonists, especially after the Church Fathers tried to weld Aristotelian and Platonic philosophy with

Christianity, sought in natural phenomena *marks* or *signs* evidencing a Designing Intelligence existing outside of creation. In the phenomena of instincts a number of writers believed they saw such marks. For Alexander Hunter, for example, instincts do not show purpose which is immanent in behaviour itself, but the purpose of a higher Mind or Planner: miracle-working almighty Providence. Clearly Hunter was no friend intellectually of his fellow Scot David Hume. Even though, to quote the early nineteenth century cleric and naturalist, the Reverend William Kirby, "it is doubtful whether the ancients had any distinct idea of that impulse upon animals, urging them necessarily to certain actions, which modern writers have denominated *instinct*" (Kirby, 1835, p. 222), it can be seen that the core of the concept of instinct which concerns us exists in the ancient world.

We have now introduced the second major species of plant psychologists, the Instinctivists. They are not necessarily independent of the Mentalists, indeed, we shall find writers talking happily both of plant sentience and instincts, but we have yet to see the Mentalist tradition at its zenith — the second half of the eighteenth century.

CHAPTER 6

The golden age of plant psychology

6.1   *Introduction*

The last two decades of the eighteenth century and the early years of the nineteenth saw the golden age of the Platonic mentalist tradition. The context of this tradition has been described: the phenomenon of vegetable irritability had been taken by some to be either itself a cognitive concept, or, if it was not itself cognitive, to be often associated with the occurrence of cognition. Its cognitivist interpretation in terms of natural perception, a concept claiming there to be a physiological order of sentience independent of brains and nervous systems, went back to Plato's concept of the sentient plant soul. These, together with a fourth concept, the doctrine of the chain of being, provided the theoretical backgrond for the interpretation of certain plant movements, some of which were modern marvels, in terms of vegetable mentality. There were several educated, respected, privileged and influential writers who were able in an articulate fashion to bring together the phenomena of vegetable "irritability" and "spontaneity" and an increasing mass of analogical observations to argue for psychological capacities in plants. In addition to George Bell, discussed in Section 5.3, there is another student of Professor Hope of Edinburgh, Thomas Percival. Percival had at Warrington Academy been a pupil of Joseph

Priestley, who was a friend of Erasmus Darwin. Darwin and Priestly were members of the Lunar Society of Birmingham, a pioneering group of Midlands gentlemen interested in natural philosophy and technology, who used to meet on the Monday closest to the full moon; Percival and Bell founded the renowned Manchester Literary and Philosophical Society, Darwin and Priestley being made honorary members of it as was Richard Watson. Thus Priestley, Bell, Percival, Watson and Darwin all had some connection with the flourishing natural philosophy of the English midlands in the second half of the Eighteenth Century, but it should be pointed out that they were few among the number of those provincial natural philosophers. In addition to these there was the surgeon and Fellow of the Linnaean Society, James Tupper. Percival, Watson, Darwin and Tupper should be singled out as the luminaries of this period of plant psychology.

6.2 *Thomas Percival*

Thomas Percival M.D. (1740-1804) was, with George Bell, a founder of the Manchester Literary and Philosophical Society in 1781. Having studied medicine at the Universities of Edinburgh and Leyden, he was not only a practising physician, but also wrote many essays on medical, experimental and humanitarian topics. At the time he was the youngest man to be elected to the Royal Society. One of Percival's friends was his former teacher, that turbulent Unitarian cleric, the Reverend Doctor Joseph Priestley, known best today as the (or a?) discoverer of oxygen. Indeed, Priestley's researches on oxygen were assisted by Percival's experimental demonstration that plant growth was enhanced by an atmosphere of carbon dioxide. Priestley, it should be noted, in 1775 in a study supporting Hartley's theory of mind, had made in his introduction a passing reference to the possibility of what would now be called a materialist theory of mind, noting baldly that "this hypothesis is rather favourable to the notion of such organical systems as plants having some degree of sensation. But at this a benevolent mind will rather rejoice than repine" (1775, p. xx).

In 1784 Percival presented to his Mancunian discussion circle the *Speculations on the Perceptive Power of Vegetables*. The essay was said by his son to "have attracted some attention, as a philosophical attempt to illustrate an ingenious but fanciful hypothesis" (Edward Percival, 1807, p. lxxiii). Percival himself described it as a *jeu d'esprit*, but evidently took it sufficiently seriously to have it published independently in 1785 (Percival, 1785 (a)) in addition to its publication in the Society's *Memoirs* that year (Percival 1785 (b)). It appears in the same volume of the memoirs as does the translation of Bell's essay.

Percival declares his aim to be to show that plants, "like animals, are endowed with powers, both of perception and enjoyment" (1785 (b), p. 115), and this is to be done by the systematic drawing of analogies of several types given the existence of "the scale of beings". The influence of Bonnet is apparent.

The first analogical basis is that of structure. Plants and animals have a structural similarity (e.g. cellular membranes, aligneous or bony substance protecting a pith or marrow) which is not found in inanimate matter. They must therefore be ascribed a "living principle" which in turn implies some degree of perceptivity. Perceptivity entails the capacity for enjoyment, which, even if lowly, will produce an increase in the aggregate of happiness. This concern with the amount of happiness, quantitive hedonism, calls to mind the utilitarianism which was "in the air" then.

Instinct, which Hunter said plants *seemed* to have, is declared unhesitatingly to exist in plants. Percival's definition is

"INSTINCT is a propensity, or movement to seek, without deliberation, what is agreeable to the particular nature; and to avoid what is incongruous or hurtful. It is a practical power, which requires no previous knowledge or experience; and which pursues a present or future good, without any definite ideas or foresight; and often, with very faint degrees of consciousness" (1785 (b), p. 117).

His concept of instinct is teleological. Although instincts are innate faculties there is no claim of any *a priori* knowledge being brought to bear on their manifestation, in fact, the possibility of innate knowledge is denied. Examples of instinct at work in animals are the suckling of the new-born calf and the swimming motions of a duckling hatched at a distance from water by a hen. Plants have instincts analogous to these — e.g. the seedling planted in an inverted position finds its leaf shoots and roots reoriented in appropriate directions (a story used by Bonnet), the Venus fly-trap's sensitive lobes close upon a foreign body and the shoots of the honeysuckle instinctively climb on supporting structures. Percival does not comment directly on a cognitive component in plant instincts, but it is a safe deduction that he allows the possibility: in animals instincts "often" are accompanied in their operation by a tiny degree of consciousness, plants are capable of cognitive activity, and plant instincts are analogous to animal ones.

Spontaneity of movement is the next analogical basis of argument. Spontaneity, which involves the impulse of discriminating or choosing, is a volitional concept, but presupposes cognition, an "innate perception" of what is helpful and harmful to the individual or species, and again the exercise of spontaneity may be accompanied by "consciousness or feeling". The anecdote, from Sharrock via Bonnet, of the plant in the darkened room which shoots towards a light-admitting hole in the wall, is adduced to illustrate the faculty at work. The sun-following behaviour of the sun-flower is mentioned; the movement of a sprig of mint suspended head downwards well shows volition:

> "In twenty-four hours, the stem formed into a curve, the head became erect, and gradually ascended towards the mouth of the vessel; thus producing, by successive efforts, a new and unusual configuration of its parts. Such exertions in the sprig of mint, to rectify its inverted position .... seems to evince volition to avoid what was evil", (1785 (b), p. 121).

The final basis of analogy lies in the ability of animals and plants to move. There are some fixed animals such as oysters and corals which have "self-moving" faculties, and, accordingly, "animality". Why deny it to vegetables which may be possessed of an equal or superior faculty of self-movement? Examples include again the ancient observation of the daily movements of water-lilies, the telegraph plant ("hedysarum") and the sensitive plant. Percival's comments on the sensitive plant are interesting because he takes issue with mechanism by seeing feeling as *manifest* in irritability. Having noted that the movements of the sensitive plant show "obvious signs" of its perceptual capabilities, and that the plant contracts to electric and non-electric stimulation alike and to volatile alkaline or sulphurous fumes he concludes

> "the powers of chemical stimuli, to produce contractions in the fibres

of this plant, may perhaps lead some philosophers, to refer them to the *vis insita*, or irritability, which they assign to certain parts of organized matter, totally distinct from, and independent of, any sentient energy. But the hypothesis is evidently a solecism, and refutes itself. For the presence of irritability can only be proved by the experience or irritations, and the idea of irritation involves in it that of feeling" (1785 (b), p. 124).

Percival thus has brought irritability back to its historical meaning, undoing the cleaning-up conceptual work of Haller. The claim that feeling is manifest in irritability, that the concept of irritability is necessarily connotative of cognition, might be expressed by using the scholastic term which we have met already and which Brentano was to revive later in the nineteenth century: immanence. To Percival feeling was *immanent* in irritability, i.e. irritability "holds within itself" the concept of feeling, the first concept is incomplete without the second.

6.3 *Richard Watson*

Richard Watson, (1737-1816) later in his career was an honorary member of the Manchester Literary and Philosophical Society.

Watson's academic promise was recognized early in his life at Oxford University: he was elected professor of chemistry there, having had no formal training in the subject, and later became regius professor of divinity, again having little claim to previous formal background in theology. He became a successful chemist, and a prominent theologian, (especially as a defender of revealed religion against atheists such as Tom Paine), and in course became Bishop of Llandaff.

Strictly speaking, Watson's essay on vegetable perception, misleadingly entitled *On the Subjects of Chemistry and their General Division* has temporal priority over Percival's. It was written in 1767 (or close to it), a little after Bonnet's work, and was published as a "review" by "X" in the *Gentleman's Magazine* in 1771. "X", later identified by Watson as the journalist and author Dr John Hawkesworth, did little more in his "review" than give pages of direct quotations, in effect publishing the whole essay ("X", 1771, pp. 410-414 and 464-466). Watson included it in the fifth volume of his *Chemical Essays* (1787), and because it is here that most readers came to it and because Watson here acknowledges the inspiration of Percival it is better regarded in its historical context as coming after Percival's essay.

Watson's theme is the "perceptivity of vegetables". He has read some earlier writers on it, including Bonnet, and knows his scale of creation (man is "the first term of a series" (1781, p. 173). There are metaphysical, physical and chemical reasons in favour of perception in plants. The metaphysical one is that if there are more percipient beings in the universe, the greater is the quantity of happiness, and accordingly the greater is the estimation of God's goodness — a type of theistic utilitarianism.

The naturalistic considerations are based on"comparative reasoning". Many plant "muscular motions" e.g. in heliotropes and sun-flowers) are as marked as those in lower sea-creatures such as corals and oysters.

"Trefoil, woodsorrel, mountain ebony, wild senna, the African marigold, etc. are so regular in folding up their leaves before rainy weather,

112

that they seem to have a kind of instinct or foresight similar to that
of ants; which however deserts many of them as soon as they have
propagated their kind, by shedding their pollen" (pp. 140-1).

Young trees and plants orient their angle of growth towards sources
of light, and the roots of plants
"are known to turn away with a kind of abhorrence from whatever
they meet with which is hurtful to them, and to desert their ordinary
direction, and to tend with a kind of natural and irresistible impulse
toward collections placed within their reach" (p. 141).

Stimulation of the anthers of some flowers will convulse them,
and movements of the sensitive plant are mentioned; those of the
Venus fly-trap are "far superior in quickness to those of a variety of
animals" (p.142).

Watson is aware that "these and other similar motions of vegetables
may by some be considered as analogous to the automatic or involuntary motions of animals" (p. 143) e.g. peristaltic bowel motions
and muscular contractions in decapitated animals, but contends that
physiologists cannot say yet whether such motions in animals may
not be caused by irritability "unaccompanied by perceptivity, or to an
uneasy sensation" (p. 143). Irritability here has become a causal agent,
(" .... irritability, if admitted as the cause of the motions of vegetables
.... " (p. 144)), it is not just the name for the fact of the particular vegetable movements, it is what brings them about.

Watson's list of animal/vegetable analogies is large. Both animals
and vegetables are capable of sexual procreation. Physiological and
structural similarities include

"expiration and inspiration, a kind of larynx and lungs, perspiration, imbibition, arteries, veins, lacteals, an organized body, and probably a circulating fluid appertain to vegetables as well as to animals" (p. 148).

Some animals share the ability of plants to live as individuals after division and to grow new limbs after amputation. Some animals and most plants are hermaphroditic. Hirsute animals shed their hair just as trees shed their leaves. Some plants, as do animals, need to sleep.

The core of Watson's case is the theme which is by now familiar: the criteria which lead to the predication of mental life to animals also lead to the predication of mind to plants. If mind is to be denied to plants then it must also be denied to animals, but this is unacceptable (except to the ultra-mechanists). Therefore mind must be predicated of plants and here Watson invokes the philosophically contentious issue of "same effects, same causes":

"Now to refer the muscular motions of shell fish, and zoophytes, to an internal principle of volition, to make them indicative of the perceptivity of the being; and to attribute the more noticeable ones of vegetables, and to certain mechanical dilatations, and contraction of parts occasioned by external impulse, is to err against that rule of philosophyzing which assigns the same causes for effects of the same kind. The motions in both cases are equally accommodated to the preservation of the being to which they belong, are equally distinctive and uniform, and should be equally derived from mechanism, or equally admitted as criterions of perception" (pp. 138-143).

Watson draws upon many more analogies between the two kingdoms than does Percival. "Instinct" for him is not an important concept in its own right, but it is worth a mention in passing. His essay lacks some of the systematic organisation of ideas which Percival's has.

6.4 *Erasmus Darwin*

His reputation was eclipsed by that of his grandson Charles, but Erasmus Darwin was a highly gifted man in his own right, and should be remembered as more than a pioneer of evolutionary thought. His main biographer, Desmond King-Hele, gives this summary of Darwin and his achievements:

"Erasmus Darwin, who lived from 1731 until 1802, was by profession a physician, widely acclaimed as the finest doctor of his time in England. By nature Darwin was a large and powerful-looking man, cheerful and healthy, and, although he stammered, he was a witty and persuasive talker. He was very sociable and had a passion for science and technology. He founded three Midland scientific societies, the most important being the Lunar Society of Birmingham. The Lunar Society was a major intellectual driving-force of the Industrial Revolution in Britain, which has led to the modern world of technology. Darwin was a compulsive inventor and with the encouragement of his Lunar friends, particularly Josiah Wedgwoood, James Watt and James Keir, he produced working inventions ranging from a speaking-machine to a horizontal windmill, and dozens of designs on paper. Darwin's most potent talent, however, was his deep scientific insight, which enabled him to make several important discoveries in biology and geophysics and to propose many scientific ideas which time has shown to be correct. He won fame late in life in a quite different sphere, as a poet: his long poem *The Botanic Garden* captivated the literary world in the 1790s. Coleridge called him "the first *literary* character in Europe", the Napoleon of literature , as it were.

Today Darwin earns most credit among scientists for recognizing and describing biological evolution, specifying the essentials of plant nutrition and of photosynthesis, and explaining how clouds usually form. And he has attracted the attention of literary critics not so much for his poems as for his immense influence on the English Romantic poets, Wordsworth, Coleridge, Shelley and Keats" (King-Hele, 1981, p. vii).

Elsewhere King-Hele gives a list of 75 "concrete examples" of Darwin's original achievements (King -Hele, 1968, pp. 199-200), but the plant psychology is not included in that list. This is under-standable because even in his own day it was regarded generally not to be a serious achievement, to be at the best, a fancy, and at the worst, an absurdity. Most writers on Erasmus Darwin have little or nothing to say about his plant psychology. To take two examples: Maureen McNeil, a recent historian and biographer, describes his plant psychology as his "botanical analogy", and indi-cates its flavour, but to present it in a wider context is outside the scope of her study (McNeil, 1987); Janet Browne's paper on *The Loves of the Plants* (Browne, 1989) brings out generally the social significance for his age of Darwin's dramatized exposition of the Linnaean doctrine of plant sexuality, and particularly the attitudes to women conveyed in the poem, but has only a passing reference to make to the plant psychology proper in it.

Darwin scholars, then, have bigger fish to fry. His plant psychology has no conceptual relation to his evolutionary theory, nor is it a scientific achievement in its own right. On the other hand it did have a wider influence than that of the direct one on plant psychologists who followed him, e.g. on some of the Romantic poets, especially Wordsworth (see King-Hele, 1977). Again, if "originality" rather than "achievement" is to be taken as the touchstone to determine whether something is to be included in a budget of memorable contributions, then "plant psychology" should be so included. It is not that Erasmus Darwin has anything conceptually radically new to offer here — he is fairly faithful to a well-articulated traditional context, tiny though it is. It is original in its embellishment. Darwin has at disposal a vast knowledge of natural philosophy in the broad, and of botany in the narrow. He lets analogy have its head. It gallops with an unmatched style and exuberance. Darwin's reservation that plants possess mental faculties "though is a much inferior degree even than the cold blooded animals" (Darwin, 1800, p. 133) is belied by his accounts: they are the most elaborate of the mentalist tradition.

Contrary to his practice in other areas of writing, Darwin tends not to make reference to other plant psychologists, prior or contemporary. He would have received an orthodox botanical education in his medical studies in Edinburgh. He knew, as any respectable natural philosopher of his day would have known, his Bonnet and his Buffon (see, e.g. King-Hele, 1981, pp. 122 and 72 for Bonnet and Buffon respectively). Galen and Harvey were cited in his writings. He purchased Watson's *Chemical Essays* for the library of the Derby Philosophical Society which he inaugurated in 1784 (Robinson, 1953). Percival's priority was acknowledged by Darwin's admirer, friend and biographer, Anna Seward, in recording her conviction of the truth of his theory of mind in plants:

"Of this theory, however, Dr Darwin is neither the source, nor the first who drew the scattered hints of former philosophers concerning it, into a regular system. The ingenious and excellent Dr Percival, of Manchester, preceded him in maintaining that system from the press. Congeniality on it's subject between a mild, a temperate and religious sage, and a bold philosopher of the modern school, who possessed the eye of a lynx for nature's arcana, leave us little reason to doubt that it is veritable" (Seward, 1804, p. 413).

The starting point for Darwin's plant psychology is to be found in his introductory remarks to his translation of Linnaeus's *Genera Plantarum* (*Families of Plants*), published in 1787 under the authorship of "A botanical society at Lichfield". This "society" never consisted of more than three people, and was, in fact, Darwin's vehicle for promotion of translations of Linnaeus (Browne, 1989). "Vegetables" wrote Darwin, "are, in truth, an inferior order of Animals, connected to the lower tribes of Insects, by many productions, whose faculties of motion and sensation are scarcely superior to those of the petals of many flowers, or to the leaves of the Sensitive plant, (*Mimosa sensitiva,*) the Moving plant, (*Hedysarum movens,*) and the Fly-trap (*Dioneamuscipula*)" (A Botanical Society at Lichfield, 1787, p. xix).

In the contention that plants are a species of animal he makes no reference to Plato, nor does he do so when he repeats the claim in later writings. There is no evidence of a direct influence of Plato on Darwin.

Four volumes of Darwin's writings are relevant to his plant psychology, but in none of them is it a dominant theme. They are *The Loves of the Plants* which was published anonymously in 1789, but Darwin's anonymity was dispelled quickly. The book was so successful that a second and a third edition followed soon, the third one (1791) being coupled with *The Economy of Vegetation* in 1791. Jointly they comprised *The Botanic Garden*, *The Economy of Vegetation* being Part I and *The Loves of the Plants* being Part II of *The Botanic Garden*. Thus the second part of *The Botanic Garden* was written before the first part. *The Loves of the Plants* introduces some ideas of Darwin's plant psychology, and references to this 1789 work will be to it as it appeared in the 1791 *Botanic Garden*. *The Economy of Vegetation* is the first work to set out formally Darwin's views, but it is not at all systematic in its presentation of them. The systematic presentation is shown in *Zoonomia*, Volume I, 1794. *Phytologia*, which appeared in 1800, recapitulates and elaborates the plant psychology, but adds nothing of substance to the essential ideas of *The Economy of Vegetation*.

The Loves of the Plants explains the Linnaean system of botany in verse. It is not at all dull or heavy-handed. As King-Hele puts it, he "baked the stodgy mass with plenty of bicarbonate, to produce the lightest of confections" (King-Hele, 1977, p. 190). Plants are discussed individually in sets of rhyming couplets in terms of the Linnaean sexual system of classification, "often charming, often ridiculous, sometimes witty, sometimes pedestrian, always accurate in its essentials and fanciful in its embellishments" (King-Hele, 1977, p. 192). Darwin uses personification throughout: each plant is humanized, its behaviour, especially its sexuality, being treated with good-humoured irony.

The couplet:

"What Beaux and Beauties croud the gaudy groves,

And woo and win their vegetable Loves"

(I, lines 9-10, Darwin 1789 (1791), p.2).

sets the tone for the rest of the poem. Darwin's personified treatment of plants should not be confused with his plant psychology. His attribution to individual plant species of human attitudes to romantic love is a poetic device and nothing more. *The Loves of the Plants* is such good fun, however, that we should pause to quote a few of his stories.

The sundew (the most common British species is the *Drosera rotundifolia*) fascinated Darwin, as it did his grandson Charles:

"Queen of the dewy vale, fair DROSERA treads

Her moss-wove banks, and rush-fringed beds;

Redundant folds of glossy silk surround

Her slender waist, and trail upon the ground;

Five sister-nymphs collect with graceful ease,

Or spread the floating purple to the breeze;

And *five* fair youths with duteous love comply

With each soft mandate of her moving eye.

As with sweet grace her showy neck she bows,

A zone of diamonds trembles round her brows;

Bright shines the silver halo, as she turns;

And, as she steps, the living lustre burns". (I, 199-210, p.20).

The five "sister-nymphs" and the "five youths" refer respectively to the five pistils ("females") and the five stamens ("males") of the sun-dew flower.

The habits of the sensitive plant are described thus:

"Weak with nice sense, the chaste MIMOSA stands,

From each rude touch withdraws her timid hands;

Oft as light clouds o'erpass the Summer-glade,

Alarm'd she trembles at the moving shade;

And feels, alive through all her tender form,

The whisper'd murmurs of the gathering storm;

Shuts her sweet-eye-lids to approaching night;

And hails with freshen'd charms the rising light.

Veil'd with gay decency and modest price,

Slow to the mosque she moves, an eastern bride;

There her soft vows unceasing love record,

Queen of the bright seraglio of her Lord. -

So sinks or rises with the changeful hour

The liquid silver in its glassy tower.

So turns the needle to the pole it loves,

With fine librations quivering, as it moves" (I, 247-262, pp. 25-26).

The telegraph plant, known to Darwin by its native name and botanically as *Hedysarum movens* is given a full twenty lines:

"When from his golden urn the Solstice pours

O'er Afric's sable sons the sultry hours;

When not a gale flits o'er her tawny hills,

Save where the dry Harmattan breathes and kills;

When stretch'd in dust her gasping panthers lie,

And writh'd in foamy folds her serpents die;

Indignant Atlas mourns his leafless woods,

And Gambia trembles for his sinking floods;

Contagion stalks along the briny sand,

And Ocean rolls his sickening shoals to land.

121

- Fair CHUNDA smiles amid the burning waste,
  Her brow unturban'd, and her zone unbrac'd;
  Ten brother-youths with light umbrella's shade,
  Or fan with busy hands the panting maid;
  Loose wave her locks, disclosing, as they break,
  The rising bosom and averted cheek;
  Clasp'd round her ivory neck with studs of gold
  Flows her thin vest in many a silky fold;
  O'er her light limbs the dim transparence plays,
  And the fair form, it seems to hide, betrays. (IV, 227-246, p. 151-153).

The "brother-youths" are stamens. Darwin gives many foot-notes explaining his allusions — e.g. "sickening shoals" refers to an incident in 1775 when huge numbers of dead fish polluted the beaches and seashores of Sumatra.

The Venus fly-trap is given no poetic attention, but it is described in a footnote and is pictured in an elegant engraved plate (facing p. 14).

There is very little plant psychology proper in this entertaining book. Irritability is mentioned in the notes in connection with the sensitive plant, the Venus fly-trap, and the experiments on the contractility of filaments supporting the anthers of certain flowers performed by dal Covolo, who is acknowledged only as "an Italian writer" (p. 11). No suggestion is made, however, that there is a cognitive aspect to irritability.

The old problem inherited from the Greeks as to whether fungi belong to the plant or animal kingdom is raised, Darwin inclining to the view that they "approach" the animal kingdom, forming an "isthmus" (p. 37) between it and the plant kingdom. There is no claim, however, that they possess animal sensitivity.

Another footnote makes reference to plant "sensibility" to heat, and to plants "acquiring habits" (e.g. this explains why grains and roots brought from southern latitudes germinate earlier than those brought from northern ones) and "learning" to accommodate to new situations (e.g. apple trees sent from Europe to New England initially bore no fruit because they blossomed too early for their new environment, but later their blossoming time became appropriate to local conditions). No comment is made on the notions of "habit" and "learning".

Darwin, however, clearly does attribute volition to plants. The spontaneity of the leaves of the hedysarum, and of others, is attributed to that faculty (p. 153); in addition the sleep of plants is explained as a suspension of voluntary power, analogous to that of animal sleep. One of the plants manifesting volition in its movements is the collinsonia (an American coarse herb known as the horsebalm or horse weed), and Darwin's account of it is worth quoting because, as we shall see, it quite captured his fancy. The collinsonia flower has two male organs and one female.

> "Two males one female. I have lately observed a very singular circum-stance in this flower; the two males stand widely diverging from each other, and the female bends herself into contact first with one of them, and after some time leaves this, and applies herself to the other" (p. 4).

The Economy of Vegetation, written two years after *The Loves of the Plants* but preceding it in *The Botanic Garden*, is a long work in rhyming couplets. It has many footnotes and is replete with additional exegetical notes. It opens with an allegorical description of the history of science and technology, then turns its attention to plants, giving,

123

with plenty of personification and classical allusions, a stylised poetic exposition of the principles of plant physiology and growth.

A great deal of it argues for vegetable counterparts of animal physiological processes: e.g. vegetable perspiration, circulation, respiration, impregnation and "glandulation". There is more plant psychology. The sleep of plants is again mentioned as evidence that they possess voluntary power: further indisputable evidence is seen in petal and leaf closure occasioned by cold, rain and other external conditions.

Darwin here introduces a clear distinction between irritability and sentience or "sensibility" in plants. Unlike Percival, Darwin retains the Hallerian mechanical concept of irritability, but allows that plants have *both* irritability and sentience. For Darwin, unlike some of his contemporaries, irritability is not a concept linking plant movements and cognition. Plant cognition occurs because plants have sense organs. Although not sharing Bonnet's vitalist conception of irritability, Darwin follows him in denying that it involves sentience. Each plant or bud is an individual psychological unit possessing a *"sensitive* sensorium or brain" (Darwin 1791, p. 149) connected by nerves to muscles. The circulation of plant juices and their absorption can be explained mechanically by irritability, but not so the movements of leaves and flowers effected by muscular changes. These are sensible phenomena. That this is so demonstrated by the facts that (1) flower closure may result from the *cessation* of light (i.e. onset of darkness), but muscles cannot be mechanically fired into action by the absence of a stimulus. Accordingly the cessation of the stimulus must produce sensations (in the sensorium) which cause petal closure in some flowers: (2) parts of some plants contract when *other* parts of the plant are irritated (e.g. the sensitive plant; in some flowers the stimulation of some stamens will cause others to move), hence a disagreeable sensation must intervene between the irritation of one part of the plant and the movement of another.

One footnote of particular interest concerns the collinsonia, not this time because of its demonstration of its volitional faculty in the movements of its female flower structures, but because of its sexual proclivities:

"The vegetable passion of love is agreeably seen in the flower of the parnassia, in which the males alternately approach and recede from the female, and in the flower of nigella, or devil in the bush, in which the tall females bend down to their dwarf husbands. But I was this morning surprised to observe, amongst Sir Brooke Boothby's valuable collection of plants at Ashbourn, the manifest adultery of several females of the plant Collinsonia, who had bent themselves into contact with the males of other flowers of the same plant in their vicinity, neglectful of their own. Sept. 16." (Darwin, 1791, p. 197).

(Sir Brooke Boothby, poet and political writer of Ashbourne Hall, Derbyshire, was one of the trio comprising Darwin's Lichfield Botanical Society).

The "manifest adultery" should not be read as an item of sexual moralizing on Darwin's part, such sententiousness would have been out of character for him. Rather, it should be seen as a piece of whimsy, a little joke which he must have enjoyed because he repeats it in *Phytologia*. Another question comes out of this footnote. Is "the vegetable passion of love" meant to be read as a mere poetic conceit (most uncommon in the footnotes) or is it to be read literally?

This question is answered unambiguously in the first volume of

Zoonomia, published in 1794. Sub-titled *"The Laws of Organic Life"* it is in prose, and is a treatise on human psychology (Darwin follows the orthodox associationist idealism of his day), human physiology and disease, and visual perception. A second volume two years later is devoted entirely to the classification of diseases. Volume I is not devoted exclusively to humans, for in Section XIII there is a chapter *"Of Vegetable Animation"* which presents a systematic version of the plant psychology mentioned in *The Botanic Garden's* footnotes.

The Platonic basis of Darwin's thinking, although not explicitly mentioned by him, is repeated in his contention that plants are "inferior or less perfect animals" (Darwin, 1794, p. 102). The tree may be compared with the coralline in that the former is a collection of many living buds, the latter of many living animals. The list of plant/animal structural similarities is enormous. The claims for plants possessing sensibility as well as irritability are advanced again, as well as the claims of their possessing voluntary powers to some degree (the old accounts of climbers seeking supports and of efforts to direct growth towards the light re-appear here); just as associationism is a principle in explaining human behaviour, so it is in those plants which show that movements can become associated in them (e.g. the sensitive plant).

The concept of "vegetable passion" *is* meant to be taken literally:
"The approach of the anthers in many flowers to the stigmas, and of the pistils of some flowers to the anthers, must be ascribed to the passion of love, and hence belongs to sensation, not to irritation" (p. 103).

The question of passion as a species of vegetable sensation is taken up in the context of a larger question of whether plants have ideas of external things. Darwin followed the orthodox Lockian heritage, and believed accordingly that knowledge of the external world was mediated by ideas of it. The original sources of ideas are sense organs, hence the question about plants having ideas of the external world becomes the question of whether they have sense organs. They do, is the answer. They sense heat and cold, moisture and dryness, dark and light, the reactions to which imply sensation or volition, not mere irritability. Furthermore a sensation of love explains why the anthers in many flowers and the stigmas in others are aware that a potential paramour is in the vicinity, and for this faculty a particular sense organ is responsible.

Darwin summarizes his "system", as Anna Seward termed it, in these words:

"Thus, besides a kind of taste at the extremities of their roots, similar to that of the extremities of our lacteal vessels, for the purpose of selecting their proper food; and besides different kinds of irritability residing in the various glands, which separate honey, wax, resin and other juices from their blood; vegetable life seems to posses an organ of sense to distinguish the varying degrees of moisture, another of light, another of touch, and probably another analogous to our sense of smell. To these must be added the indubitable evidence of their passion of love, and I think we may truly conclude, that they are furnished with a common sensorium belonging to each bud, and that they must occasionally repeat those perceptions either in their dreams or waking hours, and consequently possess ideas of so many of the properties of the external world and of their own existence" (1794, pp. 106-7).

The most developed account of his views is in *Phytologia; or the philosophy of agriculture and gardening*, published in 1800. It is a prose work consisting of three parts: the physiology of vegetation, the economy of vegetation, and agriculture and horticulture. It is in the first part that a detailed and organized recapitulation of his plant psychology themes appears. There are several chapters of "correspondences" between plants and animals, which in scope and detail go far beyond those drawn by any earlier writer.

Just to give some idea of the flavour of this writing, and of the limits to which Darwin takes analogy a couple of paragraphs may be quoted:

> "The parts, which we may expect to find in the anatomy of vegetables, which correspond to those in the animal economy, are just a threefold system of absorbent vessels, one branch of which is designed to imbibe the chyle from the stomach and intestines of animals; another to imbibe the water of the atmosphere, opening its mouths on the cuticle of the leaves and branches, like the cutaneous lymphatic vessels of animals; and a third to imbibe the secreted fluids from the internal cavities of the vegetable system; like the cellular lymphatics of animals.
>
> Secondly, in the vegetable fetus, as in seeds or buds, another system of absorbent vessels is to be expected, which may be termed umbilical vessels, ... which supply nutriment to the new bud or seed, similar to that of the albumen of the egg, or the liquor amnii of the uterus; and also another system of arterial vessels, which may be termed placental ones, corresponding with those of the animal fetus in the egg or in the womb, which supply the blood of the embryon with due oxygenation before its nativity (Darwin, 1800, pp. 5-6).

The plant's leaf-turning, and petal and calyx opening or closing are controlled by longitudinal muscles, whilst vascular ones control the

128

absorption and circulation of fluids. These muscles, and the nerves connecting them to the sensorium or brain of each individual seed, flower or bud (seated in the "internal pith") are too fine for anatomical demonstration.

The concept of the sensorium is a central one in what Darwin sees as the experimental basis of his plant psychology. He believes that laboratory demonstration points to the existence of the plant sensorium, just as Harvey believed that his conception of the human brain as a "sensorium" was grounded empirically. In this matter Darwin writes:

"Now as when one part of a leaf of mimosa is touched, the whole leaf falls, it follows, that there must be a common sensorium, or brain, where the nerves communicate, belonging to this one leaf bud. To evince this further another leaflet was slit with sharp scissors, and some seconds of time elapsed, before the plant seemed sensible of the injury; and then the whole plant collapsed as far as the principal stem. Afterwards a small drop of vitriol was put on the bud in the bosom of a leaf on another sensitive plant; and, after about half a minute, when the brain of this bud could be supposed to be destroyed, the whole leaf fell, and rose no more" (p.133).

Darwin has more to say about the nature of vegetable passion in *Phytologia* (the anecdote of the adulterous collinsonia is told again). He speculates that it may be mediated by a sense organ analogous to our sense of smell, "which in the animal world directs the new-born infant to its source of nourishment; and in some animals directs the male to the female" (p. 138). Thus plants may perceive as well as produce odours. He also takes to task "Dr Peschier of Geneva" who had claimed to disprove the notion of the "amatorial sensibility of vegetables" experimentally. "Dr Peschier" is probably Jean Peschier (1774-1831) of Geneva, who submitted in 1797 a doctoral dissertation at the University of Edinburgh on animal and vegetable irritability. Peschier found that the anthers in one flower (the rosebay willow herb — *Epilobium angustifolium*) burst and shed their pollen, even though the stigma was tied down ("and thus committed a kind of vegetable Onanism" (p. 107)), and that the stigma would arise and open although the stamens had been removed. Peschier also artificially stimulated stamens of the barberry (*berberis*) flower to rise to the stigma by subjecting them to the vapour of "nitrous acid". Darwin's prowess with analogy enables him easily to turn up trumps on Peschier, however:

> "Both these experiments rather seem to confirm then to enfeeble the analogy between plants and animals; as the emotional motions of these flowers were thus produced by internal or external stimuli; as in the healthy or diseased states of animals" (p. 107).

Two broad conclusions can be drawn about Darwin's plant psychology:

(i) It presents no new radical conceptualizations. Its theoretical framework belongs to an established tradition, articulated by earlier and contemporary writers. This is not to say that there was *no* innovation on Darwin's part. His distinction between irritability and sensibility coupled with the insistence on their joint possessions by plants equipped with sensoria and sense organs, is the obvious example here.

(ii) It is nonetheless highly original. Darwin's access to a wider pool of naturalistic data and his possession of an intellect of brilliance and great imaginative power enabled him to take analogy just about as far as it could go. In Erasmus Darwin we see vegetable mentalism at its zenith. His conception of the mental life of plants was richer in quantity and quality than that of any plant psychologist from Plato onward. Plants could do much more than merely register inchoate hedonic tones of "pleasure" or "pain": they could strive actively, they could know passion, they had access to sensations from a number of different sensory sources, by which they could have some knowledge of external things and of themselves, they could build up complete mental states by the association of simple elements. They have all the categories which Darwin applied to human psychology: irritability, sensation, volition and association. Darwin's extravagant system of plant psychology is truly baroque, he gilds not only the lily, but the whole vegetable kingdom.

6.5 *James Perchard Tupper*

James Tupper (? — 1831), a surgeon (he was Surgeon Extraordinary to the Prince Regent in 1817) and Fellow of the Linnaean Society, published in 1811 *An Essay on the Probability of Sensation in Vegetables; with Additional Observations on Instinct, Sensation, Irritability, etc.* It is a long, exhaustively argued and somewhat repetitious monograph drawing on Watson, Percival, Darwin and James Edward Smith, his teacher. Of these, Percival's influence is the strongest. Tupper's essay deserves to be singled out for attention because it attempts a conceptual clarification of the arguments for plant mentality. If we regard

Bell, Percival and Watson as pioneers in the great days of plant psychology, Darwin as the publicist and main source of later influence, then Tupper can be called the theoretician.

Tupper subscribes to the cornerstone doctrines of the chain of being, " .... the transition from the animal to the plant is effected by shades so imperceptible that it is difficult, and perhaps impossible, to determine what are those beings which actually form the last link in the scale of animal existence, and the first in the of vegetables" (Tupper, 1811, p. 5), and of the importance of analogies between animals and plants. Analogies, he says, do not prove the existence of sensation in plants, but "they are at least very presumptive evidences in favour" (p. 12).

However, analogy is not the only ground for attributing mind to plants. There are phenomena with which we become acquainted if we begin to look at plant movements. These phenomena associated with the power of movements in plants point inescapably to *instinct*, and from instinct we infer sensation. Whether or not the connection is causal, there is to Tupper at least a necessary connection between sensation and instinct. If we grant this in animals, why not in plants? It may be objected that even if we were to grant him his premises here, somewhere along the line he would have to appeal to analogy to sustain his argument.

But the important points for Tupper are:

(1)   *The concept of instinct.* This is central. Although in most animals the locomotive faculty is instinctive, it is not a necessary consequence of instinct. Many plants, which are not locomotive, display the consequences of instinct in such phenomena as inclining toward the light, climbers seeking and using structures, trees directing roots towards

sources of nourishment, the spontaneous movement of some plants, e.g. the diurnal erection of flower stalks and the opening of the flowers in water-lilies, "sleep" behaviour (a term he does not like) etc.

Instinct is defined teleologically, in what are by now familiar terms. It is a

> "particular disposition or tendency, in a living being, to embrace *without deliberation* or *reflection*, the means of self-preservation, and .... such other actions as are required by its economy, *without* having any *perception* for what end or purposes it acts, or any idea of the utility or advantage of its own operations" (p. 16).

What appears to be voluntary in many plant (and animal) actions is blindly instinctive, there is no conscious intention or rational faculty being exercised (except by "superintending Providence" (p. 19)).

In plants then there is no volition, contrary to Darwin's view, all apparently volitional plant behaviour is instinctive. Instinct for Tupper has more importance than it did for Percival. Although Tupper speaks of instinctive behaviour in plants as "spontaneous", and talks of "self-inclination" (p. 21) he urges that there is no volition involved, but sensation may be.

(2) *The concept of sensation.* This must be distinguished sharply from volition and any rational mental concepts. Plants and lower animals have no rationality or volitional powers, they are driven by instinct. There is a necessary connection between instinct and sensation: instinct may occur without sensation but sensation cannot occur without instinct. The operation of instincts in animals and plants suggests accompanying sensations.

(3) *The concept of irritability.* Tupper is most concerned to clarify this concept. Irritability is a vital notion, not a mechanical one. The mechanist's conception of irritability

> "Seems to imply only the existence of a *disposition* or *susceptibility* for action, as if that *power* were in a passive state until called forth into action by some *remote* exciting cause. But I apprehend that irritability is a particular power, which is coëval with the *living principle* itself of the individual, and *continually* operating in a greater or less degree, so long as the principle of life exists" (p. 43).

Tupper faces squarely the job of trying to define this amorphous power, and in a passage of reasoning which is more acute than that to be found in his fellows, he acknowledges that to give an account of the *effects* of some agent or entity is not to give an account of its nature, is not to say what it *is*:

> "It is in general very difficult to give in few words such a definition of any particular quality as shall be fully explanatory of the real nature of it. This is, however, the true intent of a definition; though what we often give as such, in reference to some particular animal attribute, is, for the most part, only a general statement of its effects, rather than what constitutes the real nature of essence of it; and I apprehend that *irritability* comes within the sphere of this observation. *Irritability* is one thing, and its *effects* are another. I do not, therefore, presume to explain by definition the nature itself of that power, but only aim to state, generally, the effects depending upon its existence: and, what may constitute its real nature, I shall endeavour to show that the

irritability of which plants are possessed is another, and very powerful evidence of their sensation" (pp. 44-45).

If we claim that plant irritability is different to animal irritability then we must say that plants and animals have different vital principles. This we do not want to do, because the effects of the vital principles are the same and we do not want to "ascribe similar effects to different causes" (p. 48), says Tupper, appealing in his turn after Watson to the dubious principle of "same effect, same cause".

Tupper, then, shares Percival's belief that irritability is necessarily associated with feeling, or sensation (sensation is necessary for irritability), although he keeps the two notions conceptually more distinct than does Percival.

Tupper is not worried by the fact that vegetables may not have nerves which are anatomically the same as those in animals: they may have something analogous to a nervous system which does the same job, just as gills in fish and lungs in mammals are different structures which do the same job.

As to the question of what plant sensation is like, Tupper goes with the orthodox Platonic basic hedonism rather than with Darwin's baroque extravagance: we might not be able to have "any precise idea of the particular kind of pleasure or pain of which vegetables may be susceptible" (p. 60) but we can say easily in particular circumstances which of the two sensations it must be having, for example a healthy plant pulled out of life-giving earth will soon languish, but if quickly replaced will "*feel* the salutary effects", and revive and flourish.

6.6 Some More "Ingenious Advocates" and Others

In his history of English botany from its beginning to the introduction of the Linnaean system, Richard Pulteney in 1790 spared a paragraph to summarize the arguments for the notion that "plants were sentient and "animated beings" " which was being mooted by "ingenious advocates among the moderns" (Pulteney, 1790, Vol. 1, p. 330). The majority of botanists and natural philosophers were unconcerned with these particular moderns, but some were disturbed by them and some saw the need to disagree with them.

Tupper's botany teacher, James Edward Smith (1759-1828), F.R.S., another former student under Hope, first president of the Linnaean Society, and later Sir James, read to the Royal Society *Some Observations on the Irritability of Vegetables* in 1788. He distinguishes between plant movements of an irritable kind (e.g. in sensitive plant, sundew, Venus fly-trap, the stamens of the barberry) and those which were "spontaneous" (e.g. "Rue moves one of its stamina every day to the pistillum" (Smith, 1788, p. 7)), but claims that he could find no plant which showed both irritability and spontaneity — only animals showed both. Contrary to Bonnet's belief, Smith believes that only some plants possess irritability but he did share Bonnet's distinction between irritability and sensibility. His interpretation of irritability is anti-mechanistic, but there is no hint that he supposes it to have any cognitive overtones.

The Edinburgh antiquarian, naturalist and printer (he printed the first edition of the *Encyclopaedia Britannica*), William Smellie (1740-1795) also saw irritability as a phenomenon "which cannot be explained upon any principle of mechanism" (Smellie, 1790, p. 11); he found it impossible to find hard and fast criteria to distinguish between plants and animals, but he denied finally that plants had sensation. Smellie owes a great deal to Bonnet and Buffon. As did Bonnet he thought that many phenomena in plants indicated the presence of sensation, but his conclusion was more in line with Buffon's thought: all that we can say is that plants have irritability, which is to be distinguished from sensation. His *Philosophy of Natural History* is up to date on all the phenomena and anecdotes which seemed to point away from a mechanistic interpretation of plant life, and although he baulked at the conception of vegetable sensation his *Philosophy* was a source of material for popular plant psychologists for many years — for example Smellie promoted the stories of the growing cucumber which within 24 hours will grow towards a vessel of water placed within 6 inches of it, and of the unsupported vine rod which will change the direction of the growth of its branches to cling to a pole placed at a considerable distance from it.

It should be pointed out here that Philip Ritterbush is misleading in his exposition of Smellie's views on the plant mind. Ritterbush states that "William Smellie wrote that plants were "not only conscious of their existence but enjoy degrees of happiness proportioned to their natures and the purposes they are destined to answer in the general scale of animation" " (Ritterbush, 1964, p. 152). What Smellie actually wrote was "The earth, the air, the waters, are full of living beings, who are not only conscious of their existence but enjoy degrees of happiness .... " etc. (Smellie, 1790, p. 77). There is a real difference here, because Smellie does not include plants among "living things". He takes issue with Jung and Linnaeus on this question. He grants that there are analogies between plants and animals in their structure, organs, growth, nourishment, dissemination and decay, but plants do not live. All living things must have "some degree of sensation" (p. 2), and there are problems with defining "life". Plant movements, including seemingly purposive growth movements, and other analogies with animals "excite our wonder; but they by no means prove that vegetables live, or that they are endowed with sensation, which implies a distinct perception of pleasure and pain" (p. 10). Maybe all plants, like animals, are irritable, but irritability, whilst a "vital principle" and an "inferior species of sensation", merely denotes the power of contraction of muscle fibres upon contact by a stimulus. We may feel tempted to ascribe life to muscle fibres, but they have no perception of pleasure or pain: the "inferior species of sensation" is not a cognitive concept to Smellie. "Irritability .... implies not the perception of pleasure and pain, it regulates all the vital or involuntary motions of animals" (pp. 11-12). "I mean", says Smellie, "not to insinuate, that plants can perceive pleasure or pain" (p. 11).

Ritterbush is correct when, two paragraphs later, he says that Smellie's line of argument implied that plants lacked sensation (i.e. cognition), a statement which would appear to be inconsistent with his earlier claim that Smellie believed that plants were "not only conscious of their existence..." etc.

In America the traveller and naturalist William Bartram (1739-1823) had no doubts about the psychic capacities of the Venus fly-trap, which he was privileged to see growing wild in North Carolina:

"But admirable are the properties of the extraordinary Dionea muscipula! .... Astonishing production! see the incarnate lobes expanding,
how gay and ludicrous they appear! ready on the spring to intrap

incautious deluded insects, what artifice! there behold one of the
leaves just closed upon a struggling fly, another has got a worm, its
hold is sure, its prey can never escape — carnivorous vegetable! Can
we after viewing this object, hesitate a moment to confess, that vegetable beings are endued with some sensible faculties or attributes
similar to those that dignify animal nature; they are organical, living
and self-moving bodies, for we see here, in this plant, motion and
volition" (Bartram, 1791, pp. xx-xxi).

A mechanistic counter-attack was delivered by Robert Townson
to the Linnaean Society in 1792, and was published privately by him
seven years later. Townson (dates unknown) took the degree of M.D.
at the University of Göttingen in 1795, he was a Fellow of the Royal
Society of Edinburgh, a traveller and mineralogist. Townson concedes
that the external movements of some plants could give the appearance
of perceptivity and volition, but argues that the movements can be
explained mechanistically in terms of putative processes by which
"inert fluids", necessary to plant life and growth, are absorbed:

> "This supply, so necessary, must be taken in by absorption; and it is
> this act of absorption that I shall endeavour to prove to be the effi-
> cient cause of these motions in vegetables, and thus exclude volition
> from being the cause of these phaenomena; for it is from their not
> having been explained upon mechanical principles that mind has
> been resorted to, mind is in general our last resource when we fail in
> explaining natural phaenomena" (Townson, 1799, p. 141).

Although Townson's mechanistic interpretation of plant movements was hypothetical, there were soon more experimental data

to support such an interpretation. Thomas Andrew Knight (1759-1838), an agriculturalist and plant-breeder, reported in 1806 his experiments on tropisms in plants. He demonstrated that gravity directly influenced the growth of the main stem upwards and the primary roots downwards, and, although he could not specify the mechanisms involved he was forthright in saying in a later paper "I am wholly unable to trace the existence of anything like sensation or intellect in the plants" (Knight, 1811, p. 163). Knight's work led to the exploration of different kinds of plant tropisms, including that of R.J.H. Dutrochet, who made in the 1830's systematic experiments on the sensitive plant's movements in response to external stimuli. Amongst the phenomena he investigated was the transmission of a stimulus over a distance, i.e. parts of the plant which are not touched themselves may contract or droop consequent upon the stimulation of other parts, and he recognized the involvement of a turgor mechanism in the pulvinus. Dutrochet was an unequivocal opponent of vitalism, claiming the vital force to be an occult, mystical motion.

The progress of botany as an experimental discipline whose practitioners in the main were either overt or *de facto* mechanists did not put paid to the plant psychologists' speculations, however. The vitalists amongst the natural philosophers — and as the nineteen century went on there were plenty of these, especially in continental Europe — made things easier for them. The characteristic arguments of the functionalist mentalist approach (the approach which says that mind in plants may be inferred from what they do) were to be repeated long after the great days from Percival to Tupper.

In 1811, the same year that Tupper's essay was published, *Sketches of the Physiology of Vegetable Life*, written by one identified only as the "Authoress of *Botanical Dialogues*" declared its purpose "to lay before the botanic student a sketch of those leading arguments by which it has been attempted to prove the existence or deficiency of the faculty of sensation in the vegetable world" (p. 18). The author was Maria Elizabeth Jackson, a provincial English gentle-lady. The *Sketches* consists *inter alia* of page after page of teleological interpretations of plant behaviour and structure overlaid with an assembly of arguments for plant sensation which is derived, as Mrs Jackson acknowledges, from Darwin.

One of the minor provocative acts of the colourful philosophical materialist and political agitator, Thomas Cooper, (1759-1840) was to initiate a running debate on vegetable sentience in the Philadelphia magazine *The Port Folio*. Cooper had a background in medicine and natural philosophy in England, and was a fellow Dissenter and emigré to America with his friend Priestley. In a footnote in Priestley's memoirs (Priestley, 1806, p. 316) Cooper had stated that Priestley, together with Percival, Bell, Watson and Darwin, had persuaded him that the doctrine of vegetable perception had been established. In America Cooper had a vigorous academic and political life. In his article *On Vegetable Life* in 1814 Cooper lists as the properties of vegetable life irritability, contractility, extensibility, locomotion, and *"perhaps* (for further we dare not go) sensibility and voluntarity" (T.C., 1814, p. 179). "Extensibility", by the way, is seen when a vine tendril which in the old anecdote, if there is no support for it, contorts into a spiral form, but when a support is placed in its vicinity it extends towards the support. In fact Cooper dares immediately to go further, reproducing Darwin's and Smith's material to argue for plant sentience and volition: the latter concept implies the former. This is done in a grand teleological framework. All plant behaviour and structure evinces design and intention. In a fashion owing much to Paley (he begins with the watch and watchmaker parable) Cooper sees everywhere in Nature marks of a divine artist's intelligence and skill, but then moves purpose and intention from without the organism to within it:

> "but whether in great things or in small, the general rule is the same when I see motions and exertions manifestly tending and calculated to answer a particular purpose, as means to an end, I presume that they really are intended to answer that purpose .... And in all such cases when I can discover no impulse whatever ab extra to cause the motion, I have no alternative but to refer it to some excitement ab intra" (p. 184).

In the ensuing unordered debate three other parties, "J.R.W." (1815(a), 1815(b)), "W.D." (1815) and the Editor (1815) (Charles Caldwell), joined in, with Cooper (1815(a), 1815 (b)) keeping it going. The debate became somewhat sidetracked on the question of the evidence for Christian belief, but J.R.W.'s first reply to Cooper is worth mentioning, because it makes the point in a long and detailed article that the analogically-based argument drawn from Darwin can be used to establish sensibility and volition anywhere or everywhere. J.R.W. asks

> "When the magnetic needle points to the North pole, as a means to direct the serveyor and the mariner, are we to suppose that the needle really intends it to answer that purpose? We know of no impulse from without. It must then, according to T.C. come from within; and if his reasoning .... has any relevancy to his subject, the action of the needle must be

sensible and voluntary. Besides, it greatly enlarges the field of enjoyment, and puts it into our power to communicate capacities of happiness to a most important class of minerals, nay, perhaps .... to the whole mineral kingdom" (1815 (a), p. 25).

The doctrine of plant instincts continued into the nineteenth century. In his *A System of Physiological Botany* (1816) a clerical botanist, the Reverend Patrick Keith, advanced a vitalistic conception of vegetable instincts. Whilst not allowing a sensory component to instincts he is sufficiently impressed by the telegraph plant's movements to declare them "one of the strongest indications" of sensitivity in plants (Keith, 1816, p. 464).

The London physician and pioneer epidemiologist Thomas Hancock (1783-1849) considered plant behaviour in his *Essay on Instinct* in 1824. He draws very heavily on Smellie, including the stories of the water-seeking cucumber and the support-seeking vine tendril, and echoes Smellie's conclusion that plants have no sensory or perceptual capacities. He is prepared to allow reluctantly that they might be said to have "the two natural *instincts*, if such they may be called, of nutrition and propagation" (p. 131), because their patterns of acquiring nutrition and of propagating fit his criterion of instinct in man and brute, being

"performed with every indication of design, forethought, and wisdom, which are not the result of instruction nor of individual experience, but of a power operating above the consciousness of the creature, and directing it with unerring certainty to some specific ends by means far beyond its comprehension .... (pp. 15-16).

Hancock recognises that the concept of irritability has no real explanatory power, but does not appreciate that the teleological, rationalistic concept of instinct might also lack explanatory power.

Central to teleological interpretations of natural phenomena is the notion of design. William Paley's *Natural Theology* was published in 1802, and its attempt to apply the traditional argument from design to the contemporary world attracted a number of natural philosophers, its logical deficiencies notwithstanding. As has been seen, Thomas Cooper was influenced by Paley, and it is to be expected that from the ranks of the plant teleologists there would be others who would follow Paley. The doctrine of plant instincts in particular was located easily within a naturalistic framework structured in terms of natural theology — consider, for example, Hancock's account of instinct. The Reverend John Shute Duncan's *Botanical Theology* (1826) was offered explicitly as a supplement to Paley's *Natural Theology*. Its job is to present evidence of Design in the plant world. Duncan notes the "peculiar irritability" of the sensitive and carnivorous plants but stops short of predicating sentience of them. Every grain of wheat is

> "adued with instincts, which are capable, if it be duly placed, to send
> a portion of its yet undeveloped but predestined being downwards
> in the form of a root" (p. 76).

At least Hancock allows only two instincts to a plant, not an unspecified plurality. It is hard to see how the concept of plant instinct could be more vacuous than it is in Duncan's words.

In the same line of thought, but more sophisticated and better known than Duncan's book, is the Reverend William Kirby's *On the Power Wisdom and Goodness of God As Manifested in the Creation* of Animals and in their History Habits and Instincts (1835). This volume is the seventh of the eight *Bridgewater Treatises*. The *Treatises* were published as a result of a bequest from Francis Egerton, eighth Earl of Bridgewater (1756-1828), whose aim was to employ scholars to write "On the Power, Wisdom and Goodness of God, as manifested in the Creation». The *Treatises* were to present, therefore, an overwhelming mass of data proving, in the eyes of the Earl, the existence of Design in creation. Kirby (1759-1850) was Rector of Barham, Suffolk, and was active in the Linnaean Society. His interests were primarily entomological, but also botanical.

Chapter 18 of Kirby's monograph is on instinct, which he wishes to argue is a naturally occurring phenomenon evincing design. In animals "every kind of instinct has its origin in the will of the Deity, and .... the animal, exhibiting it, was expressly organized by Him for it at its creation" (Kirby, 1835, p.229). Plant instincts are important in Kirby's scheme of things. He wants to show that animal instincts have natural causes (as opposed to immediate "metaphysical" ones), the natural causes being intermediate between the Deity and the phenomena of animal instinct. If, however, he can show analogous instinctual phenomena in plants, which are "organized beings without sense or voluntary motion" (p. 245), and are therefore subject entirely to natural causes, then why suppose that animal instincts are not also naturally caused?

Just as the most remarkable instincts of animals are those connected with propagation of the species, so the analogue of these instincts in plants is the development of those parts concerned with the production of seed:

" — so that the expanded flower and the operations going on in it is the analogue of the reproductive instinct of the animal: this is all produced by physical action upon the organization of the plant. Now if we consider the infinite variety of plants, and the wonderful diversity of their parts of fructification and that these are all produced in their several seasons and stations by the action of some physical powers upon their varied organization, and by means of the soil in which they are planted, we shall think it nearly as wonderful and unaccountable as the instinctive operations of the various creatures that feed upon them. That the same action should unfold such an infinite variety of forms in one case and instincts in the other is equally astounding and equally difficult to explain. — Compare the sunflower and the hive-bee, the compound flowers of the one, and the aggregate combs of the other — the receptacle with its seeds, and the combs with the grubs" (p. 247).

Kirby then moves from analogy drawn with plant structures to plant behaviour, where there is, he believes, something stronger than mere analogy between animal instincts and plant structures, a correspondence "in some measure" with other animal instincts. Concerning plants:

"some with a climbing or voluble stem, constantly turn one way, and some as constantly turn another. Thus the hop twines from the left to the right, while the bindweed goes from right to left; others close their leaves in the night, and seem to go to sleep; others shew a remarkable degree of irritability when touched; the blossoms of many, as the sunflower, follow the sun from his rising to his setting; some blossoms shut up, as in the anemone, till the sun shines upon them; others close at a certain hour of the day, as the goatsbeard; another, *Hedysarum gyrans*, slowly revolves" (pp. 247-248).

Then follow pages of examples of changes in plant growth habits as functions of physical location, nutrition and climate, leading to the conclusion that "as the immediate cause of the vegetable instinct is clearly *physical*, so may be that of the animal" (p. 253). At this stage instincts clearly are predicated of plants.

We find no hint of "natural theology" in Percival, and certainly none in Erasmus Darwin, who had no truck with conventional religion. It is Watson who has a theological backdrop to his speculations. With or without religious overtones, however, the influence of Watson, Percival, Tupper and especially Darwin continued, and was evident in some orthodox teaching posts.

Another botanical Smith provides an example: Edward Smith (1818?-1874), a physician and medical writer who lectured at one time in botany at London's Charing Cross Hospital. Smith's *Structural and Systematic Botany* of 1855 advises the reader that if he studies the vegetable kingdom

"not as an inferior part of God's works, but as a portion of the one and indivisible kingdom of organized existences", resemblances of structure and function between plants and animals will be found, and even though no nerves or analogues of nerves have as yet been found in plants "it is quite clear that not only is a low degree of vital sensibility as universal in plants as in animals, but in certain instances — in that of the sensitive plant, for instance — it is developed to a far greater extent than is perceptible in animals removed from the lowest point in the animal scale" (p.v.).

Smith has nothing essentially new to say but there is something new which is worthy of note. In addition to the traditional examples of plant movement from which sensation may be deduced Smith adds the locomotion of the motile cells of the lower plants, first systematically observed in the 1820's:

> " .... it is well known that the spores, or undeveloped young plants of
> *Confervae* and of sea-weeds .... move about by the action of their own
> cilia or hairs, until they have found a resting-place to which to attach
> themselves. Thus we may add a degree of locomotion to the qualities
> of plants; and say that, in some instances, they grow, live, feel and
> move. On the other hand the sponges .... in their developed state, are
> denied the faculty of locomotion, although they undoubtedly belong
> to the animal kingdom" (p. 4).

The microscopic world of the tiny moving plant cells was to become another hunting ground for plant psychologists.

To conclude this chapter, we have noted that plant psychology has intersected with other ideas of the time: there is a link with utilitarianism in the claim that the sentience of plants adds to the greater amount of happiness, there is a link with natural theology in the claim that the psychology of plants is further evidence of an Intelligence which (or who) has designed a creation, there is a link with Romanticism in the claim that there is a subjective aspect of the vegetable kingdom which is lost to any mechanistic vision of it. It is interesting to speculate what a disinterested observer might have forecast for the future of plant psychology as the nineteenth century unfolded. Such an observer may well have said that, granted that no new plant marvels emerged from the Antipodes, plant psychology would peter out: the instinctivist approach in the form it took was vapid, and the mentalist tradition surely had reached its apotheosis with Erasmus Darwin.

Such a forecast would have been wrong. The observer was not to know that the doctrine of evolution by means of natural selection was to be advanced, and that it would give a boost to the fortunes of plant psychology.

CHAPTER 7

The evolutionary impact (1)

7.1 *Taking Stock; Charles Darwin*

B y the middle of the nineteenth century the terms "scientist", "biology" and "psychology" were part of current usage. There were no independent departments of psychology in universities, but the concept of psychology as a discipline arising out of, but separate from, mental philosophy and physiology, did exist. Herbert Spencer's *The Principles of Psychology* was published in 1855, and the old issue of where, if at all, in the scale of being could a line be drawn between the presence and absence of mental faculties could now be posed as a psychological question. Spencer proceeded to do so in a passage which deserves being quoted in full (it is a fine example of orotund Victorian periphrasis). Note, incidentally, that the physiological concept of the "reflex action" is now in use alongside "instinct" as a class of behaviour.

"It is not more certain that from the simple reflex action by which the infant sucks, up to the elaborate reasonings of the adult man, the progress is by daily infinitesimal steps, than it is certain that between the automatic actions of the lowest creatures, and the highest conscious actions of the human race, a series of actions, displayed by the various tribes of the animal kingdom, may be so placed, as to render it impossible to say of any one step in the series — here intelligence begins. If, from the advanced man of science, pursuing his inquiries with a full understanding of ratiocinative and inductive processes he employs, we descend to the man of ordinary education, who reasons well and comprehensively, but without knowing how; if, going a grade lower, we analyze the thinkings of the villager, whose highest generalizations are but little wider than those which local events afford data for; if, again, we sink to the inferior human races, who cannot be induced to think, who cannot take in ideas of any complexity, and whose conceptions of number scarcely transcend those of a dog; if we take next the higher quadrumana, hosts of whose actions are quite as rational as those of school-boys, and whose language, however unintelligible to us, is manifestly more or less intelligible to each other; if from these, we proceed to domesticated animals, whose power of reasoning is conceded even by those under theological bias, with the qualification that it is special and not general — a qualification which equally holds between the different grades of human reasoning; if, from the most sagacious quadrupeds, we descend to the less and less sagacious ones, noting as we pass how gradual is the transition to those which exhibit no power of modifying their actions to suit special conditions, and which so prove themselves to be guided by what we call instinct; if, from observing the operation of the higher instincts, in which a complicated combination of motions is produced by a complicated combination of stimuli, we go down to the successively lower ones, in which the applied stimuli and the resulting motions are less and less complex; if, presently, we find ourselves merging into what is technically known as a reflex action, in which a single motion follows a single stimulus; if, from the creatures in which this implies the irritation of a nerve and the contraction of a muscle, we descend yet lower, to creatures devoid of nervous and muscular systems, and discover that in these the irritability and the contractility are exhibited by the same tissue, which tissue also fulfils the functions of assimilation, secretion, respiration, and reproduction; and if, finally, we perceive that each of the phases of intelligence here instanced, shades off into the adjacent ones by modifications too numerous to specify, too minute to describe, we shall in some measure realize the fact, that no definite separation can be affected between the phenomena of mind and those of vitality in general" (Spencer, 1855, pp. 349-350).

That Spencer's remarks show implicit nineteenth century English social prejudices is so obvious that no further comment on that point is needed. What is of interest here is that they show no advance on the traditional thinking we have been considering, and (shades of Anaxagoras) they invite the claim that if mind and vitality in general cannot be separated then plants must have mind of some sort. Spencer himself never accepted that invitation, but others did.

However, to return to the disinterested observer at the end of the previous chapter, in 1855 it might have seemed that plant psychology would peter out. Edward Smith's text of that year had no compelling new arguments for mentalism; failing the discovery in the Americas or in Australia and New Zealand of new plant species possessing previously unknown wonderful forms of irritability what point could there be in persisting with claims of plant sensation?

As it happened plant psychology did not peter out. The reason is that the biological doctrine of evolution by natural selection was sufficient to give it a distinct fillip, to stimulate it anew. In 1858 Charles Darwin and Alfred Russel Wallace presented to the Linnaean Society evidence of the role of natural selection in evolution, and Darwin's *The Origin of Species by Means of Natural Selection* in the following year attracted tremendous attention.

Charles Darwin had a two-fold impact on plant psychology. His account of evolution gave it fresh stimulation, and his work as an experimental botanist — an enterprise separate from the evolutionary theorizing — attracted the interest of the vegetable mentalists. His works pertaining to the latter impact, the botanical one, were principally *Insectivorous Plants* (1875 and with Francis Darwin 1888 (2nd edition)), which shows that the sundews (*drosera*) had the same fascination for Charles that they had had for his grandfather, Erasmus, *The Movement and Habits of Climbing Plants* (1875), and especially *The Power of Movement in Plants* (1880). He was assisted in *The Power of Movement* by his botanist son Francis, who is the third member of the Darwin family to become important in this history.

Unlike his grandfather and his son, Charles Darwin made no claims for a psychology of plants in his mature published works. As a younger man, however, he had taken the notion seriously — even flirted with it, as the evidence of some early notebooks (transcribed by P. H. Barrett and published in H. E. Gruber's *Darwin on Man* (1974)) shows. He was aware of Erasmus's claims, he knew that Buffon contended that the animal and plant kingdoms were continuous and he had read Kirby's Bridgewater Treatise. In what Charles put together as "*Old and useless Notes about the moral sense & some metaphysical points written about the year 1837 & earlier*", most of which were written in fact between 1837 and 1840 (Gruber 1974, p. 382) he speculates on the existence of two orders of sensation. The first might be defined in the absence of consciousness as contraction in "fibres united with nervous filaments" (Darwin, in Gruber, 1974, p. 384). In this sense plants have sensation, but by a distinct mechanism which is unstated. The second order of sensation is a higher one: it is conveyed over the whole body, and, when there is no consciousness present, is evidenced by certain actions which are related to the primary sensation — witness the example of a man moving a leg when he is asleep. The higher order of sensation occurs perhaps in polyps, hence one could take the lower animals as "sleeping higher animals", rather than plants as supposed by Buffon. Consciousness is higher sensation combined with memory.

The *Old and useless notes* objects to the concept of irritability being used to explain the movements of the sensitive plant, the flow of sap and the orienting of the sunflower to the sun, on the grounds that irritability "at least shows a local will, though perhaps not conscious sensation" (Darwin, in Gruber, footnote p. 392). Darwin prefers a mechanistic explanation of these processes, but sees them as raising the question of how consciousness commences. He objects too to Kirby's attribution of instinct to plants, arguing that it is "misplaced" because "instincts imply willing" (Darwin, in Gruber p. 393).

The *N .Notebook* (1838-9) raises questions about plants' knowledge of causality and space, thus evoking echoes of Erasmus, even though it does not answer the questions in the direction taken by him. Charles asks

"Origin of cause & effect being a necessary notion, is it connected with
.... the willing of the simplest animals, as hydra towards light being
direct effect of some law. — have plants any notion of cause & effect/

they have habitual action which depends on such confidence /when does such notion commence? — "

(Darwin, in Gruber, p. 332).

Shortly after:

"Has the oyster necessary notion of space — plant though it moves doubtless has not. — " (p. 333).

In a passage both presaging twentieth century behaviourist psychology and recalling his grandfather's ideas, Darwin analyses plant memory in terms of mechanical associations:

"The memory of Plants, must be association, — a certain round of actions take place every day, & closing of the leaves, comes on from want of stimulus, after certain actions, & hence become associated with them. — The establishment of this principle of Association will help my theory of sensitive Plants" (p. 339).

On this point Barrett notes that in a copy of *Zoonomia*, in a passage where Erasmus says of the sensitive plant that leaf contraction can be observed as a result of the absence of light (and argues that this must be due to sensation or volition), Charles has written in the margin "does habit imply having ideas?" (Darwin, cited by Barrett in Gruber, p. 355).

Gruber has an interesting observation to make about Charles's speculation on plant knowledge of cause and effect:

"At this point Darwin is conceding nothing in his search for continuities between man and all other living creatures .... The possibility that plants think may strike the reader as plain silly. For Darwin, entertaining the idea was just pushing a bold idea all the way. Years later he made the idea a lot more plausible with his works on the behaviour of plants — climbing plants, twining plants, and insectivorous plants" (Gruber, p. 363).

It should be borne in mind that any such plausibility here is only in the eyes of some of Darwin's readers (as will be seen) — it is not in his own eyes, for his later published works on plants clearly make no claims for a plant psychology, even though they stimulated it. In *Insectivorous Plants* he uses the terms "irritability" and "sensitiveness" without any cognitive connotations (or vitalistic ones for that matter). "Strictly speaking", he says of the sundew, "the glands ought to be called irritable, as the term sensitive generally implies consciousness; but no one supposes that the sensitive plant is conscious, and as I have found the term convenient, I shall use it without scruple" (1875 (a), p. 19). In the *Power of Movement* he begins by describing "circumnutatory movements":

"The most widely prevalent movement is essentially of the same nature as that of the stem of a climbing plant, which bends successively to all points of the compass, so that the tip revolves" (p. 1).

"Apparently every growing part of every plant is continually circumnutating, though often on a small scale" (p.3).

The book concerns itself with a number of different aspects of circumnutating movements, including those modified ones which Darwin prefers to call "nyctitropic" rather than "sleep". He objects to the likening of these movements to animal sleep.

Unwittingly Charles did a great service to plant psychology in a passage in the last chapter of *The Power of Movement*, a passage which culminates in a famous analogy:

"We believe that there is no structure in plants more wonderful, as far as its functions are concerned, than the tip of the radicle. If the tip be lightly pressed or burnt or cut, it transmits an influence to the upper adjoining part, causing it to bend away from the affected side; and, what is more surprising, the tip can distinguish between a slightly harder and softer object, by which it is simultaneously pressed on opposite sides .... If the tip perceives the air to be moister on one side than on the other, it likewise transmits an influence to the upper adjoining part, which bends towards the source of moisture" .... (further details of the diverse kinds of sensitiveness of the tip follow). "It is hardly an exaggeration to say that the tip of the radicle thus endowed, and having the power of directing the movements of the adjoining parts, acts like the brain of one of the lower animals; the brain being seated within the anterior end of the body, receiving impressions from the sense organs, and directing the several movements" (pp. 572-3).

For Darwin, this analogy was just that, an analogy, and his terms such as "distinguish" and "power of directing" were figures of speech rather than literal cognitive and volitional ones respectively, but many were to read this passage as expressing an identity between plant movements and animal ones. Plants might have nothing resembling a central nervous system, but the sensitive tip of the radicle does what the brain does. To all intents and purposes it is a brain. From here the step is very short: the tip of the radicle is a brain. Is this not a reasonable conclusion, they believed, especially when Darwin's studies had shown the extraordinary sensitivity of which plants are capable? In the sundew, for example, "a little bit of human hair 8/1000 of an inch (.203 mm.) in length, and weighing only 1/78740 of a grain (.000822 mg.), though largely supported by the dense secretion, suffices to induce movement" (C. Darwin, 1888, p. 213). Darwin was blamed by some opponents of vitalism and mentalism for misleading readers (see Macdougal, 1895); to his critics his analogy was not famous, but notorious.

The other aspect of Darwin's impact on plant psychology , the stimulation given it by the theory of evolution, is in its turn two-fold. First, there is the old problem, now recast in evolutionary terms, of where mind begins (or ends) in the hierarchy of beings. Second, there is a new problem: given that evolution occurs, its mechanics have to be explained. Amongst the competing accounts of evolutionary change at the end of the nineteenth century and early in this century was one which was psychological in character. It made memory the key to evolution. Insofar as plants as well as animals were subject to evolutionary change plants accordingly must have memories. In the rest of this chapter we shall consider the first aspect.

7.2   Mind in the Phylogenetic Scale

The hoary old problem of where mind could be said to first appear (or disappear) in the hierarchical scale of being was given a new run by being re-cast in evolutionary terms. Erasmus Darwin's evolutionary speculations had nothing to do with his plant psychology, but Charles's evolutionary speculations were seen by some to provide a plausible framework for a theory of mental processes in the vegetable world. The hierarchy of being was no longer the ordering of discrete

classes or kingdoms according to criteria such as complexity of corporeal structure or capacity for spiritual awareness and perfectibility:
to the evolutionary outlook it was literally an historical (temporal)
ordering. To speak of new species evolving out of old is to recognize
morphological continuity which extends over time: the scale of being
is a phylogenetic scale. If humans have minds then the obvious question is "where did mind evolve?". As we survey down the phylogenetic
scale do we find a point where there is only rudimentary mind and
below it a point where there is no mind at all? If we believe this to be
the case then are we not denying the evolutionary thesis of the *psychic continuity* of all living organisms? The only way to answer these
questions is to find an objective criterion of mind and to compare different species systematically according to the objective criterion, and
this is what the founding fathers of comparative psychology sought
to do in the later nineteenth century. There is nothing wrong with
the ideal of specifying an objective criterion of mind, providing that
at least in principle it can be done. But, as historians of comparative
psychology have shown (e.g. Warden, Jenkins and Warner, 1935)
the brave ideal turned out in practice again to be the application
of argument by analogy. If in a human a certain sort of behaviour
accompanied a certain type or level of mental operation, and if a brute
could perform the same kind of behaviour then, ergo, it must possess
the same mental capacity as the human. If analogy is to be our sole
guide then there is no *a priori* reason for confining our quest to the
animals, for plants have their place on the phylogenetic continuum
and if our analogical reasoning forces us to conclude that plants have
mentality of some sort, then so be it. The majority of comparative
psychologists and biologists who might have had some sympathy with

analogical reasoning in their comparative researches (i.e. compar-
ing different species in respect of an attribute or set thereof) had *a
priori* reasons for not wanting to extend their analogies too far down
the scale, and for the them there was simply no serious question of
vegetable mentality.

A characteristically tough-minded approach was that of T. H.
Huxley who believed that, although the difference between plants
and animals was one of degree, not kind, and

> "although the roots of plants direct themselves towards moisture,
> and their leaves towards air and light, — although the parts of some
> plants exhibit oscillating movements without any perceptible cause,
> and the leaves of other retract when touched, — yet none of these
> movements justify the ascription to plants of perception or of will"
> (Huxley, 1876, p. 163).

Another eminent man of letters who attempted to discourage the
credulous was George Henry Lewes (1817-1878). In a monograph
on psychology in the third series of *Problems of Life and Mind* (1879)
Lewes warns of the dangers facing "the various eminent writers who
attempted an Animal Psychology" and who have "a secret desire to
establish the *identity* of animal and human nature" (p. 122), the principal dangers being anthropomorphism and analogical argument.

Of the Venus fly-trap he asks":

> "Shall we here also recognise the presence of feelings similar to the
> feelings in the dog and ourselves? There are distinguished writers
> who attribute a soul to the plant, no less than to the animal. The
> hypothesis lies wholly beyond disproof, because it lies wholly beyond
> proof. But I would urge, that if we credit plant and polyps with souls,

we are bound by every consideration to deny that these souls are *like* our own .... The marked variation of the organic conditions presented by the various animal structures must produce marked dissimilarities in sentient phenomena. *A priori*, then, we are certain that a plant or a polyp cannot possibly feel like a dog or a man; and although we may credit it with feeling, *what* the nature of that feeling is must remain entirely inconceivable to us"

(1879, pp. 126-7).

The same kind of quandary in which Bonnet had found himself over a hundred years before claimed George John Romanes in his *Mental Evolution in Animals* in 1883. This book and the better known *Animal Intelligence* constitute the main publications by which Romanes (1848-1894) earned the title of the "father" of comparative psychology. Romanes was concerned to discover as precisely as possible where mind entered the phylogenetic scale, he was sure on analogical grounds that other species besides the human did have minds. The big problem was the finding of an objective indicator of mind and Romanes had difficulty with this problem. In *Animal Intelligence* (Romanes, 1882) he suggested that learning, defined as the ability of an organism to make new adjustments of behaviour to the environment, or to modify old ones, as a result of individual experience, was the objective evidence of mind. Conceptually this was an advance on the notion of choice, or the power of discrimination, as the mark of mind ("consciousness"), which was the criterion which most appealed to him and which he advanced in *Mental Evolution in Animals*. Romanes conceded that whilst all mind involved choice, not all *apparent* choice involved mind. One of the unfortunate outcomes of allowing choice to be evidence of mind would be that plants would have to be admitted to have minds, for on his own line of reasoning this conclusion seemed inescapable.

The mark of mind is consciousness. Consciousness in action is seen in choice, and choice is manifest behaviourally in acts of *discrimination*. Romanes sets his evolutionary context:

> "Now if the power of choice is the distinctive peculiarity of a mental being, and if .... every change of Mind is associated with some change of Body, it follows that this distinctive peculiarity ought to admit of being translated into some physiological equivalent. Further, if there is any such physiological equivalent to be found, we should expect to find it much lower down in the scale of physiological development than in the functions of the human brain. For not only do the lower animals manifest, in a long descending scale, powers of choice which gradually face away into greater and greater simplicity; but we should be led *à priori* to expect, if there is a physiological principle which constitutes the objective basis of the psychological principle, that the former should manifest itself more early in the course of evolution than the latter" (1883, pp. 47-48).

Discrimination is found to be co-extensive with excitability (the capacity to respond to appropriate stimulation, taken to be the characteristic sign of vitality) and

> "it is this function that I regard as the root principle of Mind .... If we consider all the faculties of mind, we shall observe that the one feature which on their objective side they present as common, is this power of discriminating among stimuli, and responding only to those which irrespective of relative mechanical intensity, are the stimuli to which responses are appropriate" (1883, p. 52).

Mental Evolution in Animals has a large and detailed chart inspired by Haeckel's evolutionary genealogical trees showing at what place in the evolutionary scale a given level of mental functioning is to be found. Evidence of consciousness Romanes finds in animals as far down as the echinodermata (the spiny-skinned marine invertebrates such as starfish and sea-urchins) and coelenterata (a term which in Romanes's time included marine creatures such as sea anemones, corals and comb jellies). After mentioning the ability of sea-anemones to discriminate between the stimuli of bubbles and a solid body in an aquarium tank he notes the "similar power of discriminative response" in plants, referring specifically to the work of Charles and Francis Darwin. Attention is drawn to their observations which show "the extraordinary delicacy of discrimination" of the leaves of some plants "between darkness and light of the feeblest intensity" (p. 49) and especially their studies on insectivorous and climbing plants. For example the sundew and the Venus fly-trap not only respond to external stimulation but seem to discriminate between stimuli: the sundew secretes its viscous fluid when a fly lands on it but not when a drop of rain does, the fly-trap closes up on a fly but not on rain, a phenomenon which cannot be explained simply in terms of brute mechanical force because the rain drop may be heavier than the fly.

It would seem at this point that given Romanes's premises and given that the application of his criterion is accurate then it must follow that (at least some) plants possess mind. Here Romanes baulks, but is honest in recognizing the quandary in which places himself:

"The difficulty is that I began by showing it necessary to define Mind as the power of exercising Choice, and then proceeded to define the latter as a power belonging only to agents that are able to feel. Yet, on looking at the objective side of the problem, I pointed out that the physiological or objective equivalent of choice is found to occur in its simplest manifestations at least as low down as the insectivorous plants, which are certainly not agents capable, in any proper sense of the term, of feeling. Therefore it seems that my conception of what constitutes Choice is in antagonism with my view that the essential element of Choice is found to occur among organisms which cannot properly be supposed to feel. And this antagonism, or inherent con-tradiction, is a real one, though I hold it to be unavoidable .... There are two ways of meeting the difficulty. One is to draw an arbitrary line, and the other is not to draw any line at all; but to carry the terms down through the whole gradation of the things until we arrive at the terminal or root-principles. By the time we arrive at these root-principles, it is no doubt true that our terms have lost all their original meaning; so that we might as well call an acorn an oak, or an egg a chicken, as speak of a Dionaea *feeling* a fly, or of a Drosera *choosing* to close upon its prey. Yet this use, or rather .... abuse, of terms serves one important purpose if, while duly regarding the change of mean-ing which during their gradual descent the terms are made gradually to undergo, we thus serve to emphasize the fact they refer to things which are the product of a gradual evolution — things which come from other things as unlike to them as oaks to acorns or chickens to eggs. And this is my justification for tracing back the root-principles of Feeling and of Choice into the vegetable kingdom. If it is true that the plants manifest so little evidence of Feeling that the term can only be applied to them in a metaphorical sense, it is also true that the power of Choice which they display is of a similarly undeveloped character" (1883, pp. 54-55).

In this passage the material following Romanes's recognition of the difficulty he is in is nothing more than special pleading, for it follows logically from Romanes's line of argument that some plants must have minds. If one does not side with Percival, Watson, Erasmus Darwin and others and welcome the conclusion, or at least side with Bonnet and give it the benefit of the doubt, then one must call into question either the accuracy of one's observations on plants and/or the truth of one's basic premises.

Often contrasted with Romanes is another pioneer of comparative psychology, Conway Lloyd Morgan (1852-1936) whose introductory text on the subject in 1894 should have put paid to the question of plant psychology if his famous canon of parsimony had been heeded:

"In no case is an animal activity to be interpreted as the outcome of the exercise of a higher psychical faculty, if it can be fairly interpreted as the outcome of the exercise of one which stands lower in the psychological scale" (Lloyd Morgan, 1894, p. 53).

If Lloyd Morgan's canon is relevant to animals then *a fortiori* it is relevant to plants (later he was to attack plant psychology). He made it clear that he was not going to travel on Romanes's inexorable road to dilemma:

"I feel bound to lay stress on the necessity for the greatest caution in the psychical interpretation of insect activities; and I feel justified in restricting myself, in this work, to a consideration of the psychical states which we may infer to be associated with the functional activity of the cerebral hemispheres in the higher vertebrates" (1894, p. 41).

Lloyd Morgan held to an evolutionist conception of mind, and although with hindsight we may say that critics who held that Lloyd Morgan himself violated his own principle of parsimony had a point, (the behaviourist revolution in psychology passed him by, he was in 1930 writing still of "mind" in higher animals, the conceptual justification of which he sought in an emergentist philosophy), the fact remains that the wielding of Occam's razor was most appropriate at the time. Amongst the botanists who could be selected for shaving with this razor was the German plant physiologist Gottlieb Haberlandt. Haberlandt's *Physiological Plant Anatomy* (1884) claimed that organs sensitive to a few types of external stimulation (contact, mechanical, gravity and light, but not taste, smell or thermal stimuli) had been found in plants, and that these organs should be regarded as sense-organs proper. Accordingly plants may be considered to possess "sensation" and "perception", and the possibility of their possessing psychical processes is an open question, but not one subject to empirical test. Haberlandt was sufficiently parsimonious, however, to deny intelligent purpose to plants.

In the present context two other botanists who might have done well to consider whether Lloyd Morgan's canon had application to their thinking are worthy of mention.

David Starr Jordan, President of the Leland Stanford Jnr. University, as it was called then, and a systematic botanist and zoologist, argued (Jordan, 1898) that mind evolved out of basic cellular irritability. Whilst mind is collective function of the brain or sensorium in higher animals, and therefore only these are capable of consciousness, they are, with the plants, colonies of co-operating cells each one of which is irritable. Plants and the lowest animals are not conscious, then, but have consciousness immanent in them, a conclusion which is reminiscent of Percival's thinking. Jordan's reference to the importance of cells should be seen in the context of biological debate about the emergent significance of the organism (an aggregate of cells) which was current then.

Whereas the comparative psychologist Robert Yerkes had seen the problem of finding a criterion of the existence of mental states in non-human organisms as one which had no cut-and-dried answer — different criteria were of different value in different situations

(R. M. Yerkes, 1905) — his botanist wife Ada was content with the traditional analogically-based argument for mind in plants. In 1914 she reviewed a little of the history of the subject, and, after considering such telling characters of plant behaviour such as "modifiability" (she relays an old anecdote of the sensitive plant which will remain open after becoming habituated to continual jarring), she concludes that

"the unprejudiced observer must admit that instinctive activities appear in the plants and animals, and like similar responses to stimuli possess essentially the same characteristics in both. As for the instinct — consciousness, if the observer considers fairly the evidences upon which his admission of consciousness rests, he will find it easier to acknowledge affective consciousness in plants than to deny it or disprove its existence" (A. W. Yerkes, 1914, pp. 642-643).

Both Jordan and Ada Yerkes appealed to Charles Darwin's plant radical tip/brain analogy to add lustre to their claims.

If we look at orthodox psychologists' responses over the next few decades to the general problem of mind in evolution as posed by Spencer, Romanes and Lloyd Morgan we find that there are differences. In particular it is of interest to note that some were prepared to take the hypothesis of the plant mind seriously enough to raise it, even if they were to reject it.

Wilhelm Wundt had nothing to say about the plant mind. He castigated Romanes and his anecdotalist case for the animal mind, conceding that basic cognitive phenomena (e.g. knowing their proper food, recognizing the location of food) might occur in higher brutes but not in the lowest (Wundt, 1894). Within the ranks of the classical structuralist/introspectionist psychologists it was E. B. Titchener who directly addressed the issue of mind in plants. Titchener's *Outline of Psychology* in 1896 made no reference to plants, but two years later it seems that the topic of the plant mind was sufficiently in the air to provoke a passing mention in *A Primer of Psychology*. More generous than Wundt to the lower animals, Titchener allow that they might have primitive minds because they show the beginnings of "impulsive action", and having agreed to this he has to fact the prospect of vegetable mind:

> "It has been seriously argued by some psychologists that mind appears whenever life appears; not only in the animal kingdom, but in the vegetable as well. This is a question which we cannot stop to discuss here. At any rate the plant mind, if there is such a thing, must be so extraordinarily rudimentary and so totally different from our own that it is hopeless to try to form any idea of it" (1898,p.17).

Titchener's *A Text-book of Psychology*, which appeared in two parts in 1909 and 1910, was intended to replace the *Outline*, and by now Titchener is willing to at least pause to discuss the question. Whilst, like Haberlandt, he is willing to talk of plant sense-organs, he is not willing to talk now of a rudimentary plant mind. But he does not actually close the question: the final verdict is that plants do not *appear* to have minds. In his words:

> "Indeed it is difficult to limit mind to the animals that possess even a

rudimentary nervous system; for the creatures that rank still lower in the scale of life manage to do, without a nervous system, practically everything that their superiors do by its assistance. The range of mind thus appears to be as wide as the range of animal life.

The plants, on the other hand, appear to be mindless. Many of them are endowed with what we may term sense-organs, that is organs differentiated to receive certain forms of stimulus, pressure, impact, light, etc. These organs are analogous in structure to the sense-organs of the lower animal organisms: thus, plant 'eyes' have been found, which closely resemble rudimentary animal eyes, and which — if they belonged to animals — might mediate the perception of light: so that the development of the plant-world has evidently been governed by the same general laws of adaptation to environment that have been at work in the animal kingdom. But we have no evidence of a plant-consciousness" (1909, pp. 27-28).

George Trumbell Ladd, another prominent American psychologist at the end of the nineteenth century, believed that the lowest animals had a psychic life and he therefore could not easily cavil at plants having one. Biologists, he wrote,

"cannot understand or explain the phenomena of living animal forms (and, perhaps, not those of living plant forms) without appealing to the science of psychical phenomena" (Ladd, 1896, p. 296).

In contrast to the woolly thinking of the tradition-bound analogical comparative psychologists that of Madison Bentley of the Cornell University showed a Huxleyan tough-mindness which anticipated in 1902 the behaviourist outlook in psychology:

"It is, one may admit, not difficult to construct hypothetical con-sciousnesses for the amoeba, the jelly-fish, the bee and the beaver; consciousnesses which shall explain beautifully the reactions of these animals. But the question arises whether there hypothetical minds really exist .... The recent history of genetic psychology is filled with fictitious minds which are worse than useless to the psychologist, whatever their value may be to the biologist. One proof of their unsat-isfactoriness, even as agents of natural selection, is given, I am inclined to believe, in the well-marked tendency within biology to explain reactions of the simpler organisms in terms of "tropism" and "taxis" instead of in terms of "volition" and "reason" (Bentley, 1902, p. 389).

Although a believer in the existence of consciousness, Mary Calkins in 1905 took a stand against the evolutionists' arguments from continuity. It proves too much she said, if it demonstrates that the lowest animals and plants have mental lives then it demonstrates that iron fillings in their movement towards a magnet must have a mental life (Calkins, 1905). Her example is similar to that of Thomas Cooper's critic, J.R.W., ninety years before.

William McDougall's attitude to the plant mind showed some of the ambivalence which we have seen especially in Romanes. McDougall's "hormic" system of psychology saw all human and brute behaviour, *qua* behaviour, as intrinsically teleological and unamenable to mechanistic analysis. In *An Outline of Psychology* (1923) he raises the question, which he felt he could not answer, whether plants show the true behaviour (i.e. purposive) characteristic of living things:

"About plants we are in doubt. When a tree sways in the breeze, we do not speak of its motions as behaviour; but when a flower turns its face toward the sun, or opens and closes its petals, or when a climbing plant seems to reach out and grasp a support, we are more inclined to speak of its behaviour. And science cannot yet tell us whether such language is justified. In the opinion of some leading botanists it is" (McDougall, 1923, p. 43).

Just as Romanes (and many before and after him) sought objective, functional criteria of mind in the activities of organisms, so does McDougall seek objective, functional "marks of behaviour", i.e. properties of organisms' activities which would show the goal-directed character central to behaviour (as opposed to mere mechanical activity). The first five marks of behaviour he advances are a certain spontaneity of movement; persistence of activity independently of the continuance of the impression (stimulus) which may have initiated it; variation of direction of persistent movements; coming to an end of the animal's movements as soon as they have brought about a particular kind of change in its situation, and preparation for the new situation toward the production of which the action contributes. Assuming for argument's sake that these are objectively identifiable marks (an assumption which is open to question) we can ask whether they are to be found in the vegetable world's activities. According to McDougall "No movements of lifeless things combine these five peculiarities; and it is just because the movements of plants do not unmistakably show them that we hesitate to ascribe Mind to plants" (p. 46). Any plant psychologist worth his salt would have been able to tell McDougall that insofar as the marks of behaviour may be said to apply to some animal movements they certainly all apply to some plant movements, but perhaps what to McDougall was "unmistakable" in animals was not unmistakable in plants.

7.3   *The Psychic Life of Micro-organisms*

In the previous section references have been made to the simplest animals, but specific reference has been excluded deliberately to one aspect of the evolutionary quest for mind in the phylogenetic scale because it is of sufficient importance to be treated as a topic in itself. This is the debate on the psychic life of micro-organisms. We shall follow the biological nomenclature of the period and use the term "protista" to cover all single-celled ("unicellular" as they were known) organisms, i.e. the micro-organisms. The protista are members of a kingdom between the animals and the plants, they may be "protozoa" (unicellular animals) or "protophyta" (unicellular plants). By the end of the nineteenth century considerable scientific work had been undertaken on these organisms, and it was inevitable that the principle of continuity in nature, given new life by the doctrine of evolution, should lead comparative psychologists and mentalistically-oriented biologists to ask whether micro-organisms possessed psychic faculties.

Measured by the volume of literature generated, the topic is a fairly large one, and we must pay some attention to it because in that some micro-organisms are single-celled plants ("protophyta"), it intersects with plant psychology. There is no aim, however, at a comprehensive outline of the whole debate.

The first person to be mentioned here is one of the famous psychologists, Alfred Binet. In *The Psychic-Life of Micro-organisms*, subtitled

A Study in Experimental Psychology, which was published in French in 1887 and in English translation in 1889, Binet (1857-1911) claimed to show by methods of objective experiment rather than subjective anthropomorphic interpretation that animal and vegetable unicellular organisms were possessed of "a psychic life, the complexity of which transcends the limits of cellular irritability" (Binet, 1889 (a), p. 109). He was opposed to what would now be called physico-chemical reduction in biology, endorsing the widely held view that biological processes involved a vital quality, one, which although irreducible was not metaphysical. Binet objected to his countryman Richet's argument that irritability is the sole mark of the psychic life of micro-organisms, and to Romanes's view that the organisms had no developed psychic faculties beyond mere excitability. Romanes, he held, had drawn the line between the mental and nonmental arbitrarily at too high a point in his diagram of mental evolution. The most important phenomenon showing mind in micro-organisms is "the existence of a power of selection, exercised either in the search for food, or in the manoeuvres attending conjugation" (pp. 108-9); a large part of the book is devoted to details of feeding and fecundation. This "power of selection" Binet saw as satisfying Romanes's criterion of a discriminative faculty as the functional mark of the mind.

Most of Binet's data are derived from studies of the animal micro-organisms, the protozoa (especially infusoria), but he asserts that "we have shown that in both vegetable and animal micro-organisms phenomena are encountered which pertain to a highly complex psychology .... " (p. 106). Two vegetable examples are: (i) in a chapter dealing with sexual cells (which he sees as being analogous in their behaviour to complete unicellular organisms) he refers to *Ectocarpus siliculosus*, one of the algae which reproduce through union of mobile zoospores; the male spores are initially "indifferent" to the female spore, but, as external conditions change, they "make towards it" and in their interaction with it "perform .... real acts" of physical feeling (p. 85); (ii) the *Volvox* is a genus of green algae in which the many cells form a spherical colony; each cell communicates with the others "in order that their flagella may move in unison and that the entire colony may act as a unit and in obedience to a single impulse"(p.57).

Binet was careful to distinguish between consciousness and psychic life, for on the point whether the various acts indicative of psychic functions involve consciousness he declared himself forced, for the present, to suspend judgement.

In the pages of *The Open Court* (a journal "devoted to the work of conciliating Religion with Science"), Romanes was quick to take Binet up (Romanes, 1889). *The Open Court* had published *The Psychic Life of Micro-organisms* in the previous volume. Romanes feels that Binet cannot literally mean to endow the protista with mental faculties which Romanes reserved for zoologically advanced animals, that the activities seen by Binet as psychic in genesis could be explained mechanistically in terms of natural selection, and that Binet does not realize that he (Romanes) had left it as an open question whether micro-organisms showed evidence of a mental life. A series of interchanges followed (Binet, 1889 (b); Romanes, 1890; Binet, 1890) which centred on the concept of "consciousness" in both men's comparative psychologies. Romanes comes off the better here because of his insistence that Binet's conception of the psychic life of micro-organisms smuggles in sophisticated mental notions such as "intelligence" and "consciousness", despite Binet's protestations to the contrary.

174

Binet's interest in mind and micro-organisms was not peculiar to him. It was part of a wider interest, especially in German physiology. For example Max Verworn (1863-1921) had given English readers access to his ideas a few years earlier (Verworn, 1893-4). Verworn saw the old metaphysical vitalism in physiology as a product of a dualist conception of the mind-body relation. He called for a monist conception, which, he believed, in recognizing that all organisms are "ensouled", that material bodies are also psychic, replaces the old vitalism with a new naturalistic one. This new vitalism is not inimical to chemical and physical explanations of physiological phenomena, because the material and the mental are in reality parts of the whole. His monism was a "psychomonism": the physical world is contained in the psychic. He advocated a cellular approach to physiology, calling especially for study of the free-living unicellular organisms, the protists. His *Psycho-physiologische Protisten-Studien* (*Pychophysiological Studies of the Protists*) was published at the same time as the English version of Binet's book, and in it Verworn urged that all protists show in their movements and physiological processes unconscious psychic processes which are the germ of the highest psychic phenomena of man and other higher animals (Verworn, 1889).

Verworn's cellular theories were themselves much influenced by one of his mentors, Ernst Haeckel (1834-1919). Haeckel, the crusading Darwinist who had come to zoology from botany proclaimed under the banner of monism the "psychological unity" of the organic world. Haeckel saw his scientific enterprises in the context of a world-view which, although it might be claimed to be an evolutionary science-based one, could also be called a new post-Leibnizian monadology with its roots in the naturalistic doctrines of Aristotle and Plato.

For details of his vitalist system, with its religious overtones, see Holt (1971). Haeckel acknowledged the influence of Gustav Fechner on the doctrine of plant "soul-life". To Haeckel different types of "souls" were associated with forms at the different evolutionary levels, the most elementary being the "cell-soul", the basic unit of evolutionary psychology or the most elementary kernel of consciousness. He summarized four decades of thinking on this topic in *The Riddle of the Universe* (1899, first English translation 1929), which acknowledges Verworn's *Psycho-physiological Studies of the Protists*. Under the heading "Cellular theory of consciousness" Haeckel writes that consciousness

" .... is a vital property of every cell. The application of the cellular theory to every branch of biology involved its extension to psychology. Just as we take the living cell to be the "elementary organism" in anatomy and physiology, and derive the whole system of the multicellular animal or plant from it, so, with equal right, we may consider the "cell-soul" to be the psychological unit, and the complex psychic activity of the higher organism to be the result of the combination of the psychic activity of the cells which compose it .... I was led to a deeper study of this "elementary psychology" by my protracted research into the unicellular forms of life. Many of these tiny (generally microscopic) protists show similar expressions of sensation and will, and similar instincts and movements, to those of higher animals; that is especially true of the very sensitive and lively infusoria. In the relation of these sensitive cell-organisms to their environment .... we seem to have clear indications of conscious psychic actions. If, then, we accept the biological theory of consciousness .... and credit every psychic function with a share of that faculty, we shall be compelled to ascribe it to each independent protist-cell. In that case its material basis would be either the entire protoplasm of the cell or its nucleus, or a portion of it .... I now feel compelled to agree with Max Verworn in his belief that none of the protists have a developed self-consciousness, but that their sensations and movements are of an unconscious character" (Haeckel, 1899, p. 145).

In denying that psychic functioning is co-extensive with consciousness Haeckel states that consciousness is dependent upon the possession of a central nervous system. Haeckel's account of the "plant-soul", to which he gave the name the "phytopsyche" reminds us irresistibly of Plato's account, but Plato's plant soul is less well developed psychologically than is Haeckel's. Haeckel says that whilst plants (and other lower organisms) have no such thing as consciousness, their behaviour nonetheless gives evidence of emotion, will, memory and association of ideas. For instance, tropisms in creatures at the lowest levels show "elementary feelings of like and dislike", hence "emotion". These phenomena are predominantly unconscious and "instinctive" in lower orders, whereas in higher animals they are conscious and "rational". Some plants have more developed souls than do some animals (cf George Bell (1785): " .... there are plants, which surpass some animals in vital power, and, perhaps, in sensation"); for instance, the psychic life of sponges (animals) "for which no special organs have been differentiated — is far inferior to that of the mimosa and other sensitive plants" (1899, p. 131). Haeckel perceives, however, that those who want to grant consciousness to the lower animal forms must grant it, if they follow their own logic, to plants:

"In truth, the remarkable stimulated movements of the leaves of the sensitive plants (the mimosa, drosera and dionaea), the automatic movements of other plants (the clover and wood-sorrel and especially the hedysarum), the movements of the "sleeping plants" .... are strikingly similar to the movements of the lower animal forms: whoever ascribes consciousness to the latter cannot refuse it to such vegetal forms" (p. 144).

Under the influence of Romanes, Haeckel, Verworn and Binet some comparative psychologists began to take up micro-organismic psychology. For example in a paper on protozoan psychical life in the *American Journal of Psychology*, G. P. Watkins hypothesized that *learning by experience* is a sufficient but not necessary condition of consciousness. Consciousness may exist in protozoa. Further, " .... a specialized nervous system or a high organization is *not* a precondition to mentality .... mentality in some sense is a property of the original cell" (Watkins, 1900, p. 166). Watkins takes it for granted that one can speak of psychic processes in protozoa without mentioning them in protophyta.

The main spokesman for the hard-line mechanist interpretation of micro-organismic movements was the physiologist Jacques Loeb (1859-1924), who, influenced by botanists such as Thomas Knight, borrowed the botanical concept of "tropism" to use it as a basic zoological category. Loeb was a staunch enemy of teleology (Gussin, 1962). Movements of the lowest organisms, instead of being labelled as evincing various psychic faculties and instincts were to be seen as mechanical tropisms. Of course to name the phenomenon is not to explain it: to talk of a sequence of movements as a tropism is not to say how it comes about. In his 1901 book on comparative brain physiology and comparative psychology Loeb writes:

"Some physiologists and psychologists consider the purposefulness of the psychic action as the essential element. If an animal or an organ reacts as a rational man would do under the same circumstances, these authors declare that we are dealing with a phenomenon of consciousness. In this way many reflexes, the instincts especially, are looked upon as psychic functions. Consciousness has been ascribed even to the spinal cord, because many of its functions are purposeful. We shall see .... that many of these reactions are merely tropisms which may occur in exactly the same form in plants. Plants must therefore have a psychic life, and, following the argument, we must ascribe it to machines also, for the tropisms depend only on simple mechanical arrangements. In the last analysis, then, we would arrive at molecules and atoms endowed with mental qualities" (Loeb, 1901, pp. 10-11).

Loeb's advocacy of theoretical parsimony did result in some restraint on the part of comparative psychologists (his main influence on psychology was an indirect one, through J. B. Watson), even when, as did the zoologist H. J. Jennings, they felt that he was stretching the concept of tropism too far when dealing with all micro-organismic movements. Jennings' *Behaviour of the Lower Organisms* (1906) at least acknowledges that some of the lower organisms are plants:

"Since the book is written primarily from a zoological standpoint, it would appropriate in some respects to entitle it "Behaviour of the Lower Animals". But the broader title seems on the whole best, since the treatment of unicellular forms involves consideration of many organisms that are more nearly related to plants than to animals" (Jennings, 1906, pp. vii-viii).

The observational data, however, on unicellular organisms concern mostly protozoa, although there is a chapter on bacteria which then generally were considered to be protophyta, and the theoretical discussion is in terms of animals (protozoa and metazoa). Jennings' theoretical restraint is shown by his admission that consciousness in lower organisms is unamenable to controlled, objective study; assertions about it "are not susceptible of verification" (p.v.); psychic states are by definition subjective and we must be careful of analogical reasoning. A true-blue mechanist would see this as merely token restraint, for Jennings does indicate his general sympathy with attributing provisionally psychic states to lower organisms — we would be more likely to make such an attribution, he says, if the organisms were bigger: consider an amoeba as big as a whale — and then we would find in them the behavioural criteria or marks which in the higher animals we would accept as signs of perception, discrimination, choice, attention, fatigue, desire (e.g. for food), pain, fear, memory and habit, and intelligence. We have only rippled the surface of the aquarium, so to speak, in discussion of the psychic life of microorganisms, but there is little extra here that is of specific relevance to the protophyta.

The sensitive plant (*Mimosa pudica*)

Venus fly trap (*Dionaca muscipula*)

Sundew (*Drosera* family)
(above and below)

Aristotle, 384BC–322BC

Plato, 428BC–347BC

Willian Harvey, discovered the circulation of blood.

Gustav T. Fechner

Erasmus Darwin

Charles Darwin

Sir Francis Darwin

Maurice Maeterlinck

Samuel Butler, author of *Erewhon*
and *The Way of all Flesh*.

John Broadus Watson

Richard L. Gregory

CHAPTER 8

The evolutionary impact (2)

8.1 *The mechanics of heredity*

This chapter will discuss the second way in which the theory of evolution influenced plant psychology. After Darwin and Wallace had produced sufficient empirical data to indicate at least the plausibility of the evolutionary hypothesis the question of the mechanics of heredity took on a new importance. The key to evolutionary change lies in heredity. As was said in the previous chapter, one of the competing accounts of the nature of evolutionary change was a psychological one, making memory the central concept. Insofar as plants — as well as animals — must possess memories of some kind then this version of evolutionary theory intersects with plant psychology.

The hypothesis that evolution proceeds by natural selection draws attention to the fact that organisms which are better able to cope with the exigencies of their environments are more likely to survive to breed and thus to pass on inherited characters, but it has nothing to say about how inherited characters are passed on, nor indeed which characters are inherited.

The philosophical "monism" emanating from Germany, which attracted a number of physiologists and some psychologists in the late nineteenth and the early twentieth centuries, was conducive to the hypothesis that hereditary characters are transmitted from parents to offspring by unconscious units of memory. For example Haeckel believed that consciousness extended downwards not only to individual cells, but to their components ("plastidules") and further to individual atoms. At the lower levels such "consciousness" was in fact unconscious, and was manifest in elementary psychic qualities of sensation and will. The plastidules of cells are capable of learning, and learning is impossible without memory. The monistic view sees that whatever is passed on in heredity is both material and psychic, and the obvious psychic character is memory.

An important influence on Haeckel's conception of the fundamental role of memory, and on the conceptions of a number of later thinkers was the essay *On Memory* (1870) by the physiologist Ewald Hering (1834-1918). Most psychologists remember Hering for his work in sensory physiology and visual perception. Hering had no particular theory about the relationship between mind and body beyond claiming that there was a necessary "functional interdependence" between them. During its lifetime, Hering argued, an organism learns things. It cannot learn without continuity in its psychic life and the faculty of memory makes that continuity possible. Most memory, even in humans, is unconscious. Not only do we learn much without consciously striving to do so, but we are generally not conscious of what we have learned — for example, upon command we may be able to call into consciousness the fact that Paris is the capital of France, but we do not go around constantly mulling consciously over this. Sequences of motor acts, speech, thought and so on in which we indulge repeatedly eventually become "automatic", i.e. we run them through without consciously striving to do so, the classical example here is the experienced pianist who can play a complex score without "thinking about how he does it". The explanation of habit therefore is that the elements of the habitual sequence have become deeply committed to unconscious memory. Then, says Hering (as translated by his main supporter in Britain, Samuel Butler),

> "after both conscious sensation and perception have been extinguished,
> their material vestiges yet remain in our nervous system by way of
> change in its molecular or atomic disposition, that enables the nerve
> substance to reproduce all physical processes of the original sensation,
> and with these the corresponding psychical processes of sensation
> and perception" (Hering, 1870, p. 69).

The "germ" material we pass on to our offspring thus contains our originally conscious experiences, but these are unconscious, they are immanent in the molecular and atomic changes they have made in our nervous system. It is really no greater mystery that a child may inherit some parental unconscious memory than that an old man may carry around memories belonging to his youth decades ago. "Not only is there a reproduction of form, outward and inner conformation of the body, organs and cells, but the habitual actions of the parent are also reproduced. The chicken on emerging from the eggshell runs off as its mother ran off before it; yet what an extraordinary complication of emotions and sensation is necessary in order to preserve equilibrium in running. Surely the supposition of an inborn capacity for the reproduction of these intricate actions can alone explain the facts" (Hering, p. 81).

Habits may be transmitted from an individual to a generation, from generations to the "race" or species. ("As habitual practice becomes a second nature to the individual during his single lifetime, so the often-repeated action of each generation becomes a second nature to the race" (Hering, p. 81)).

Now according to evolution there is literal continuity between different species and thus there must be an evolutionary transmission of habits (based upon memories) through species. Natural selection describes the fact that those unconscious phylogenetic habits which are no longer necessary to survival will not be called upon by circumstances, and therefore will lapse through want of practice. Those necessary for species survival will continue by being repeated.

"We must bear in mind", says Hering, "that every organised being now in existence represents the last link of an inconceivably long series of organisms, which come down in a direct line of descent, and of which each has inherited the acquired characteristics of its predecessor. Everything, furthermore, points in the direction of our believing that at the beginning of this chain there existed an organism of the very simplest kind, something in fact, like those which we call organised germs. The chain of living beings thus appears to be the magnificent achievement of the reproductive power of the original organic structure from which they have all descended. As this subdivided itself and transmitted its characteristics to its descendants, these acquired new ones, and in their turn transmitted them — all new germs transmitting the chief part of what had happened to their predecessors, while the remaining part lapsed out of their memory, circumstances not stimulating it to reproduce itself" (Hering, p. 80).

Proponents of this theory of the mechanics of heredity and

evolutionary change have a ready explanation of instinct. "Instincts" are simply those habits which are "automatic" in a species, having been acquired as unconscious memories by the species earlier in its history or in an earlier species from which it is descended. The habits have been so long practised that the actual events giving rise to them have long ago become dissociated from them, just as the skilled pianist has long forgotten the processes of his learning to play.

We call this account of heredity a psychological one because a psychological category, memory, is central to it. It is also a Lamarckian account because it teaches that what is inherited are acquired characters. (Lamarck himself never stated how the inheritance of acquired characteristics is possible). The characters, whether behavioural or structural, are learned (acquired) somewhere in the evolutionary history of the organism. It should be pointed out, however, that it is only a *species* of Lamarckianism, that other, non-psychological, Lamarckian theories of heredity were in existence. The doctrine of the inheritance of acquired characteristics does not entail necessarily that the key factor in the mechanism of heredity be memory. It would be possible, for example, for a thorough-going anti-mentalist to argue that characters are acquired through some somatic change in the organism, a change which has nothing to do with any "psychic" properties of either the organism or its constituent parts. Of course most Lamarckians have not been "psychological" Lamarckians in the Hering tradition, although the psychologist James Ward maintained that on Lamarck's views a psychological component in evolution was necessary (see Ward, 1899, Vol. I, p. 273).

Lamarck, by the way, had no sympathy for plant psychologists of his day (or of any day, for that matter) for in *Zoological Philosophy* (1809) he denied even the existence of vegetable irritability:

"Plants are organised living bodies, not irritable in any of their parts, incapable of performing sudden movements several times in succession, and the vital movements of which are only performed by means of external stimuli, that is to say, by an exciting cause provided by the environment and acting chiefly on the contained and visible fluids of these bodies.

In animals, some or all of the parts are essentially irritable, and have the faculty of performing sudden movements which may be repeated several times in succession. The vital movements are in some performed by means of external stimuli, and in others by a force developing within them" (Lamarck, 1809,p.195).

"When I touched the extended branches of the sensitive plant (*Mimosa pudica*), instead of a contraction I observe in the joints of the disturbed branches and petioles a relaxation, which permits these branches and petioles of the leaves to droop, and causes the leaflets themselves to sink down upon another .... I cannot see in this phenomenon any relation to the irritability of animals" (p. 52).

The psychological hereditarian approach to plant psychology shares with the dominant approach dealt with in earlier chapters the fact that it is based on the notion of some kind of continuity between species which allows them to be ranked or scaled according to their possession of certain structural or functional capacities. Whereas that dominant approach is analogical and *a posteriori* in character (plants being predicated with psychological properties upon their being observed to exhibit the same behaviour which in animals is taken to be sufficient evidence of their possession of mind) the approach here is not analogical, it is *a priori*. The basis of the predication of mentality to plants does not lie in the observation of their movements, it lies in the hypothesized psychological mechanics of evolution and heredity, such hypotheses being drawn alike from botanical and zoological phenomena. The psychological hereditarians did not see their accounts as being *a priori* in a rationalist philosophical sense, rather they saw them as being derived empirically from biological observation, but the accounts are *a priori* in the sense that a prior theory dictates that plants must have memories of some sort. It is easier to appreciate that the one approach is *a priori* and the other *a posteriori* by realizing that the former predicates mind of all the plant kingdom but that the latter does not necessarily do so, it is an open question as to whether all or only some plants possess mind.

The "purest" of the psychological hereditarians vis-a-vis plant psychology (e.g. R. Semon and J. Ward, who will be discussed later) predicated mind of plants only in the formal sense of hypothesizing the germ of heredity to be "memory". The conception of "memory" here is a distinctly *ad hoc* one, an hypostatized principle lacking the richness or flavour of the account of memory given by the associationist psychologists such as Locke. As such it does not have much interest for students of plant psychology, the plant "memory's" being consists entirely in its *ad hoc* explanatory function which applies universally to animate species. Therefore it becomes as empty a concept as the souls which animists suppose all live things to have.

However when the psychological hereditarian bolsters his accounts by appealing to other psychological properties possessed by plants, or by characterizing the plant memory as something more complex and richer than a mere formal principle, his views become of more interest to students of plant psychology. This is exemplified well by Francis Darwin and Samuel Butler, each of whom deserves a separate section.

8.2 *Francis Darwin*

Francis Darwin (1848-1925) is often introduced as a son of Charles. For our purposes it would be more appropriate to introduce him as a great-grandson of Erasmus. Francis has a secure place in the history of orthodox botany. He studied under von Sachs in Germany, was assistant in botanical researches to Charles Darwin, after whose death he took up an academic career in Cambridge. As a pioneer vegetable physiologist Francis Darwin was noted for his work on plant movements and responses to such stimuli as gravity and for his work on the transpiration of water in leaves. Recognition of his botanical contribution included Fellowship of the Royal Society and in 1913 a Knighthood. Less well known were his theories on the psychological nature of plant life, and orthodox biographical summaries tend not to mention them. Although Francis came to embrace the psychological theory of heredity, which is why he is included in this chapter, he was not himself greatly interested in evolution and did not direct his researches to problems in this area.

His first important work on vegetable psychology was a paper in *Nature* in 1878, two years before the publication of *The Power of Movement in Plants*. The paper (*The Analogies of Plant and Animal Life*) was right in the tradition of his great-grandfather. It uses contemporary observations to illustrate its claims that there are significant similarities in respect of sensitiveness, instinct, memory and habit between plants and animals. He is aware that he can be criticized for analogical reasoning, but maintains that "Nevertheless I have tried to show that a true relationship exists between the physiology of the two kingdoms: it is a mistake to grant that plants are "alive" in rather a meagre sense" (F. Darwin, 1878 (b), p. 414).

"Sensitiveness" is defined in an animal as meaning "that an animal must be capable of being affected by changes which, considered as mere physical agents, are insignificant" (p. 412), and Francis cites studies from Charles's *Insectivorous Plants* to show an analogous sensitiveness in the sundew and Venus fly trap to that in animals.

"Sleep" and other periodic movements of plants call to Darwin's mind habit. Erasmus, it will be recalled, wrote of habit in plants (Francis, by the way, makes no reference to Erasmus). We see the parallel of habit in man in the sensitive plant, when, having been placed under constant illumination, it for the first few days continues to act as if under outdoor illumination, "waking" in the equivalent of morning and "sleeping" in the equivalent of evening, just as a man on holidays wakes up at his usual waking hour for work for a few days until he settles into a holiday routine. This "habit" in the plant progressively dissipates under continued constant illumination. The crocus shows periodicity of habit. It is very sensitive to changes in temperature: normally a change of 1° F can be sufficient, e.g. a crocus open in the sunlight will close when a cloud moves over the sun, and will re-open when the cloud moves away. But if it had shut for the night a big rise in temperature during the night will not make it open up. Lowering the temperature has less of an effect in the morning than in the evening. Therefore we see here that the crocus's movements are not determined solely by external conditions, internal ones have to be taken into account as well. Thus we see that in the crocus, as in man, "similar external causes do not produce like effects" (p. 414).

The phenomenon of habituation, exemplified by the factory boy who can sleep in an iron boiler while riveting is going on, is demonstrated in the sensitive plant by fastening a thread from a leaf to a metronome. Initially as the metronome beats it pulls the leaf which then shuts, but after a while the leaf remains open despite the periodic pulls from the metronome.

Although Erasmus did not describe plant behaviour as instinctive, Francis does, citing examples of growth in relation to the force of gravity ("geotropism") and in relation to light ("heliotropism") as two indispensable plant instincts. For example in a seedling "both the young stem and the young root have an instinctive knowledge as to where the centre of the earth is — one growing towards the point, the other directly away from it" (p. 390).

We noted that earlier in the nineteenth century "instinct" was used by the Reverends John Shute Duncan and William Kirby within the context of natural theology. Darwin's concept of instinct has no link with natural theology, hardly a surprise given his family background, and we find that plant instinctivists later in the century generally used the concept without giving it theological overtones — e.g. the anonymous author of «*Plant Instinct*» in the popular Scots *Chambers's Journal* simply repeats Charles Darwin's classification and description of climbing movements in plants, whilst claiming such movements to be explicable as instinctive (Anon., 1883, pp. 500-502).

Francis Darwin cannot resist one little anecdote, even though he recognizes it to be fanciful, and in so recounting it shows an incipient romanticism, although nothing compared to that of Erasmus. Francis writes:

> "There is one — but only a fanciful resemblance — between the sleeping plants and animals, viz. that both have the power of dreaming. I have been sitting quietly in the hot-house at night waiting to make an observation at a given hour, when suddenly the leaf of a sensitive plant has been seen to drop rapidly to its fullest extent and slowly rise to its old position. Now in this action the plant is behaving exactly as if it had been touched on its sensitive joint; thus some internal process produces the same impression on the plant as a real external stimulus. In the same way a dog dreaming by the fire will yelp or move his legs as if he were hunting a real instead of an imaginary rabbit" (p. 413).

It is a moot point whether this anecdote is much more fanciful than some which Romanes was going to publish in good faith about animals.

There is one important feature of this 1878 paper which points to a trend which Darwin's thought was to take later. So far there is nothing basically new in what he says, but there is one observation he makes which will become more important to him, and it foreshadows the basis of his inclusion in this chapter. That observation is that there is only a tiny step between habitual phenomena and *memory* in plants. Surely the habit of the sensitive plant in "shutting down" at the early phase of constant illumination at its "normal" hour in the outside world bespeaks memory. Between habit and memory, says Darwin, there is "hardly any distinction" (p. 413).

Over twenty years later, in another paper in *Nature*, this time on the movements of plants, memory becomes a pivotal concept for Darwin. He addresses the question whether "there is anything in which we may recognise the faint beginnings of consciousness, whether plants have the rudiments of desire or of memory, or other qualities generally described as mental" (F. Darwin, 1901, p. 43). The paper is conceptually more sophisticated than was the 1878 one, and it moves away from the old-fashioned analogically based arguments of that paper. It is not a total move, however — witness the appeal to Charles's animal brain/plant root-tip analogy.

The tone is ambivalent, a feature we have found in other writers such as Bonnet and Romanes, but Darwin comes down in favour of "the value of consciousness in the economy of living organisms" (p. 44). Although aware of the dangers of anthropomorphism and violation of the principle of parsimony, aware too of Huxley's epiphenomenalist strictures against allowing organisms to have causally efficacious minds, Darwin has become too much under the influence of Hering and Samuel Butler to surrender to the conceptual blandishments of a mechanistic botany.

Having discussed plant growth curvatures which result when plants are displaced from the vertical, and which stop when the direction of growth attains its usual relation to the vertical, Darwin observes that they

"seem to me only explicable on the theory that gravitation does not act as a mechanical influence, but as a signal which the plant may neglect entirely, or, if it notices, may interpret in any way; that is, it may grow along the indicated line in either direction or across it at any angle. You may say that this is no explanation at all, that it only amounts to saying that the plant can do as it chooses. I have no objection to this, if you will first define the meaning of the word "choice" " (p. 42).

It is not clear how the last sentence of this passage would assuage the fears of those readers alarmed by the naked voluntaristic and cognitive language, but Darwin then proceeds to justify that language by placing the notion of "signals" to which the plant may respond variously within the Hering-Butler framework of evolutionary unconscious memory:

"The characteristic element in what is done by memory or by that "unconscious memory" known as habit is the association of a chain of thoughts or actions each calling for the next.

What I wish to insist on is that the process I have called action by signal is of the same type as action by association, and therefore allied to habit and memory. The plants alive today are the successful ones who have inherited from successful ancestors the form of curving in certain ways when, by accidental deviations from that normal attitude, some change of pressure is produced in their protoplasm. With the pianist the playing of A has become tied to, entangled or associated with the playing of B, so that the playing of A has grown to be a signal to the muscles to play B: similarly in the plant the act of bending has become tied to, entangled or associated with, that change in the protoplasm due to the altered position. There is no mechanical necessity that B should follow A in the time; the sequence is owing to the path built by habit in the man's brain. And this is equally true of the plant, in which a hereditary habit has been built up in a brain-like root-tip" (p. 43).

There is a concession to mechanism, however. Darwin now wishes to replace the term "instinct" by "reflex", because the former usually connotes an undoubted mental basis. Even so he cannot bring himself to embrace mechanism and finds support in Ward's arguments for the ubiquity of mind in life.

The next relevant paper of Darwin does not show the ambivalence of the 1901 one. It protests against Cartesian "automatonism" on the grounds that it does not lead to any useful research (even granted the relative popularity of vitalism in some botanical circles of the day there would be little support for this contention). Plants, as well as animals, respond to the echoes of the ancestral past by memories:

" .... even in plant physiology we want the idea of an individuality, a something on which the past experience of the race is written and in which the influences of the external world are weighed. I do not of course imply conscious weighing, nor do I mean that the plant has memory in the sense that we have memory. But a plant has memory in Hering's and S. Butler's sense of the word, according to which memory and inheritance are different aspects of the same quality of living things. Thus in the movement of plants, as in the instincts of animals, the spontaneity of the individual has disappeared, the balance of profit and loss has been struck during the past experience of the species, and the individual acts by that unconscious memory we call inheritance" (F. Darwin, 1906, pp. 199-200).

Now Darwin is able to claim more theoretical support for his position by appealing to Semon's mnemic theory. The process of ecphorisis (the activation of associated engrams) takes place without any conscious memory component.

Semon was invoked again in Darwin's 1908 Presidential Address to the British Association for the Advancement of Science. Darwin is concerned mainly to defend Lamarckian principles of inheritance in plants. This time habit in plants is illustrated by the scarlet-runner (*Phaseolus*), the leaflets of which tend to the horizontal by day but sink down at night. Its response to light and darkness is not on the same mechanical level as that response in sensitive photographic plates or radiometers, because the sleeping plant placed in a dark room raises its leaflets next morning and lowers them that evening, thereby demonstrating habit.

Unperturbed by the possibility that vegetable physiologists might show the physico-chemical bases of morphological changes in plants, Darwin believed he could serve the memory hypothesis because "memory will be none the less memory when we know something of the chemistry and physics of its neural concomitant" (F. Darwin, 1909, p. 10). He answers honestly the charge that his views imply some sort of consciousness in plants.

> "It is impossible to know whether or not plants are conscious; but it is consistent with the doctrine of continuity that in all living things there is something psychic, and if we accept this point of view we must believe that in plants there exists a faint copy of what we know as consciousness" (p. 11).

8.3 *Samuel Butler*

Although he is remembered generally today as the author of *Erewhon* and *The Way of all Flesh*, Samuel Butler (1835-1902) saw as his greatest achievement his few books on evolution, which were "unread save by a very few" (G. D. H. Cole, 1961, p.21). His evolutionary views did impress a number of people, however, including some with formal scientific backgrounds. As we have seen Francis Darwin was one such person, indeed he knew Butler personally. Butler's first main evolutionary work, *Life and Habit* (1877, dated 1878), took issue with Charles Darwin's views on evolution, to which Butler had become converted after his break with established religion. He claimed that Charles had failed to acknowledge and appreciate the rightful place of Erasmus as the source of contemporary evolution-ary theory. Erasmus had seen, more clearly than had Lamarck, the role of psychological factors in evolution. Now, as a neo-Lamarckian and bitter opponent of "Charles Darwinism", Butler began to insist on the role of will, plan, memory and cunning rather than luck or chance in evolutionary change. For an account of Butler's personal relations with Darwin, and the origins of the component of hostil-ity in his ambivalent attitude to Darwin, see Coleman (1974). Just as *Life and Habit* was ready to be published he read Hering's essay which he recognized to have anticipated his own evolutionary views. Thereafter he gave priority to Hering, including him with Buffon, Erasmus Darwin and Lamarck as the true prophets of evolution as against the false prophets Spencer, Charles Darwin, Lewes and Romanes.

His main other evolutionary works were *Evolution, Old and New* (1879), *Unconscious Memory* (1880) and *Luck, or Cunning?* (1887). *Unconscious Memory* contains his translation into English of Hering's *Memory as a Universal Function of Organised Matter*. The core notion of unconscious memory as the material of heredity and the key to evolutionary variation even lay behind Butler's well known aversion to "reason" and his distrust of doctrines which run contrary to "common sense". As Breuer and Howard put it in their introductory notes to their 1981 edition of *Erewhon*,

> " .... there is a biological continuity between parent and offspring, the experiences and needs of all past generation are transmitted to each new generation in the form of an unconscious memory, the seat, in short, of all instincts which manifest themselves also as "common" sense. Hence, the least deliberate and most unselfconscious, or "unreasoned" activity, is the result of successfully repeated efforts of countless previous generations" (Breuer and Howard, 1981, p. 28).

Butler has more to say about the mental faculties of the plant kingdom than the mere attribution to it of memory as a formal neo-Lamarckian principle. In saying more he shows himself to be an ingenious and most amusing writer, altogether a worthy follower of Erasmus Darwin. His two main works relevant to plant psychology in the fuller sense (i.e. in his words "vegetable intelligence") are *Luck, or Cunning?* and the third edition of *Erewhon*.

The nucleus of his view occurs earlier than those two works, being contained in the travel book *Alps and Sanctuaries of Piedmont and the Canton Ticino* (1881). In it Butler remarks in passing on the "schism" in the ranks of protoplasm which gave rise to the "sects" of animals and plants, the former believing that it is better to go in search of prey and the latter believing that it is better to stay put and see what comes. Plants do have wit "of a limited kind indeed, but still wit .... within their own bounds they know the details of their business sufficiently well — as well as though they kept the most nicely-balanced system of accounts to show them their position" (Butler, 1882, p. 197). Incidentally *Alps and Sanctuaries* shows a considerable love of flowers.

The last chapter of *Luck, or Cunning, as the Main Means of Organic Modification?* introduces some comments on "vegetable intelligence": because, says Butler, many of those who accept his account of evolution as true for animals would cavil at it for plants unless he can show that plants, too, are intelligent:

> "Many who feel little difficulty about admitting that animal modification is upon the whole mainly due to the secular cunning of the animals themselves will yet hesitate before they admit that plants also can have a reason and cunning of their own" (Butler, 1887, p. 298).

Butler has a two-fold response. The first is that we tend mistakenly to regard what is intelligent as that which is understandable by our lights as intelligent. What we must do is not to use our own interests whereby yardsticks of intelligence are created, but to see whether plants are efficient in pursuing their own interests, such efficiency being a sign of intelligence. Perhaps contemporary psychologists who deal in intellectual assessment would call this a "species-free" definition of intelligence.

> "Once admit that the evidence in favour of a plant's knowing its own business depends upon the efficiency with which that business is conducted than either on our power of understanding how it can be conducted, or on any signs on the plant's part of a capacity for understanding things that do not concern it, and there will be no further difficulty about supposing in its own sphere a plant is just as intelligent as an animal, and keeps a sharp look-out upon its own interests, however different it may seem to be to ours" (p. 298).

Butler does not take up the practical problems of how we know what a plant's own interests are and how we detect its efficiency in pursuing them, but the second part of his response to demands for evidence of vegetable intelligence might give some indirect guides to solving these problems. Now Butler cites what are, as far as we can determine, the first experiments set up with the aim of showing that plants "were .... endowed with some measure of reason, fore-thought, and power of self-adaptation to varying surroundings" (p. 299). The experiments were conducted by Butler's deceased friend Mr Alfred Tylor. Butler gives Tylor's resumé of his work, but it is of little use to the reader because it does not say what was done in the experiments; it reports only the theoretical conclusions derived from them. Butler was enthusiastic in his endorsement of Tylor's experiments, he continued to mention them and every indication is that he regarded them as decisive. The 1908 re-issue of *Luck, or Cunning?* was dedicated to Tylor. The dedication credits him with "establishing" that plants are endowed with "intelligential and volitional faculties". Therefore it is appropriate to digress briefly to outline Tylor's work.

Alfred Tylor (1824-1884), brother of the anthropologist E. B. Tylor, was a manufacturer and colliery owner who was interested in tech-nical and scientific subjects, especially geology and evolution. His experiments were conducted at Carshalton, Surrey, in 1883-4. They were written up to be read before the Linnaean Society in 1884, but Tylor himself was too ill to attend the meeting (in fact he was on his death-bed). The secretary read his paper for him, but without includ-ing its background theoretical hypothesis. Butler was present, and spoke for Tylor in the question-time. The paper received a very poor reception, but was published posthumously as a monograph in 1886;

the monograph, which is now very rare, is entitled *On the Growth of Trees and Protoplasmic Continuity.*

The background theoretical hypothesis which was not communicated to the Linnaean Society meeting was that plants possess a "protoplasmic continuity" between cells whereby a link exists between one part of the plant and all other parts, enabling the plant to function as a single unit. This is true also for the larger woody trees. An interesting aspect of Tylor's work, by the way, is that it is not concerned with the plants which caught traditionally the curiosity of generations of plant psychologists, but largely with woodland trees, and common garden shrubs and plants. As a single unit "the plant is something more than a mere assemblage of parts .... There is a whole, an individual, an *ego*, in plant life as there is in that of animals, and only by taking into consideration the behaviour of a plant as a whole, can we adequately appreciate its powers" (Tylor, 1886, p. 6).

Tylor makes some preliminary observations on tree and branch growth: trees always grow to form a symmetrical outline distinctive of the species; there are no spreading branches in the middle of clumps or pairs of trees because the trees act as if they were one, sending out branches only where they are needed to form a spheroid shape overall, and voluntarily abstaining from branching elsewhere; trees voluntarily determine the curvature of their branches and trunks, e.g. a beech, overshadowed by an elm, will flatten itself out to grow away from the elm with which it would otherwise collide, and the horse-chestnut allows its limbs to curve upward until they assume its characteristic stately candelabra shape, but then flattens out their grown so that the curve will not become a circle. Observations such as these lead Tylor to surmise that the growing movements "show a certain degree of power of adaptation, or a low class of intelligence, and could not all be explained by the direct influences of gravitation, light, heat and air" (p. 5).

In turning to the details of the experiments themselves we find that they are not reported systematically, and that the details are disappointingly meagre. At least this is the case with the published report, the actual presentation was accompanied with quite a few lantern slides and diagrams which are not available in the publication. The "experiments" consisted of :]

(i)   Observations (sketches, measures and records) made of the growth behaviour of trees and plants when obstacles were in their line of growth. Sometimes the obstacles were there naturally e.g. a branch of a horse-chestnut tree growing towards the trunk of a beech. Sometimes the obstacles were placed deliberately in the line of growth of vigorous branches of trees, e.g. boards or tree-trunks were placed at a distance of "several inches" from horse-chestnut branches. Tylor outlines the study of "Mr. Massee" (presumably George Massee, an expert on fungi) in which a fungus (*agaricus junonius*) was removed from the spot on wood where it had sprouted, and placed close to an obstacle. In a few days the original fungus had curved around the obstacle, and new shoots it had sent out also avoided the obstacle. Tylor was aware that critics might attribute the deviation of the horse-chestnut branches to the influence of light (i.e. the nearer they get to an obstacle, the less ambient light they receive). In an attempt to meet this criticism he conducted something approaching a formal experiment with geraniums. He took three pairs of geraniums, those in each pair being equal in size and having strong branches growing

at an angle. Each pair was planted in a separate box in such a position that if the branches continued to grow as they were, they would
meet. The first two pairs were placed in an open garden under "hand
lights", one pair being oriented North — South, and the other East
— West. The third pair, oriented North — South, was placed in a
vinery receiving light from the West and from above. The distances of
the growing points apart were 15mm for pair 1, 12mm for pair 2 and
10mm for pair 3. The study began on April 13, 1884. By May 21 the
branches in pairs 1 and 2 had not lengthened, but numerous leaves
were put out, some of which touched. In pair 3 the branches turned
up at a sharp angle "to avoid meeting". The leaves touched. "Both
branches were bending outwards towards the light, and the eastern
shoot was weakly and growing slowly. In June all the shoots had bent
upwards, and in no instances did the branches ever touch. In these
cases the light was made to fall in all possible directions and yet the
result was the same, it seems clear that the bending was independent
of light and is for the sake of avoiding contact" (Tylor, 1886, p.11).

(ii) Observations made of the growth behaviour of trees and plants
when they were tied down in different ways, always in pairs,so that
the growing points would meet if they continued in their original line
of growth. In no case did they do so. In these studies Tylor used the
climbers stephanotis, honeysuckle and tropæolum ("nasturtium" to
the gardener), the shrubs laurel, geranium, coronopus (swinecress),
rhynchospermum (one of the *compositae*, daisy family) and arbutilon,
unnamed others, and the trees chestnut, elder and ash.

Tylor concluded that "I may say that the result of all my work
shows that all plants endeavour, and a great many succeed in avoiding

obstacles, and that the action takes place generally before the branch touches the obstacle" (p. 10).

It would be improper to dignify these studies with the name of "experiments". In the printed account there are insufficient details to allow anyone who might care to do so to replicate them; no overall quantitative data are given, and the results are reported in an impressionistic anecdotal way — in only a few instances are measurements cited; apart from the attempt to test the "influence of light hypothesis" in the geranium experiment (and in it some transluscent glass obstacles should have been included), there is no recognition of the need for control conditions, such as having control plants of the same species and stage of development as experimental ones observed under similar conditions but without any obstacles in the way of a growing branch. It is no wonder that the Linnaean Society meeting did not receive the paper well — Tylor's studies show a failure to grasp the requirements of experimental method, an ignorance which may be contrasted with the elegance of the experiments of some of the other Victorian workers in the field of plant movements, such as the Darwins.

Samuel Butler, however, was persuaded by Tylor's claims, claims, after all, which were most important to establish the basic plausibility of Butler's whole approach to evolution.

His most entertaining account of vegetable intelligence comes in the third, the revised edition (also called the "ninth" edition) of *Erewhon* in 1901. Amongst the additional chapters in that edition are ones on animal rights and vegetable rights. Considered together their aim is to satirize the way in which rigid puritanical adherence to the letter of moral law can lead to absurd violation of common sense. We need make no apology for quoting extensively from the chapter on vegetable rights because it sets out Butler's theories of plant intelligence and its relation to neo-Lamarckianism in a lively literary style.

The background is that philosophers by their relentless logic had long ago convinced the Erewhonians that to eat animals would be to flout basic rights animals possessed. The Erewhonian populace paid lip service to the proscription but tended to disobey it in the privacy of its homes. From time to time new laws would be drafted aiming at clamping down on the immoral practice of eating animal flesh, but, being out of touch with the reality of the people's eating practices, they became in their turn largely unobserved, until a new fanatic would appear and "re awaken the conscience of the nation" (Butler, 1901, in Breuer and Howard, 1981).

> One such crusading moralist was exceptionally vigorous.
> "Many think that this philosopher did not believe his own teaching, and, being in secret a great meat-eater, had no other end in view than reducing the prohibition against eating animal food to an absurdity, greater even than an Erewhonian Puritan would be able to stand" (p. 262).

This he did by persuading the people that vegetables had rights and that therefore it was sinful to eat them. When animal rights (to which he paid great respect) had been proclaimed, he said, not as much was known about plants as was now. Accordingly moral attitudes and practices should be brought into line with the new knowledge of plants. This devious philosopher, a botanist,

> "had arrived at a conclusion now universally accepted among ourselves
> — I mean, that all, both animals and plants, have had a common

ancestry, and that hence the second should be deemed as much alive as the first. He contended, therefore, that animals and plants were cousins, and would have been seen to be so, all along, if people had not made an arbitrary and unreasonable division between what they chose to call the animal and vegetable kingdoms" (p. 263).

Butler now introduces his evolutionary thesis:
"He declared .... that there is no difference appreciable either by the eye, or by any other test, between a germ that will develop into an oak, a vine, a rose, and one that (given its accustomed surroundings) will become a mouse, an elephant, or a man.

He contended that the course of any germ's development was dic-tated by the habits of the germs from which it was descended, and of whose identity it had once formed a part. If a germ found itself placed as the germs in the line of its ancestry were placed, it would do as its ancestors had done, and grow up into the same kind of organism as theirs. If it found the circumstances only a little different, it would make shift (successfully or unsuccessfully) to modify its development accordingly; if the circumstances were widely different, it would die, probably without an effort at self-adaptation. This .... applied equally to the germs of plants and of animals.

He therefore connected all, both animal and vegetable develop-ment, with intelligence, either spent and now unconscious, or still unspent and conscious; and in support of his view as regards vegetable life, he pointed to the way in which all plants have adapted themselves to their habitual environment. Granting that vegetable intelligence at first sight appears to differ materially from animal, yet, he urged, it is like it in the one essential fact that though it has evidently busied itself about matters that are vital to the well-being of the organism that possesses it, it has never shown the slightest tendency to occupy itself with anything else. This, he insisted, is as great a proof of intelligence as any living being can give" (pp. 263-264).

Examples of how plants so successfully attend to their own business in ways which are beyond our intelligence are then given:
"Look at the earth, air and water — these are all the raw material that the rose has got to work with; does it show any sign of want of intelligence in the alchemy with which it turns mud into rose-leaves? What chemist can do anything comparable? Why does no one try? Simply because every one knows that no human intelligence is equal to the task. We give it up. It is the rose's department; let the rose attend to it — and be dubbed unintelligent because it baffles us by the miracles it works, and the unconcerned business-like way in which it works them" (p. 264).

Plants protect themselves against their enemies:
"They scratch, cut, sting, make bad smells, secrete the most dreadful poisons .... cover their precious seeds with spines like those of a hedgehog, frighten insects with delicate nervous systems by assuming portentous shapes, hide themselves, grow in inaccessible places, and tell lies so plausibly as to deceive even their subtlest foes" (p. 265).

The insectivorous plants
"Lay traps smeared with bird-lime, to catch insects, and persuade them to drown themselves in pitchers which they have made of their leaves, and fill with water; others make themselves, as it were, into

living rat-traps, which close a spring on any insect that settles upon them .... " (p. 265).

Flowers can deceive. For example those orchids which
"make their flowers into the shape of a certain fly that is a great pillager of honey, so that when the real fly comes it thinks that the flowers are bespoke, and goes on elsewhere" (p. 265).

Personal identity continues between a rose seed and the plant whence it comes, making an infinite regress of seed and bush:
"it is impossible to deny continued personality between any existing rose-seed and the earliest seed that can be called a rose-seed at all" (p. 266).

Thus there is ancestral memory in the rose:
"the rose-seed did what it now does in the persons of its ancestors — to whom it has been so linked as to be able to remember what those ancestors did when they were placed as the rose-seed now is. Each stage of development brings back the recollection of the course taken in the preceding stage, and the development has been so often repeated, that all doubt — and with all doubt, all consciousness of action — is suspended" (p. 266).

The evidence for memory is that, like animals, plants perform "an ineffably difficult and intricate action, time after time, with invariable success, and yet not knowing how to do it, and never having done it before". The behaviour "will become unconscious as soon as the skill that directs it has become perfected" (pp. 266-267).

The Erewhonian philosopher-botanist concludes that if it is sinful to kill animals, so to it is to kill plants. Only dead leaves or fallen fruit (*not* living grain) should be eaten. The upshot was that his argument was successful. The populace rebelled against the proscriptions against eating plants and animals, so too did a few hardy Puritans who tried vainly to live on a "kind of jam" made of apples and yellow cabbage leaves.

The object of Butler's satire is not the notion of vegetable intelligence, he was serious about this. It is, rather, the policy of letting reason override common sense.

8.4 *Two Other Neo-Lamarckians*

As has been mentioned, Francis Darwin appealed in his later thought to Richard Semon for theoretical justification of his views. The German zoologist Semon (1859-1918) provided in his "mnemic" theory a conceptual haven for many early twentieth century neo-Lamarckians, although Semon himself saw his theory of heredity as being consistent with Mendelism.

Semon was a student of Haeckel, but it was Hering to whom he gave the main credit for the intellectual inspiration of his book *The Mneme*, published in 1904. Semon acknowledged an indebtedness to Butler, but on the balance saw him as doing more harm than good. He had a high opinion, however, of Francis Darwin, to whom he dedicated the English edition of his book in 1921.

According to Semon memory, habit and heredity are all manifestations of a common principle, the mnemic principle. Stimuli applied to irritable organic substances produce both an immediate reaction and a capacity for an after-effect. This capacity is the *mneme*. The enduring but mainly latent modification in the irritable matter produced by stimuli is an *engram*. Certain stimuli thus have an *engraphic effect* on some organic substances. *Ecphory* is the process of "awakening the mnemic trace of engram out of its latent state into one of manifested activity" (Semon, 1921, p. 12).

Plants as well as animals and protista retain engrams which may be revived. Mnemic laws cover all kinds of "organic reproduction" — they subsume the phenomena of memory, habit, training, ontogenetic development, inherited periodicity and regeneration.

In addition to seeing his principles as compatible with Mendelism, Semon insisted that they were not vitalistic nor teleological, and emphasized that mnemic phenomena do not connote conscious memory. Whether mnemic biology is compatible with Mendelism and determinism, indeed whether it is even testable, are arguable points, but Semon had nothing more to say about plants specifically.

James Ward (1843-1925), credited with the establishment at Cambridge of the first psychological laboratory in England, and known with G. F. Stout as a British act-psychologist for his break with classical associationist psychology, gave the Gifford Lectures at Aberdeen University (1896-1898) on the topic *Naturalism and Agnosticism*. Here a Lamarckian teleological philosophy of natural history is advanced, in which he urges that the principle of continuity in evolution could be used either in a "levelling-down" method, i.e. if psychical factors are not necessary at one point in the evolutionary scale they are not necessary elsewhere, or in a "levelling-up" method, i.e. if psychical factors are necessary at one point they are necessary everywhere. Ward advocates "levelling-up"; even though we cannot imagine what the mental life of creatures far below us could be like, we can appreciate that mind is concomitant with life, and that all behavioural movements are "determined by feeling" (Ward, 1899, p. 296).

"It would hardly be going too far to say that Aristotle's conception of a plant-soul .... is tenable even to-day, at least as any such notion can be at a time when souls are out of fashion" (p. 287),

said Ward, a statement which was later quoted by Francis Darwin. Ward in turn appealed to the weight of Francis's opinion in his *Heredity and Memory*, a lecture delivered in 1912. Ward sees psychology as the basic science of heredity ("from .... a spiritualistic and not from the usual naturalistic standpoint, psychology may shew us that the secret of heredity is to be found in the facts of memory" (Ward, 1913, p.6)). The lecture defends the doctrine of the inheritance of acquired characters against the inroads of Weismann's claims. The analysis of the role of memory in heredity follows Hering, Butler and Francis Darwin. He takes exception to any physicalist version of the mnemic theory, saying that it is "meaningless to talk of memory unless we are prepared to refer it to a subject that remembers" (p. 55). Plants, as well as protozoa, exhibit plasticity of behaviour, hence retentiveness, a retentiveness based on ancestral memories. Ward has nothing more detailed to say about the nature of mental faculties in plants.

To finish this chapter we may note two historical papers which display contrasting attitudes to evolutionary speculations on mind in plants. Lloyd Morgan's *The Beginnings of Mind* (1902-3) identifies mind with "consciousness" or intelligence" and, in opposition to epi-phenomenalism, as a causal agent. Lloyd Morgan cites J. M. Baldwin's principle of organic selection to show that mind may be active in concert with natural selection in evolutionary development in a non-Lamarckian way. Unlike Romanes, Lloyd Morgan cannot say where mind first appears on the evolutionary scene, but it can be presumed to be present in those individual organisms which show that they can learn (profit by experience). Animals as low as crabs, octopuses and spiders thus show evidence of mind. Plants and micro-organisms do not. Both Binet and Francis Darwin are roundly criticized. Plants, whether they be forest oaks or marsh marigolds, lack the nervous system which is necessary for mind. Botanists who want to talk of plant perception should be reminded that

"Now there is, at present, not the smallest shred of evidence that in the hypothetical sentience of plants anything like a conscious situation is developed or that they ever have any experience which can acquire "meaning", or, in other words, that there is the most rudimentary form of perception in the sense in which psychologists employ this term. All that we can say is that they react to certain stimuli, often with much delicacy of co-ordinated response" (Lloyd Morgan, 1902-3, p. 335).

On the other hand G. Stanley Hall, best remembered now for his pioneering work in America in developmental psychology, showed a general sympathy for the views of Haeckel, Verworn and Semon (and also Fechner, J. Bose, Loeb and Jennings — Francis Darwin and Binet are not mentioned) in his *A Glance at the Phyletic Background of Genetic Psychology* (Hall, 1908). Because Hall treats both proponents

and opponents alike of plant psychic life favourably one might conclude either that the paper exudes a generous eclecticism or that it
characteristically lacks critical ability.

CHAPTER 9

A miscellany of romantics

9.1 *Introduction*

It may well be objected that to single out a group of plant psychologists as "romantics" is ingenuous, because to believe in vegetable mentality at all is to be romantic: they are all romantics. There is a point to this objection. On the other hand, we can distinguish between accounts of plant mentality according to the degree to which it is supposed to resemble human mentality. At the one extreme are those views of the plant mind which see it as being more or less akin to the human mind, at the other are those which see the plant mind as having no significant resemblance to the human mind, as being incomprehensible or unimaginable to us. The romantics, as the term will be used here, are those at the former extreme: they take a relatively extravagant view of the nature of vegetable mental life. Whilst plant minds are not as fully developed as humans' are, they are similar, often having some capacity for self-awareness. Another possible label for this sub-set of plant psychologists is "anthropomorphists", but this provokes the same kind of objection as "romantics" does, i.e. that to argue for any conception of plant mentality is to be anthropomorphic.

The romantics in this chapter are nineteenth and twentieth century writers some of whom belong to no natural science tradition, even though they might be influenced by writers who claim their speculations to be based on naturalistic observation and scientific method. Their inspiration lacks that discipline which should accompany an objective orientation to the world. Typically the romantics claim nature to be their inspiration, but their apprehension of nature is distorted systematically by those needs and yearnings, not necessarily conscious, which the romantic temperament projects onto the external world. The romantic attitude to nature is encapsulated in Wordsworth's famous couplet:

"And 'tis my faith that every flower
Enjoys the air it breathes". (From *Lines Written in Early Spring*).

This was written under the direct influence of Erasmus Darwin, but Darwin is not included in this chapter, having been located previously in the main naturalistic tradition of plant psychology. Erasmus could well have been included here, and this brings us to the observation that it will be arbitrary in some cases as to whether an individual is classified as a romantic. There is little temptation to include, for example, Francis Darwin here because he allowed that plant minds cannot be understood as being like human ones. Erasmus, however, clearly can be called a romantic when he allows plants enjoyment of an amorous character and knowledge of the external world. However, Erasmus fits well into a tradition which considered itself to be naturalistic, and he saw his own romantic tendencies as being confined to his verse: the prose writings on plant psychology were part of the scientific corpus of his work. I have decided then to leave Erasmus where he is and to confine this chapter to the post-Erastian romantics.

Some of those identified as romantics have a formal scientific background, but even if they claim that their speculations are licenced by the principles of scientific method, it is apparent that only lip service is paid to the objective requirement of science. Thus the writers in this chapter are a heterogeneous lot. The only thing they have in common is their relatively inflated conception of the plant mind. Often it is not clear within these ranks to what extent the writers should be taken literally, and sometimes it is not clear to what extent they were not joking. On these points it is sometimes necessary to distinguish between what a theorist declares his principles to be and what in practice he actually shows them to be: in his writing he might be flagrantly anthropomorphic, but would declare if taxed on this question that he was using metaphor, other poetic devices or wit. Despite his protestation one cannot help feeling, however, that he has become ensnared by his poetry or his joke.

9.2   Gustav Theodor Fechner

Survivors of most university undergraduate courses in experimental psychology have a firm misunderstanding of G. T. Fechner (1802-1887). They see him only as the pioneer of the field of experimental psychology called psychophysics. They do not realize that to Fechner his work on psychophysics was a minor thing, serving only to show that a precise quantitative method of establishing the psychological identity of the physical could be attained. Of far more importance were his philosophical works which argued for a grand, teleological panpsychist ontology. Of these philosophical works *Nanna, oder über das Seelenleben der Pflanzen* (*Nanna, or the Soul Life of Plants*), published first in 1848, was one of the more significant in his eyes and it deserves to be called one of the classics of plant psychology. As has been noted, Fechner was one of the influences upon Haeckel. Fechner was influenced by the *Naturphilosophie* of the early nineteenth century in Germany. Associated especially with Friedrich von Schelling, *Naturphilosophie* advanced a system of transcendental pantheism in which all natural processes could be unified or subsumed as aspects or manifestations of the ultimate Spirit. When applied to natural science this conception embraced teleology and sometimes led to the use of wild analogy, the exploitation of coincidences and similarities at the expense of differences in natural phenomena, to yield cosmic designs and principles of disarming simplicity and enchanting grandeur. Its tenor is well captured in this passage by one of the prominent members of the group, Lorenz Oken, who, according to the translator, is giving a practical application to the plant kingdom of themes pronounced by Schelling:

> "The plant is a radius, that towards the centre becomes identical, towards the periphery divides or starts asunder. The plant is not therefore an entire circle or globe, but only a section of such, a cone, whose apex has been turned towards the centre of the earth, or would become earth-centred. It can therefore have no middle point. It will on the contrary demonstrate that the animal is the totality of radii, is consequently diameter, and has therefore a centre of its own, or is entire globe. As the whole earth is surrounded by plants, and all their roots turn towards the centre; the whole vegetable kingdom only forms a sphere, composed of infinitely numerous cones. On the contrary every individual animal forms a sphere for itself alone, and is therefore worth as much as all plants taken together. Animals are entire heavenly bodies, satellites or moons, which circulate independently about the earth; all plants, on the contrary, taken together

are only equivalent to one heavenly body. An animal is an infinity of plants" (Oken, 1810, p. 207).

Fechner was capable of more than matching spectacular leaps of the imagination like this. For example in *Zend-Avesta* (1851) we learn of the animate nature of the Earth and other planets, the sun and other stars, and of their identity with the angels, principalities and powers of the hierarchy of celestial beings.

Nanna is the old Nordic goddess of purity, blossoms and vegetation, and wife of Baldur, the god of light. The thesis of *Nanna* is that plants have minds and feelings, and that this is so is suggested by analogy with humans and other animals. Fechner's use of analogy has a rather different style than that of the writers in the natural philosophy tradition of Bonnet, Percival, Watson and their intellectual descendants, his style is that of the rationalist poet-philosopher. For example consider the charge that we know that in animals nerves are necessary for the occurrence of sensation. Plants have no nerves and therefore cannot have sensation. Fechner's reply is that to maintain this would be like maintaining that because violins, pianos and lutes need strings to produce tones and melodies then instruments such as flutes, trombones and organs which have no strings would not be able to produce music. He refused to be daunted by analogy, arguing that it is all one has to go by in this field of enquiry, indeed, it is only by analogy that we declare our brothers to have souls as we ourselves do. The terms "mind", and "spirit" generally do not have sharp differences of meaning for Fechner, and the discussion of their place in the vegetable kingdom in *Nanna* takes place in a context of teleological panpsychism. One little story well conveys the flavour of *Nanna*:

"I stood once on a hot summer's day beside a pool and contemplated a water-lily which had spread its leaves evenly over the water and with an open blossom was basking in the sunlight. How exceptionally fortunate, thought I, must this lily be which above basks in sunlight and below is plunged in the water — if only it might be capable of feeling the sun and the bath. And why not? I asked myself. It seemed to me that nature surely would not have built a creature so beautiful, and so carefully designed for such conditions, merely to be an object of idle observation — or not even that, seeing that thousands of water lilies bloom where no one can observe them. I was inclined rather to think that nature had built it thus in order that all the pleasure which can be derived from bathing at once in sunlight and in water might be enjoyed by one creature in the fullest measure" (Fechner, in Lowrie, 1946, pp. 176-177).

Fechner elaborates his thesis of the sensate plant soul by argu-ing that although plants might lack the higher functions of the soul — are less developed spiritually than are animals — their sensuous faculties are better developed than are those of men and brutes. For example plants have to assimilate raw earth, water, air and decaying matter, i.e. a heterogeneous array of dead substances, whilst animals assimilate matter which has been alive already. Therefore plants have to put greater vital effort into the task than do animals, and the more apt this is to arouse sensation. Accordingly "plants in the process of assimilating their food will experience not less sensation than we do but more" (Fechner, in Lowrie, 1946, p.184). Other aspects of the relatively highly developed sensuous life include the taking of pleasure (*Lust*) in adorning themselves with magnificently coloured blossoms, and a sensual capacity: they may have sexual feelings similar to those of animals. Both feeling and impulse are present in the plant's sensory experiences:

"Judging by all the indications we have, the sensuous life of the plant has in common with the animals the double aspect of feeling and impulse. In both cases, too, the impulses are in a similar way stimulated or released by feeling. We see that in response to the stimulus of food, air, light, etc. the plant produces buds, blossoms and branches, turns, bends, twists, winds, opens and closes its flowers. All this reciprocal action of feeling and impulse is exhibited, however, far more simply in the plant than in the animal, in correspondence with the simpler laws to which it is subjected. The teleological reason for this is to be found in the simpler conditions of the plant's life, and the organic reason in the greater simplicity of its construction" (Fechner, in Lowrie, 1946, p. 207).

The question of the plant soul does not hinge on that of freedom. Plants are in the same position as brutes in this respect: if the latter are free, so are the former; if the latter are not, neither are the former. Fechner himself inclines to the view that the fact that plant movements in branching, putting out leaves, buds and blossoms, point to freedom, but in the end all that is required for the attribution of soul is the capacity to feel as one's own the impulse to certain activities.

Fechner summarizes his hypotheses about the cognitive capacity of the plant mind in this passage:

"It is probable that the life of the soul of the plant is even more sensitive than that of animals; animals lack rationality as well as plants, but they have memory of past happenings and a certain foreknowledge (expectation) of the future, whilst the life of the plant lacks these, being lived fully in the present. Yet they do not lack separateness of the soul. Instead, however, of being less developed than the soul of animals it may even be more fully developed." Even if plants do not have higher thought processes they nonetheless have some kind of conscious life. "A kind of instinct will develop which makes plants reproduce their own life in the creation of the young plant in the seed. .... One could say that the development of the plant in the seed represents the only thought the plant is able to produce in which it combines its whole life in a new being.

One may say that the analogous process in man is not accompanied by consciousness, yet as in the other growth processes of the plant .... these processes have an entirely different meaning. What is first in man is last in plants and vice-versa. As the flowering of the plant is only the summit of growth in an outward direction, so the fruit and seed production is return of the plant into the self. .... Plant and animal worlds seem also in this sense to complement each other and the process of self-reflection in the plant is divided into two different processes which is important in a psychological sense. What happens in an animal unconsciously is in the plant the most relevant part of its conscious life. Certainly it may only be a play of the imagination, yet the fruit generally stands at the head or the top of the plant and is generally enclosed in a hard cortex (crust) like the skull of man; it can often be compared to a man's brain, e.g. the walnut fruit resembles it even in outward shape" (Fechner, 1848, unpublished translation by M. Clouston).

To dwell on the fact that Fechner's scientific contemporaries generally regarded *Nanna* in its entirety as a "play of the imagination" would be to labour the obvious. William James, who preferred the "thick" flavour of Fechner's metaphysics to the "thin" flavour of that of British neo-Hegelians, stated of him that "his means were always scanty so his only extravagances could be in the way of thought, but these were gorgeous ones" (James, 1908, p. 68). *Nanna* was not translated into English and therefore was not generally known to English readers, unlike some of his other metaphysical treatises. It had one enthusiastic supporter a century after its publication in the American Episcopalian clergyman, Walter Lowrie. Lowrie, who introduced Kierkegaard to many English speaking theologians, wrote a fulsome eulogy of Fechner in 1946, entitled *Religion of a Scientist*. Lowrie has a tendency to overstate his case (e.g. "I believe that on the continent of Europe since some time before the First World War there has been no scientist of repute who has espoused the Darwinian theory" (Lowrie, 1946, p. 62), by which he means a non-Lamarckian mechanistic theory of evolution) but his book contains selections from *Nanna* and the other major religious works of Fechner. It includes also Lowrie's own comments on the soul life of plants, which claim that more recent research, such as that of Bose, supports Fechner.

In addition Lowrie's book contains passages translated from Raoul H. Francé's *Die Seele der Pflanze (The Soul of the Plant)*, an undated but post 1909 work. Although the Viennese-born Hungarian botanist praises Fechner, his conception of the plant soul is much more pallid than Fechner's. Apart from the passages in *Religion of a Scientist* Francé (1874-1943) had three works on plant life translated into English: *Gems of Mind in Plants* (1905), *The Love-Life of Plants* (1926) and *Plants as Inventors* (1926). He is an ardent advocate of vitalism and teleology but does not follow Fechner's elevated conception of the plant soul: "It is only a few feeble sparks, but still a beam of the light which is analogous to our mentality or consciousness glows within the plant" (Francé, 1926, pp. 45-6); "plants have the same instinctive life as animals of the lowest order" (p. 52). His books are collections of "just-so" stories illustrating metaphorically the supposed inability of mechanism to account for the instinctive wisdom and design in the plant kingdom. For example symbiotic plant-insect interactions in which insects depend upon plants for food and plants depend upon insects for fertilization are seen as "alliances for mutual help" (p. 49).

9.3   *John Ellor Taylor*

Francé's "just-so" tales are by no means the only ones we find in the period from the late nineteenth century to well into the twentieth century. There were other collections of popular teleological botanical anecdotes in circulation. In his history of comparative psychology C. J. Warden, having noted in later Victorian England the significant extent of romantic attitudes in animal studies, pointed out that plant behaviour was "usually thought of as being purely physiological and as lying entirely outside the pale of psychology, and hence it escaped for the most part the evil influence of anecdote and anthropomorphism" (Warden, in Warden, Jenkins and Warner, 1936, p. 18). But to escape "for the most part" is not to escape entirely, as we by now are well aware.

A good example of the "evil influence" in plant behaviour is J. E.

Taylor's *"The Sagacity and Morality of Plants"* (1884). Taylor (1837-1895) had little formal schooling but rose through his own efforts, especially attendance at evening classes in Manchester, to become a popular writer and lecturer on science. He was elected a Fellow of the Linnaean Society in 1873. The *Sagacity and Morality of Plants* attempts to show that the vegetable kingdom embodies those moral attitudes and values which conform to the modern stereotype of Victorian propriety.

We should not take at face value Taylor's disclaimers that "the reader may if he so chooses .... consider both the title of this Book, and much of its contents, as a Parable" (Taylor, 1884, p.v.). He defends himself against possible charges of projecting human attributes onto plants by appealing to contemporary botanical language: "A new language has been developed .... Whether we believe in the consciousness of plant life or not, this language almost implies such a belief. We speak of plants adopting this habit or that device — always and only when such habits and devices are beneficial to them — as if they did it of set and intelligent purpose .... Who knows — perhaps there can be no life, animal or vegetable, unaccompanied by consciousness" (p.2). Taylor's tone indicates certainly a wanting to believe in plant consciousness, even if his scientific constraints prevent him from such an avowal, and it becomes clear to the reader that in being invited to "choose" whether what he is reading is merely a Parable there is a definite expectation of what the choice will be.

In Taylor Lamarckianism once again comes to the aid of the plant psychologist. The doctrine of the inheritance of acquired characteristics opens the door for plant instincts and the psychological categories of experience and memory as explanatory concepts in plant psychology. "It may some day be shown", says Taylor, "that life is conditioned by psychological action, and that there is in plants the equivalent of "instinct" in animals — the power of gaining individual experience, and of transferring such experience to descendants to profit thereby, not altogether unconsciously!" (p.5).

In chapters headed Floral Diplomacy, Co-Operation, Social and Political Economy of Plants, "Defence, Not Defiance", Robbery and Murder *inter alia*, Taylor gives many examples of how plants have acquired instinctive sagacious and moral attributes. Sagacity can be seen, for instance, when one considers climbers making use of forest trees to get up to direct sunlight and energy.

" .... and that they would not have attained the positions we find them in unless high woody trees had acquired their present magnitude first, our admiration for the methods adopted by them increases. The mere statement of this fact carries with it to the mind of the botanist the knowledge that such successful climbing habits have been *acquired*. The devices thus developed undoubtedly partake of the character we should call *sagacious* if animals had displayed them" (p. 46).

" .... in most the climbing plants have beaten the tall, strong, woody trees and shrubs in the contest for light, heat and gaseous food. They have conquered by sheer wit, or the equivalent of it; and there is little doubt if animals had been similarly successful in their endeavours to achieve a certain end, we should have spoken of them as "clever"" (p. 55).

Morality is manifest, for example, in plant co-operation, whereby plants can benefit in growing together in clusters in a way they could not if they grew singly:

"The *Umbelliferae, Dipsaceae,* and *Compositae* have carried out this idea with the completest success, and with certain modifications of a most suggestive character; some of the members of their floral community being altered for the benefit of the community. This alteration has been carried to the extreme point of even sacrificing the individualities of some members for the well-being of the rest! .... The large flowers of the common Honeysuckle are usually grouped to the number of about half a dozen on the flower-head; whilst the smaller individuals in the Elder (*Sambucus Nigra*), Wayfaring Tree (*Viburnum Lantana*), and Guelder Rose (*Viburnum Opulus*), are clustered in great numbers. The grouping of the latter species is remarkable for the *increased size* of the outer circle of flowers .... But in the natural state all these larger outer flowers are *barren.* Their size has been increased for the benefit of their brethren, so as to render them more conspicuous to insects, but they have sacrificed their own fecundity. Floral *altruism* is a fact in the vegetable kingdom, only found in the most differentiated floral societies; just as we meet with it only in the highest developed of humanity" (pp. 167-168).

Given such examples of high virtue one asks immediately whether vegetable immorality ever occurs. Taylor has no hesitation in saying it does, nor in providing examples. Plants parasitical on others are robbers and potential murderers. Amongst the villains of the plant world are the sinister gangs of mildews, rusts and various blights.

9.4   *Thomas George Gentry*

Thomas Gentry (1843-1905) was a Pennsylvania biology teacher who wrote books and papers in several areas of enquiry, including ornithology and botany. In 1897 he had published in Philadelphia *Life and Immortality — or Soul in Plants and Animals* which re-appeared as *Intelligence in Plants and Animals* in 1900, published this time in New York.

That plants and animals indeed possess intelligence is his theme. Plants are conscious beings (although their consciousness may be only a small degree of that of animals), they are capable of purposive acts and at least some give active evidence of memory.

There are some echoes of Fechner in his style. Gentry is an antimaterialist. He runs together biological speculations with religious ones, but, unlike Fechner, his religious standpoint tends to that of a more orthodox Christianity, but he is persuaded that not only man and the brutes but plants as well will partake of eternal life after death. Another example which calls Fechner to mind is this passage:

> "Our evening primrose does not bloom in the dark hours for mere sentiment or moonshine, but from a nature which lies figuratively speaking, much nearer her heart .... From the first movement of her wooing welcome it would seem that our evening primrose listens for murmuring wings, and awaits that supreme fulfilment with joyous expectancy, for it will invariably be found that these blossoms, which open in the twilight, have adapted themselves to crepuscular moths and other nocturnal insects .... " (Gentry, 1900, p. 338).

Gentry has two lines of argument for the existence of consciousness in plants. The first is that considerations of evolutionary survival demand it. E. D. Cope, the doyen of American neo-Lamarckians, is cited here as stating that acts of self-preservation in organising entail at least a modicum of sensation to external stimuli, i.e. consciousness, and consciousness is necessary to a rising scale of organic evolution.

The second is that observations of plant behaviour indicate the presence of consciousness. Particular attention is drawn to the behaviour of radicles (e.g., if necessary, of their own mental effort they can change their direction of growth if they meet an underground obstacle, such as a stone, demonstrating thereby that they do not grow just in response to gravity). References to Charles Darwin's studies of plant growth and movement include the animal brain/plant radicle tip analogy. Gentry explains here how it is that psychological factors are involved:

"Whatever be the nature of any movement, whether the projecting of portions of its own body-substance as pseudo-podia in the primitive animal, the movement of flagella or cilia in more specialized forms, or the turning of the radicle of a plant-seedling in overcoming some obstacle, there is no resisting the conclusion that the functions of these organs, when once called into existence, are due to stimuli not unlike those which affect the motions of the limbs of the higher animals, and that the preliminary to all such movements, which are not automatic, is an effort. And as no adaptive movement is automatic the first time it is performed, effort, therefore, may be regarded as the immediate source of all movement. Now, effort is a conscious state, and implies a sense of resistance to be overcome .... How this resistance is overcome, there seems to be some diversity of opinion among physiologists and metaphysicians, but it is generally believed that some such mental state as a sensation or desire, which may or may not stimulate a natural process as an intervening element in the circuit, is concerned in its subduement. That sense-perceptions are stimuli to the immediate appearance of structural changes or movements is shown by the production of colour-changes in animals through changes in the condition of the organs of sight and in the bending of the radicle of a seedling-plant a short distance above its tip in obedience to a communication from the tip of a sensation of hardness, caused by contact with a stone experienced in its downward progress in the ground" (pp. 330-331).

The hoary old tale of the tendril of the climber which inherently "seeks out" a nearby support is told, but something new is also recounted: Gentry points out that the extreme sensitivity of the sundews means that there can be no question "that these plants manifest a comparatively high order of consciousness" (p. 332), and asserts that this claim is supported by Mrs. Treat's experiments.

Just as Butler had appealed a few years before to the experimental data of Tylor to support his view we now have Gentry appealing to experimental corroboration of his theories. The experimenter this time is Mrs. Mary Treat of New Jersey. Mrs. Treat (1830-1923) was an amateur naturalist whose publications included several papers on carnivorous plants. Charles and Francis Darwin cited her in the second edition of *Insectivorous Plants* in 1888. The experiment to which Gentry appeals (he does not give its source, nor do later writers who borrowed from him) was reported in her paper *Observations on the Sundew*, published in 1873 in *The American Naturalist*.

The plant Mrs. Treat reports on in that paper is the *Drosera*

filiformis, a sundew which has long thread-shaped leaves. After recording the plant's responses to being "fed" with various items such as
pieces of chopped beef, Mrs. Treat writes:

> "July 11th, 10 o'clock, A.M., I pinned some living flies half an inch
> from the leaves, near the apex, of *D. filiformis*. In forty minutes the
> leaves had bent perceptibly toward the flies. At twelve o'clock the
> leaves had reached the flies and their legs were entangled among the
> bristles and held fast. I then removed the flies three-quarters of an
> inch farther from the leaves. The leaves still remained bent away from
> the direction of the light toward the flies, but did not reach them at
> this distance.
>
> Whether the action of the flies' wings maybe created sufficient
> force to bring the leaves near enough to entangle the flies is a question
> I have not yet satisfactorily settled in my own mind, for dead flies did
> not seem to have the same power as living ones" (Treat, 1873, p. 706).

This tantalizing little study, like Tylor's, is presented in a skimpy
way. There are some quantitative data, but no information about
number of plants, flies and leaves nor degree of displacement of the
leaves. Other details such as the species of flies and the method of
pinning them, are insufficient to allow one to undertake confidently
a faithful replication. Apparently Mrs. Treat had some awareness
of the necessity of using controls, for she tried to get the effect with
dead flies. There is no mention of other control conditions, e.g. the
use of living flies shielded from the plants, the use of non-moving
but "acceptable" food targets such as pieces of beef, the inclusion of
a base-line condition where observations of leaf displacement are
made in the absence of any nearby targets. At the best, then, this is

a suggestive formal demonstration which needs, as Asa Gray put it in his comment on it, "ample confirmation" (A. G., 1874, p. 598). So far as is known no-one has attempted to replicate it.

It should be pointed out that Mrs. Treat did not offer her study as a formal experiment. How much she knew about the formal requirements of experimental method we cannot say, but other researchers in the area at the time did appreciate the basic requirements. Francis Darwin, for example, reported in *Nature* (F. Darwin, 1878(a)) an elegant little experiment contrasting the growth and health of "starved" and "fed" common English sundews (*D. rotundifolia*).

More importantly perhaps it should be pointed out that Mrs. Treat suggested no theoretical explanation of the effect (if it is assumed to be real). Asa Gray (A. G., 1874) saw it as evidence for purpose as a botanical category, but did not suppose that cognition was involved. Gentry, however, began to develop an elaborate explanation, deeming no mechanical account of the movements of the leaves adequate. They

"felt within them a desire for food, and it was this desire that led the leaves to bend away from the light and in the direction of the objects whose presence created in them that sensation. But how were they able, in the absence of any visible sense-organs, to determine the presence of these objects is difficult to surmise. That they are sensitive to contact is generally conceded and in them, no doubt, the sense of touch is keenly developed. Granting this to be the truth, then they see, as a blind-man sees, by the sense of feeling. Currents of air, established by the vibration of the insect's wings, impinging upon the epidermis of the leaves, affect the cells beneath, and a nervous influence is started, guided by some central agency, of which we know nothing, causing the leaves to bend in the proper direction. But why the leaves do not thus bend when impinged upon by currents other than those produced by insects, I am unable to say. Even as a blind man, through deaf, is able through the sense of touch to discriminate moving objects by the currents of air they excite, so it may be presumed that the leaves of Drosera are endowed with the same wonderful and intelligent capacity. Such a feeling once experienced would be apt to be known again, for it would become fixed in consciousness by a process of memory" (Gentry, 1900, pp.33-334).

9.5 *Maurice Maeterlinck*

"The wonderful and intelligent capacity" of the sundew noted by Gentry was shared by all the floral kingdom according to Maurice Maeterlinck (1862-1949). "A great volume might be written on the intelligence of the plants, even as Romanes wrote one on animal intelligence" said Maeterlinck in his essay *The Intelligence of the Flowers* (Maeterlinck, 1907, p.237).

This essay was published in a volume entitled *Life and Flowers*, which was translated into English directly upon Its publication in 1907. In addition to his literary works Maeterlinck published popular biological ones, including accounts of the lives of bees, ants and termites. His scientific views were influenced by, in addition to Romanes, Charles Darwin, Huxley, and the entomologist Lubbock. The excursions into biology did "with the vision of his genius, Maeterlinck saw that the scientific and the poetic imagination are akin. And so he painted them in *La Vie des Abeilles* and *L'Intelligence des Fleurs*, with the result that neither science nor poetry will claim either for Its own"

(Clark, 1915, p.291). Another biographer, W. D. Halls, quotes Andre Gide's scathing comment on *The Intelligence of the Flowers*: "when I see Maeterlinck so enraptured, I have some difficulty in finding him as intelligent as his flowers" (Halls, 1960, p.87).

Maeterlinck wrote only an essay on the intelligence of flowers, rather than "a great volume", but the essay is replete with instances of floral wisdom. It may be read in two ways, either as a portrait of a basically Aristotelian teleological conception of plant life, with the central concept of "instinctive intelligence" overlaid with a poeticized conceit employing metaphor and lyrical prose ("secondary elaboration" as psycho-analysts understand the term); or as a romantic whole in which there is no clear distinction between scientific fact and poetic imagination, literal truth and poetic truth are one. Inclination toward the latter reading explains why Maeterlinck is included in this chapter. We know that he was susceptible to occult claims, for example he was taken Iin thoroughly by "demonstrations" of the telepathic powers of the "intelligent" horses of Elberfeld, Gemany. Horses belonging to the skilled charlatan, Herr Krall, appeared to answer mathematical questions by tapping out the right number with their hooves. In fact they were responding to tiny bodily cues emanating from human observers. If we read him in the former way then we would not understand him as attributing mental powers to plants, but if we read him In the latter way we would find quite a Fechnerian conception of vegetable life.

The intelligence of the plant world is intelligence to a high degree. It is used by plants to overcome the confines of their rooted earth-bound existence. The proofs of intelligence are "innumerable and continual, especially among the flowers, in which the effort of vegetable life towards light and understanding is concentrated -- all exert themselves to accomplish their work, all have the magnificent ambition to overrun and conquer the surface of the globe by endlessly multiplying that form of existence which they represent" (Maeterlinck, 1907, pp.205-206).

Our usual notion of the tranquil tempo of life in vegetation Is wrong:

"This vegetable world, which to us appears to placid, so resigned, in which all seems acquiescence, silence, obedience, meditation, is, on the contrary, that in which impatience, the revolt against destiny and the most vehement and stubborn. The essential organ -- its root, attaches it dissolubly to the soil. If it be difficult to discover among the great laws that oppress us that which weighs heaviest upon our shoulders, in the case of the plant there Is no doubt: it is the law that condemns it to immobility from its birth to its death -- The energy of its fixed idea, mounting from the darkness of the roots to become organized and full-blown in the flowers, is an incomparable spectacle. It exerts itself wholly with one sole aim: to escape above from the fatality below, to evade, to transgress the heavy and sombre law, to set Itself free, to shatter the narrow sphere, to invent or invoke wings, to escape as far as It can, to conquer the space in which destiny encloses it, to approach another kingdom, to penetrate into a moving and active world --

The flower sets man a prodigious example of insubmission, courage, perseverance and ingenuity" (pp. 207-8).

In citing a couple of examples of plant intelligence in action we should first quote the story of the heroic laurel. It is a good example of Maeterlinck's style, showing him in full flight. The story concerns the "heroism given me the other day in Provence, in the wild and delightful gorges of the Loup -- by a huge centenarian Laurel tree. It was easy to read on its twisted and, so to speak, writhing trunk, the whole drama of its hard and tenacious life. A bird or the wind ..... had carried the seed to the flank of the rock, which was as perpendicular as an iron curtain; and the tree was born there, two hundred yards above the torrent, inaccessible and solitary, among the burning and barren stones. From the first house, it had sent its blind roots on a long and painful search for precarious water and soil.

... The young stem had to solve a much graver and more unexpected problem: It started from a vertical plane, so that its top, instead of rising towards the sky, bent down over the gulf. It was obliged, therefore, notwithstanding the increasing weight of its branches, to correct the first flight, stubbornly to bend Its disconcerted trunk in the form of an elbow close to the rock and thus, like a swimmer who throws back his head, by means of incessant will, tension and contraction to hold its heavy crown of leaves straight up to the sky.

Thenceforward, all the preoccupations, all the energy, all the free and conscious genius of the plant had centred around that vital knot. The monstrous, hypertrophied elbow revealed, one by one, the successive solicitudes of a kind of thought that knew how to profit by the warnings which it received from the rains and the storms. Year by yea, the leafy dome grew heavier, with no other care than to spread itself out in the light and heat, while a hidden canker gnawed deep Into the tragic arm that supported it in space. Then obeying I know not what order of the instinct, two stout roots, two fibrous cables, issuing from the trunk at more than two feet above the elbow, had come to moor it to the granite wall. Had they really been evoked by the tree's distress, or were they perhaps waiting providently, from the first day, for the acute hour of danger, in order to increase the value of their assistance? Was it only a happy accident?" (pp.215-217).

It is among the orchids that are found "the most perfect and most harmonious manifestations of vegetable intelligence" (p. 255). Some orchid flowers have a complex, intricate machinery which functions to ensure pollination. It is poised for the entry of an insect to set it in motion. A number of examples from common European orchids illustrate the flower's calculating skill, for in the complex programme of fertilization "the orchid has minutely calculated the time needed for the insect to suck the nectar and repair to the next flower; and it has ascertained that this requires, on an average, thirty seconds" (p. 259), the thirty seconds being the time required for contraction of the parts of the flower which is necessary before pollination can occur.

Although few took Maeterlink's speculations about floral intelligence seriously, he was not entirely without influence as will be seen when Jean Piaget's views on vegetable life are discussed.

9.6   Clifford H. Farr

Maeterlinck's reference to the orchid flower's calculating ability was a passing one, but Clifford Farr (1888-1928) Professor of Botany at the University of Iowa in 1922, placed a great deal more emphasis on the calculating abilities of plants. He did so in his paper *The Psychology of Plants* published in *The Atlantic Monthly*. *The Atlantic Monthly* is not a professional or academic journal, and it may be that Farr's essay is an exercise in humorous journalistic licence and is not meant to be taken literally or too seriously. On the other hand its general tone suggests otherwise; also the magazine published many serious articles and Farr may have felt that he could express in *The Atlantic Monthly* arguments in favour of a theoretical position which he took seriously, arguments which he could not expect to be published in orthodox botanical journals. His conceptual framework is consistent with epi-phenomenalism, for he does not deny that physico-chemical explanations of plant behaviour exist, but does not see why this should exclude psychical experiences accompanying the behaviour. Whatever Farr's motivation was, he produced an entertaining paper.

In a confident, even brash manner, he lines up in the traditional ranks of plant psychologists by declaring that "I can demonstrate just as well that the plant has a mind as that you have a mind. Both are matters of analogy of structure and behaviour" (Farr, 1922, p.777). He rebukes E.B. Titchener for not having studied plants sufficiently to know that the mind of the plant, "far from being extraordinarily rudimentary, is really extraordinarily well-developed" (p. 775).

Farr predicates of plants sensations, habit, memory, volition, intelligence, reason and feeling. He not only introduces variations on old arguments but brings to bear some novel considerations. His writing has the refreshing directness which is often found in those who commit themselves without equivocation to minority causes. His account of "habit" in plants reminds one of the notion of habit held by Erasmus and Francis Darwin. Farr, however, illustrates it by reference to an oxalis species, which, having been placed in a greenhouse under conditions of reversed day-night illumination, at first preserves its usual "sleeping" pattern, i.e. it "wakes" when it is day outside but it is in darkness.

Memory is shown "if I expose a pot of oat-seedlings, the sheaths of which have not yet broken, for twelve seconds to one-sided illumination, and then cover them from the light, they will curve over in the course of about forty minutes, so that the tips will come to point in the direction from which the light had been received" (p. 780).

Feeling is exhibited by the mimosa when it departs from or approaches to equilibrium, feeling having been defined as the mental process accompanying changes in states of equilibrium. Taking gratuitously the "sleeping" position of the mimosa as its state of equilibrium, Farr sees the unfolding of its leaflets to light and the dropping of its leaf-stalks to blows as indices of unpleasant or painful feeling. The folding of the open leaves in response to gentle stroking is an indication of pleasure. "So that, when I stroke the leaf gently it is pleased, and when I strike it sharply, it experiences pain; just as my dog is pleased when I pat his head, and pained when I kick him" (p. 781).

That plants in a single act select the substances in the soil appropriate for their nutrition and ignore those which are inappropriate indicates that they possess volition. "The clover plant absorbs just five and two thirds times as much calcium as does the barley plant growing beside it; and the barley takes up just eighteen times as much silicon as does the clover" (p. 782). Phototropic responses of white-mustard seedlings show their "will-power".

It is on the matter of plant calculation that Farr really comes into his own. What he seeks to do is to show that plants possess reason. He argues that to be mathematically competent is to exercise reason. Accordingly he demonstrates the mathematical competence of plants:

" .... let us first inquire whether or not plants display reason.

237

Mathematics constitutes the most extensive and ideal system of logic. Let us see if the plant mind is mathematically inclined.

The basis of mathematics is addition and subtraction, and it can readily be shown that plants perform both these operations. If, in place of exposing .... oats continuously, I had exposed them for six seconds, then waited a short time and exposed them six seconds more, they would have reacted in exactly the same way as in the case noted above. Or, if I expose them for four three-second periods, or twelve one-second periods, they will add up the individual periods and, if the sum is twelve, they will react. Or they will add periods of unequal length, such as a three-second period, a four-second period, a two-second period, a one-second period and another two-second period, and if that makes twelve, they will react. It if is less than twelve, they will refuse.

Furthermore, if I expose them for fifteen seconds on one side and four seconds on the other, they will subtract and, finding the answer to be eleven seconds, will not respond. But if I expose them for seventeen and one-half seconds on one side and five and one-half on the other, they will respond, because the answer to that problem is twelve" (p. 781).

Only a churl would call into question this delightful example by pointing out that a similar procedure using weights could be followed to demonstrate the mathematical knowledge of kitchen balances.

9.7   *The problem of Jagadis Chunder Bose*

Earlier this century Jagadis Bose, the Indian physicist and plant physiologist, was world famous, but he is largely forgotten now. Bose

(1858-1937) took his higher education in England (Sir Francis Darwin was one of his teachers and was later a friend) and was professor of physical science at Presidency College, Calcutta from 1885 to his retirement in 1915. This was not the end of Bose's scientific work, for he founded and directed the Bose Research Institute in Calcutta in 1917. He was knighted in 1917 and elected to the Royal Society in 1920. In his travels he visited Harvard University's Departments of Philosophy and Psychology, and was welcomed at Clark University by G. Stanley Hall, who was interested in his work.

In his early research Bose noted that stimulation of certain inorganic substances (e.g. some metals) produced responses, defined as variations in galvanometer readings, which resembled those of irritability in animal tissues. He interpreted this similarity as evidence of the continuity between the organic and inorganic domains, and the sufficiency of inorganic categories of explanation for the inorganic world. "Thus", he wrote "living response in all its diverse manifestations is found to be only a repetition of responses seen in the inorganic. There is in it no element of mystery or caprice, such as we must admit to be applied in the assumption of a hypermechanical vital force, acting in contradiction or defiance of those physical laws that govern the world of matter" (Bose, 1902, pp. 189-190).

These studies prompted him to compare animal tissue and plant tissue, out of which grew years of botanical experiments. Bose showed in 1906 that not only may both organic and inorganic substances give positive readings when electrodes are attached to them (emit electrical "responses" in Bose's word), but that all parts of all plants do so. Bose tested not only the sensitive plant, but other traditionally "inert" ones as well. (The sensitive plant and the telegraph plant became his favourite demonstration plants over the years.) He argued further that all the important characteristics of responses exhibited by even the most highly differentiated animal tissues were to be found in plants. Electrical signs of "excitatory responses", he was surprised to find, were not the only ones which could be detected. "Motile responses" existed also in ordinary plants, not just in the sensitive and spontaneously moving species. Bose raised the question of whether the plant movements were to be understood mechanistically or whether they demanded explanation in terms of some non-material, non-lawful principle. He recognized the temptations of vitalism but concluded "I have attempted to show that the plant may nevertheless be regarded as a machine .... " (Bose, 1906, p. viii). He denied that "spontaneous" or "autonomous" plant movements, such as those of the telegraph plant (*desmodium gyrans*) were literally spontaneous: they had a mechanical origin and were not caused by some vital force.

Although at this stage a number of physiologists still took exception to what they saw as the misuse of some technical terms in their discipline by an interloping physicist, there is nothing to indicate that Bose's theories were inimical to a thoroughly mechanistic approach to plant physiology. Bose might be called a monist for seeing continuity between the mineral, animal and vegetable kingdoms, but his monism was of a materialist character.

Why then, is Bose being discussed here? Because (1) he demonstrated, as had no-one before, the range, the variety and the sensitivity of plant movements and (2) he indulged in such descriptive metaphorical language that his work on plant movements exerted an irresistible attraction to those who held romantic, anthropomorphic conceptions of vegetable life. True, he did talk of plants as being sensitive to an enormous range of stimuli, was prepared to listen to speculation about the presence of consciousness in them and wrote of them as if they possessed human feeling-states, but he never claimed that any but mechanical causes underlay plant behaviour, and he always baulked at attributing consciousness to plants. Perhaps a case might be made that at heart he was an anthropomorphist, a romantic in spite of himself. Certainly a case can be made that it is his own fault that many have taken him to be such.

Bose's researches on plant movements and growth were unique in their day because he invented instruments which allowed reliable automatic recording of movements, instruments, moreover of enormous sensitivity. Minute changes could be picked up by them, magnified, recorded and quantified. Bose was able to show, for example, that it was not just the sensitive plant, the telegraph plant, the Venus fly trap, and a few others which moved, but that all plants produced "spontaneous" movements. Most of them are too small to be seen by the naked eye. All plants respond to stimulation, whether it is mechanical, electrical, radiant or chemical, but mostly the naked eye is unable to observe the responses.

For our purposes Bose's two most important works are the book *Plant Autographs and their Revelations* (1927) and the popular paper in the Century Magazine, *Is the Plant a Sentient Being* (1929).

If an advocate of the doctrine of developed mental faculties in plants had been inspired by Farr's demonstrations that they possessed mathematical abilities, and wanted to show that they also were capable of language, then it is to *Plant Autographs and their Revelations* that he would turn. Plants have no vocal apparatus, of course — neither do they have fingers to count on — but they can, our advocate would argue, express their inner feelings in writing, i.e. the graphs made by automatic recording pens of Bose's machines.

The word "revelations" might connote to the religiously inclined apocalyptic visions, or to the reader of tabloid newspapers prurient or scandalous titillation. Bose's plant revelations have no such dramatic characters. The central revelation is the monistic one of the unity of life, "there is no characteristic of the higher animal which has not been foreshadowed in the plant" (1927, p.22). *Plant Autographs and their Revelations* aims to give a popular account of Bose's work. It presents his physiological evidence for plants possessing hearts, nervous systems and circulatory systems — these of course have a functional identity with the same systems in animals, not a structural one. That is to say that Bose's arguments are analogical. It is not since the work of Erasmus Darwin that anyone has presented in such detail analogies of plant and animal function, but the physiological processes to which Bose appeals do not have the speculative character of many of Darwin's, they are real. The only question to be raised with Bose is whether the analogy is appropriate, but there is no question that every living plant is not an arena of microscopic physiological activity which is immediately and highly responsive to changes in the external world.

Bose faces the question of plant consciousness. His answer is interesting because it might appear to be read at first as allowing the possibility of the imputation of consciousness to plants, but a closer reading shows that he comes no closer to affirming it than equivocating, and in fact pushes the question aside. First he says "The difficulty lies in defining consciousness and in drawing a line below which consciousness does not exist, and above which it enters the domain of life" (p. 21).

Then he refers to Bergson's vitalism, stating

"If .... at the top of the scale of living beings, consciousness is attached
to very complicated nervous centres, must we not suppose that it
accompanies the nervous system down its whole descent, and that
when the nerve stuff is merged into the yet undifferentiated living
matter, consciousness is still there, diffused, but not reduced to nothing? Theoretically, then, everything living might be conscious. *In
principle* consciousness is coextensive with life" (p. 22).

The last two sentences in that quotation take us back to ancient
Greek metaphysics. The final part of his answer is that he wishes to
stick to experimental facts and to eschew "metaphysical questions on
which authorities are so greatly divided" (p. 22).

When one reads passages such as the following from *Is the Plant
a Sentient Being* one can understand why many supposed Bose to
attribute consciousness to plants (again, in this paper he nowhere
says that they have a conscious life):

"We will now try to discover whether the ordinary plants are inert
and insensitive as they are supposed to be. The plant when struck
does not show any movement, but this absence of movement is due
to a quite different cause from that of insensitiveness.

The living tissue is attached to wood, which is inflexible. To find
out whether the plant perceives and reacts to a shock, the stem is
placed between a fixed rod and a moveable magnifying lever, the
movement of which is further magnified by optical means to something like a million times. .... A very feeble electric shock was sent
through the plant, and through one of the leading physicians who
was in the same circuit. The human being felt nothing but the

Contraction Recorder showed that the plant gave a shuddering twitch under the shock. Ordinary plants are not only sensitive, but they are able to register impressions which are far below the range of human perception. How blind we are, how limited our knowledge! The little we can see is nothing, compared with the vastness we cannot.

What happens when the shock is no longer feeble, but terrible in its intensity?

The plant was strapped in the electric chair, with moist sponge to facilitate the passage of the current. The plant became quiescent after a while, as indicated by the stationary line of bright light reflected from the magnifying recorder. By switching a key, a high voltage current drones like thunder through the machine.

This produces a convulsion in the plant, the line of light being jerked violently to the left — it is not dead as yet. There is once more the growl of the destroyer, followed by another convulsion, the line of light having gone right round toward that from which there is to be no recovery. The plant is probed again. It answers no more, being stilled with the stillness of death" (Bose, 1929, p. 388).

Two examples of the popular impression which Bose left may be given.

The first is from the article *What Plants Feel* by W. Kaempffert, in *McClure's Magazine* in 1915. Kaempffert's essay is based on Bose's 1913 book, *Researches on Irritability of Plants*. Kaempffert's style is not unlike that of Bose.

"His ingenious recorders", writes Kaempffert, "are pens of incredible lightness with which lillies or cabbages may write down their impressions of the outer world in a script that we can understand. Use these instruments intelligently, and vegetation, hitherto mute, will whisper its story" (Kaempffert, 1915, p. 70).

Then comes an irresistible story:

"A plant responds to intoxicants in the same human fashion. When Dr. Bose subjects a mimosa to the influences of alcohol, he does not administer the liquid but vapour. Confined in its little chamber, mimosa drinks in the fumes. The effect is almost ludicrous. The plant is evidently intoxicated. It cannot lurch and reel, but it can and does indicate its intoxication by means of the resonant recorder in an inebriate script. In behaviour, a drunken mimosa differs in no essential from a drunken man. Its script shows exaltation alternating with maudlin depression which seems almost repentant. A whiff of fresh air and mimosa is once more restored to sobriety" (p. 73).

The second comes a number of years after Bose's death. In 1972 Charles Musès and Arthur M. Young edited an anthology which they called *Consciousness and Reality* (Musès and Young, 1972). They included an excerpt from *Plant Autographs and their Revelations*. The excerpt is headed "Awareness in Plants". Nowhere in that piece does Bose predicate awareness of plants, but the casual reader might be forgiven for supposing that he does.

It should be remembered, however, that for all the anthropomorphic metaphor Bose used in writing of plant life he never repudiated mechanism. To speak strictly he does not belong in this monograph.

CHAPTER 10

Alternatives to mentalism : some more instinctivists and the behaviourists

10.1 *Introduction*

None of the writers considered in this chapter predicate mind of plants, they belong to the two other approaches to vegetable psychology identified at the beginning of this monograph: the instinctivists and the behaviourists.

10.2 *Some more instinctivists*

We have discussed already those who, after Matthew Hale in the seventeenth century, have employed "instinct" as an explanatory category of plant growth and movement. As we have seen the term "instinct" in the present context has a fairly uniform meaning. Writers implicitly or explicitly draw a distinction between mere mechanical movements (e.g. the shaking of leaves of grass in the wind) and instinctive movements ("true behaviour" in modern psychological usage), and they have a teleological conception of the latter. Plant (and animal) movements occur "in — order — to" bring about some state of affair, some goal (e.g. some movements of the sundews and the Venus fly trap are aimed at catching insects). Such movements are immanent with design, occur under conditions of no previous learning and under no rational guidance. Although resembling rational behaviour, the instinctive innate movements only mimic it — after all humans are the only rational beings. We may call this rationalistic metaphysical conception of instincts Aristotelian because of its teleology. Although "instinct" is not a Greek word, the doctrine of instinct with which we are concerned can be seen as a Renaissance counterpart of Anaxagoras's *nous* : i.e., in the unfolding of plant (and animal) instincts we see Intelligence or Mind manifested. We are not concerned in this chapter with changes in the meaning of instinct in modern psychology, especially those attributable to the animal ethologists such as Lorenz and Tinbergen.

We have seen also that for some instinctivists instinct and mind have not been mutually exclusive categories, being both predicated of plants (e.g. Percival, Tupper, Francis Darwin), whilst others have used solely instinct as an explanatory category (e.g. Hunter, Hancock and Duncan). None of the instinctivists to be considered now are mentalists.

It is no surprise to find that many instinctivists are vitalists. They see instincts as vital principles supervening in material processes — a mechanistic account of plant movements can never be sufficient in principle. On the other hand, instinctivism does not necessarily have to be vitalist (as will be seen in the case of Bekhterev), for instincts could be regarded as immanent in material processes, having no existence outside them. There are problems with this account, just as there are problems with the vitalist account (e.g. , how can the materialist offer a qualitative definition of "instinct" which would characterize it independently of its functions? Would not the materialist be forced to ascribe instincts to inanimate "goal-seeking" machines such as guided missiles?).

Mind and Brain: Or, the Correlations of Consciousness and Organization is the best known work of Thomas Laycock (1812-1876), British physician and physiologist, who is mainly remembered in psychology as a pioneer of the notion of unconscious mental activity. Laycock advances in it the doctrine of "Primordial Instincts", which are "the most general vital energies .... by which the continued existence of the organism in time and space is maintained" (Laycock, 1860, Vol. II, p. 190). They are universal and fundamental, other instincts grow out of them, and in animals they may be accompanied by consciousness, but not so in plants. The Primordial Instincts can be divided into the Absolute ones, which are concerned with living, gaining nutriment, surviving and reproducing, and the Contingent or Relative ones, concerned mostly with adaptation, protection, cure or repair of damage. The Relative ones evolve finally in man into the "rational instincts". Laycock, who was of a systematizing bent, proceeded to sub-divide the instincts and to coin names for them, but his taxonomy went unnoticed by physiologists.

The notion of plant instincts generally is more attractive to a vitalist than a mechanist, and, while most vitalists in botany in the nineteenth and early twentieth centuries did not use "instinct" as a category, one notable theorist who did was the Austrian Anton Kerner von Marilaun. In his very popular *The Natural History of Plants*, published originally 1887-91, and in English translation 1894-5, Kerner von Marilaun (1831-1898), having argued for the necessity of the concept of "vital force" in the life sciences, goes on to introduce his account of plant instincts:

"Were we to designate as instinctive those actions of the vital force which are manifested by movements purposely adapted in some manner advantageous to the whole organism, nothing could be urged against it. For what is instinct but an unconscious and purposeful action on the part of a living organism? Plants, then, possess instinct .... *Linaria Cymbalaria* (ivy-leaved toadflax, T. McM.) .... raises its flower-stalks from the stone wall over which it creeps towards the light, but as soon as fertilization has taken place, these same stalks, in that very place and amidst unchanged external conditions, curve in the opposite direction, so as to deposit their seeds in a dark crevice" (Kerner von Marilaun, 1894, vol. 1, pp. 52-53).

Here the ivy-leaved toadflax exhibits instinctively a marked reversal of a behavioural tendency as a consequence of change of object: to the teleologist this is clearly purpose unfolding.

In the history of psychology Vladimir Bekhterev has been overshadowed by I. P. Pavlov, but in his own right Bekhterev (1857-1927) is an interesting theorist, in addition to his being a researcher of great achievement in psychiatry, physiology and psychology. In contrast to Kerner von Marilaun's contention that the doctrine of plant instincts is necessarily vitalistic, Bekhterev's contention is that it must eschew vitalism. Opposed to vitalism, Bekhterev saw plant instincts as instantiated solely in behaviour. Historians of psychology tend just to note his "objectivism" and mechanism, they refer to his anti-psychological stance in claiming that psychic (mental) categories should be replaced in an objective science by the physiological behavioural reflex. Wolman, for example, notes that "causation and motivation, learning and thinking became reduced to a mechanistic model of the human organism which resembled the mechanistic parts of Descartes's theory" (Wolman, 1960, p. 65). They do not bring out clearly the fact that Bekhterev's mechanism was not thoroughgoing, in that, although he rejected vitalism and mentalism, he was explicitly a teleologist.

This outline of plant instincts comes from the English translation of the fourth edition (1928) of Bekhterev's *General Principles of Human Reflexology*, the first Russian edition of which was published in 1918. (It is referenced in this monograph under the name Bechterev, following the usage of the translators, Emma and William Murphy. To-day "Bekhterev" is the preferred rendition of the Cyrillic alphabet). In this theoretical exposition of his system Bekhterev's starting point is the claim of reflexology to be objective. In dealing with human personality from a strictly objective "bio-social" standpoint it makes no reference to subjective psychic processes. The latter can be expressed in terms of reflexes of varying levels of complexity.

Instincts have no separate existence. They are "organic reflexes", which may be modifiable according to individual experience, and which are more complex than ordinary reflexes, but less so than the "association" ones involved in learning (Pavlov's conditioned reflexes). However, the difference between them is of degree rather than kind.

Reflexology is teleological: Bekhterev, for example, objects to Loeb's tropistic mechanism; he quotes approvingly from William McDougall's *Outline of Social Psychology* (1908); he states that teleology is seen in the activities of the simplest animals and even plants, citing Jennings and Francis Darwin respectively (the zoologist Jennings, as was reported in Chapter 7, flirted with the idea that all micro-organisms possessed psychic faculties). An objective behavioural version of neo-Lamarckianism is hinted at in the claim that complex inherited organic reflexes also reproduce ancestral experience.

Aggression and defence are the two basic instincts for Bekhterev, and they are exhibited by both animals and plants: "the fundamental activities of all living beings are acts of aggression and defence: in other words, they are aggressive and defensive reflexes, which are to be found not only in the lower animals, but even in plants which are tied by nature to a definite spot and get food from the environment" (Bekhterev, 1928, p. 116). A footnote on the same page reads: "As is well known, plants are capable of the activity of sucking in, sometimes even of seizing (for instance, the well-known fly-trap, fish-catching seaweeds, and the like) and acts of defence in the form of drooping, shedding leaves in autumn, so-called gall nuts, etc."

These basic organic reflexes distinguish the animate from the inanimate: "It is scarcely necessary to say that aggression and defence, inasmuch as they are fundamental functions of the organism, must represent the earliest reflexes in animal phylogenesis, and, consequently, as we have seen, we find these reflexes in the simplest unicellular organisms, beginning from the amoeba, and even in plants" (p. 117).

The ancient concept of irritability is invoked by Bekhterev, for him it is a "special reflex activity" which in "the vegetable kingdom represents acts of defence or aggression" (p. 119). He mentions J.C. Bose's experimental demonstrations that all plant organs are irritable to some extent, and concludes his treatment of plants by reference to the by now thoroughly historically sanctified sensitive plant, telegraph plant and the carnivorous sundew.

Some attention to the general question of the conceptual adequacy of teleology in organismic behaviour will be given in the next chapter.

10.3 *The behaviourists: plant psychology becomes orthodox*

The rise of comparative psychology in America early in this century, and the connected broadening of the denotation of "psychology" to include "behaviour", enabled plant psychology to become part of psychological orthodoxy for about three decades. Its orthodoxy consisted in its being given room in official journals and its inclusion in academically reputable books as a legitimate branch of comparative psychology.

We turn now to the third approach to plant psychology; the behaviourist. Those in this group wish to predicate only "behaviour" of plants, and they see such behaviour as a proper datum of psychology. Their general line of argument is that psychology is the science of organismic behaviour, plants are behaving organisms, therefore the study of plant behaviour is a legitimate field of psychology. Such an approach refuses to make reference to mental states, sometimes on pragmatic, sometimes on philosophical grounds. It includes, but is not co-extensive with, Behaviourism (with a capital B), by which is meant Watsonian and post-Watsonian mechanistic stimulus-response behaviour theory (e.g. C.L. Hull, K.W. Spence and B. F. Skinner).

The conception of "behaviour" advanced by John B. Watson in *Psychology as the Behaviourist Views* (1913), would seem to allow legitimization of plant psychology into psychological orthodoxy, even though Watson and most of his intellectual descendants took it more or less for granted that Behaviourists studied man and lower animals. Insofar, however, as Watson's interpretation of behaviour permitted him to acknowledge the activities of amoebae as behaviour, it appears that there could be no theoretical objection to the notion of behaviour as a psychological category in plants: "From the viewpoint of behaviour here suggested the facts on the behaviour of amoebae have value in and for themselves without reference to the behaviour of man", Watson said, and, after noting that the laws of behaviour in amoebae may not be general, went on to state that they must be studied if "the phenomena of behaviour are ever to be brought within the sphere of scientific control" (Watson, 1913, p. 177).

A few years before, in a paper whose influence was in inverse proportion to that of Watson's , the psychologist Edward Kirkpatrick (better known as a writer on child development) had made a proposal which sought to unify all the life sciences into a single discipline. This discipline, "organosis", would recognize behaviour as its datum and ignore issues of the existence of consciousness, issues which only confused matters. The influence of American functionalism with its evolutionary basis (e.g. that of James Angell) is apparent in Kirkpatrick's paper:

> "The end of the functioning of all organisms is the preservation and
> perpetuation of the organism, and all behaviour adapted to secure
> that end may (if we think of intelligence as the adaptation of means
> to ends) be regarded as intelligent, whether or not it is conscious".
> Because "intelligence" has connotations of consciousness and what is
> wanted is a term which will include unconscious as well as conscious
> adaptation of means to ends, he suggests " "organosis" to signify the

253

adaptive functioning of any organism or organ without reference to whether the activity involved is conscious or unconscious, and without reference to whether the organ is nervous or non-nervous, or the organism vegetable or animal. Such a general term and conceptions are necessary because certain fundamental characteristics of the behaviour of all living organisms, from the plant and the amoeba to man, are the same (nervous tissue having them only in a greater degree), because there are no means of knowing whether some of these are conscious or not, and because there is good reason to believe that any organ may at one time function with consciousness and at another time without. We need therefore to recognize a science of behaviour of organisms and organs, or organosis" (Kirkpatrick, 1907, pp. 544-545).

Although the proposal for a discipline of "organosis" was never taken up, we see in it, and in Watson's paper of which it could be regarded as a forerunner, clear evidence that plant behaviour might be seen as being locatable under the rubric of a broadly-based psychology.

The precursor of *Psychological Abstracts*, the *Psychological Index*, listed some plant papers in the early 1900's under the sub-heading *Comparative Psychology* in the general section headed *Genetic, Individual and Social Psychology*. In 1911 that general section became *Organic Evolution: Behaviour in other species*, and the sub-heading *Plants; organs and responses* was introduced. This sub-heading continued when the general title of the section changed in 1915 to become *Mental Evolution: Behaviour and the Animal Mind*, and again in 1925 when it became *Plant and Animal Behaviour*. *Plant and Animal Behaviour* with *Plants; organs and responses* as a sub-category was continued by the *Psychological Abstracts* when it began publication in 1927. The overwhelming majority of plant publications listed under these headings during those years were German and they were in the area of plant physiology. Thus plant psychology was respectable scientifically, being seen as that part of comparative psychology which shares with plant physiology the objective study of plant movements.

Mention has been made in this book's opening chapter of the paper by the botanist H. J. Fuller in the *Journal of General Psychology* in 1934. Fuller complains that "unfortunately, psychology has been so engrossed in .... animal investigations that it has neglected one extensive field for comparative research — namely the study of plant responses" (Fuller, 1934, p. 379). Fuller takes it for granted that plant behaviour is a legitimate domain for the psychologist, and his paper is devoted to descriptions of plant reactions, some of which were quoted in Chapter 1. He is careful to use inverted commas around the word "memory" in his observation of the "sleeping behaviour" of oxalis under reversed illumination conditions.

Carl Murchison's now classic *Handbook of Social Psychology* appeared in the mid-30's (Murchison, 1935). It came from Clark University where G. Stanley Hall early in the century had given favourable notice to plant psychologists. The first chapter was on the *Population Behaviour of Bacteria* by the microbiologist R. E. Buchanan. It gave quantitative accounts of the influence of experimentally controlled conditions on the size of bacteria populations. Chapter 2 was on *Social Origins and Processes among Plants* by the botanist F. E. Clements. It presented an outline of some of the principles of plant ecology. Evidently in both Buchanan's and Clements' cases it was not deemed necessary even to pose the question of what these chapters were doing in a text on social psychology. Incidentally, other chapters included the topics of insect societies, bird societies and the behaviour of mammalian herds and packs.

Most comparative psychologists accepted without question the view that the province of animal comparative psychology was the behaviour of non-human animal species, even if they no longer talked in terms of the "animal mind" as, for example, Margaret Floy Washburn had done (Washburn, 1908). But not so C. J. Warden, T. N. Jenkins and L. H. Warner in their massive three volume *Comparative Psychology* which was brought out between 1935 and 1940. The first volume was on the principles and methods of comparative psychology and the third volume was on the vertebrates. The second volume, a very large one in its own right, was on the comparative psychology of plants and invertebrates. Chapter 1 was on protista, isolated cells and tissue cultures. The plant material was in Chapter 2 ("Metaphyta", prepared by Warden). It was organized in two sections, receptive capacities and reactive capacities. The authors claimed their psychological orientation to be "organicist", i.e. to be concerned with the functioning of the organism as a whole. They were opposed to vitalism and the approach of Russian reflexologists. They had some sympathy for the approaches of Perry, Woodworth and Gestalt psychologists, but they rejected the Gestaltists' use of mentalistic concepts such as insight. Behaviour they proclaimed as their focus of study. It is interesting to note that they did not attempt to justify the appearance of a psychological volume substantially on plant behaviour; it appeared without any fuss as if it had a right to be there in the natural order of things.

Thus in the mid-1930's there was a clear, if small, place for a behavioural plant psychology in psychological orthodoxy, but it disappeared as if overnight, and its disappearance, if not unmourned, certainly was not mentioned.

The *Psychological Abstracts* had listed the heading *Plant and Animal Behaviour* up until 1937. In that year the heading was dropped and the editorial note said:

"Some changes have been made because the number of publications on a particular topic, for example statistics or emotion, hardly justifies a separate heading. A major change has been the dropping of the heading *Plant and Animal Behaviour*. The use of this rubric in the past has resulted in much confusion, because while most animal studies were classified here others were assigned to different sections on the ground that they concerned such topics as the nervous system, receptive processes of learning. Animal studies were so widely used .... that to segregate all of them in a separate section seems no longer practicable or justifiable" (Editorial Note, 1937, p. 1).

No specific reason is given for the dropping of a Plant abstract heading. Certainly only a few plant abstracts had been published up until then, but now apparently no more were to be published.

Lindzey's new version in 1954 of the Handbook of Social Psychology (Lindzey, 1954) contained only one "comparative" chapter, viz. Hebb and Thompson's *The Social Significance of Animal Studies*. Gone were the plants, along with the bacteria, insects and birds. There was no reason given for the change of policy, other than the unqualified statement that Murchison was out of date and out of print.

Texts of comparative psychology since Warden, Jenkins and

Warner make at the most only the occasional passing reference to plant behaviour, it is not a topic in itself.

One could speculate on the reasons for the silent demise of behavioural plant psychology. There is probably no single reason. One possibility, which is hard to substantiate, is that the orthodox-trained psychologists always felt a certain theoretical awkwardness with the notion, even though their discomfort was never articulated. They did not like the concept, but their theoretical lights, such as they were, were unable to find fault with it. Hence they bided their time, and when the chance came to drop it, drop it they did, in much the same way as a high *bourgeois* family might drop a legitimate but embarrassing member.

A more prosaic possibility is just that the vast majority of experimenters were so entrenched in the unquestioned belief that the subjects of psychology were denizens of the animal kingdom that they did not realize that the behaviourist approach logically allowed the extension of psychology to plants.

Other possible reasons are purely pragmatic ones which do not call into question the probity of orthodox psychologists: the systematic study of plant responses was just too difficult to do in relation to the study of the responses of other organisms, such as rats. Rats are easier to handle and maintain than are plants. They are easier and faster to work with and they have a much larger repertoire of responses. The kinds of plants whose responses are amenable to laboratory experiments of interest to comparative psychology are hard to get in sufficient numbers, expensive to buy and relatively difficult to keep under controlled conditions.

Another possible reason is that as time went on it became clear that plants cannot learn, whereas animals, or at least most of them, can. Now one could conclude this section by saying here "whether plants can learn all depends on what is meant by learning", but in preference a little story can be told which may have some significance, but it is a story about conditioning rather than learning.

Warden, Jenkins and Warner's three volume work was published also as an abridged single volume. The abridged version appeared in 1934 *before* the main opus. Volume I of the master work did not come out until 1935, Volume III appeared in the following year, and Volume II, the Plant and Invertebrate one, appeared last of the series in 1940. In the 1934 abridged volume there were two references to the possibility of establishing conditioned responses in plants:

> "Darwin, (Charles — T. McM.) reports also that the tendrils of the passion flower, when stimulated by contact at too frequent intervals, came to show little or no response in time. These and similar facts would seem to suggest the possibility of establishing simple conditioned responses in connection with growth movements.
>
> The evidence for modifiability of behaviour is much more definite in the field of turgor movements. Pfeffer reports that the tendrils of the sundew, *Drosera*, cease to respond to a mechanical stimulus that is repeated a number of times within a short interval. A similar decrease in irritability, or negative adaptation, occurs also in *Mimosa* under like conditions. The response of the Venus fly trap seems to depend to a large extent upon the existing conditions of nutrition. Darwin found that the response was sluggish for a day or two after the ingestion of an insect. A purely mechanical stimulus induces closure followed by an immediate re-opening of the leaf. In such

cases, a second response can be elicited at once. These variations in behaviour suggest the likelihood that conditioned responses could be established in the insectivorous plants" (Warden, Jenkins and Warner, 1934, pp. 237-8).

In the same section of the master volume of 1940 there is now no mention at all of conditioned growth responses in plants, there is a parenthetical mention that "strangely enough no one has a yet attempted to develop conditioned responses in such insectivorous plants or *Dionaea* in which rapid movements occur" (Warden, Jenkins and Warner, Vol. II, 1940, p. 284). Maybe, then, in the period between 1934 and 1940 orthodox psychologists lost any time they might have had for the vegetable kingdom because that basic phenomenon of the behavioural approach, conditionability, had not been demonstrated in it.

The invocation of Charles Darwin's name by Warden, Jenkins and Warner in the context of plant conditionability is quite apposite historically. It has been stated in Chapter 7 that Charles's youthful speculations on plant psychology in the *N. Notebook* (1838-9) analysed plant memory in terms of mechanical associations of movements. In his *M. Notebook* of 1838 he asked among his many questions "Would a sensitive plant if irritated very regularly at one time every day naturally close at that time after a long period — " (Darwin, in Gruber, 1974, p. 296).

10.4 *Conditioning and learning in plants*

It was not until the 1960's that attempts were made to condition plant responses and these attempts were instigated by physiologists. The plant used in all the studies was the sensitive plant.

At first sight it would appear that this is an obvious plant to select for conditioning studies. There are no great problems about obtaining unconditioned responses and unconditioned stimuli.

The unconditioned response (UCR) could be either the closure of the leaflets and/or the drooping of the leaf stems, which occur readily and are easy to observe. They are also easy to quantify, the simplest being the counting of the number of movements which occur. Another simple measure is latency, the time elapsed between the stimulus occurrence and the appearance of the response.

There is a choice of unconditioned stimuli. Because the plant responds to a range of stimuli, the most likely unconditioned stimulus (UCS) would be one of a touch to the leaflet, a shaking of the plant, the onset or offset of light, and the application of electric current. Quantification and observation of these is easy.

The choice of a conditioned stimulus (CS) presents a problem, however. In the ideal conditioning paradigm the conditioned stimulus should be one which is capable of eliciting responses, but does not, under ordinary conditions, elicit the desired response, i.e. the connection between the conditioned stimulus and response must be novel. In Pavlov's experiments, for example, dogs can hear buzzers readily, but normally the noise of the buzzer does not elicit salivation until after the conditioning process has occurred. What could be an appropriate CS for a *mimosa*, and, for that matter when we think about it, for any plant? The stimulus to become associated with leaf-closure/stem drooping must be one which ordinarily is not associated with that response but is associated with other readily observable responses. One cannot think of any ready candidate.

It would seem then that at the best there is only the possibility of an approximate demonstration of conditioning; there are experimental designs which might yield data suggestive of conditioning, but nonetheless whose interpretation is ambiguous. For example, say that we know that the leaflets of the sensitive plant fold up relatively quickly to being touched and relatively slowly to the onset of darkness. We might then decide to train a group of mimosas (the experimental group) by plunging the plants into darkness and shortly afterwards giving their leaflets a good hard touch. We might take a second group of plants (the control group) and touch their leaflets just as often as we did those of the first group, and plunge them into darkness just as often as we did those of the first group, but having this time a random relationship between the onset of darkness and the occurrence of the touching. Then we might make a test by subjecting all the plants to darkness suddenly, but not touching any of them. We would count the numbers of folded leaflets at the time they would have folded had they been touched. There would be evidence of conditioning if the experimental group had more leaflets folded up than had the control group. Such an experiment, were it to succeed, could not be called a rigourous demonstration of conditioning, however.

To move from the hypothetical experiment to the actual experiments reported is to discover that the evidence for plant conditioning is contradictory and inconclusive.

The experiments were instigated by E. Holmes (Holmes and

Gruenberg, 1965; Holmes and Yast, 1966). The results were nega-tive, which is just as well because no controls were used. In the first experiment a light touch (producing little or no leaflet folding) was the CS, it was followed quickly by a sufficiently powerful electric shock to produce folding (the UCS). When after this training the light touch was given by itself no folding occurred. In the second study the CS was brushing with a light brush, the UCS was a strong jarring to the leaflets.

R. E. Haney (Haney, 1969) used two experimental groups. One had the onset of darkness as the CS, the other the onset of light. Both had a strong enough touch to produce folding as the UCS. A control group had just alternating light and dark, no UCS was applied to it. Haney claimed positive results for the light-onset CS group: i.e. when light onset alone was presented after training, it showed more leaflet responses than did the controls (and the other CS group). This is a rather odd result because leaflet folding and stem drooping are contrary to the normal response of the plant to light. Haney's control conditions were deficient (e.g. no control group received randomly paired light and touch stimuli). Haney's positive finding was not rep-licated in the following year (Levy, Allen, Caton and Holmes, 1970).

Armus in 1970, in a paper which was published in a text by H. R. Denny and S. C. Ratner on comparative psychology (Armus, 1970) claimed to have conditioned leaflet folding but not stem drooping to darkness onset as the CS, the UCS being manual striking of the main stem, but the study again is open to charges of inappropriate controls. There are some data to support such charges. An attempt to replicate Armus' study with the addition of a blind observer (i.e. an observer who did not know to which group, experimental or control, the plants belonged) gave negative results (Blau and Walthall, 1976). In the same paper Blau and Walthall reported negative results in another experiment which attempted to maximise the opportunities for conditioning to occur by including more conditioning days in relation to test days than did the first experiment. Their preferred interpretation of Armus' results is that they are artefacts of the experimenter's perceptual bias.

The choice of appropriate controls is a point emphasized by Applewhite, who surveyed studies on learning in bacteria and fungi as well as the plant conditioning ones. The conclusion which Applewhite reaches is that "from a behavioural standpoint, it must be concluded that conditioning has not been clearly demonstrated in single-celled organisms, in Metazoa which lack a nervous system, in fungi, or in plants" (Applewhite, 1975, p. 185).

A theoretical review of classical conditioning in plants (Simón, 1978), having noted both the enormous range of animal species in which conditioning has been shown and the fact that neither the whole nor any part of the central nervous system is necessary for conditioning, urged that a much greater attempt to condition plants should be made. In Simón's view the area has been "barely explored" (Simón, 1978, p. 39).

We can come back to the question raised earlier in the chapter of whether plants can learn. Now we will say "it all depends on what is meant by "learning" ". This chapter is not concerned with cognitive approaches to learning, earlier chapters have reviewed claims that plants learn by undergoing certain cognitive changes. The question here is whether plants can learn as "learning" is understood from a behaviourist orientation.

If learning is identified with conditioning in the strict sense then there is no good evidence that plants can learn. But to identify learning exclusively with conditioning would be to beg the question, because there are many behaviour theorists who see conditioning as just one species of learning; in particular they allow habituation to be another species. R. A. Champion, for example, who is a behaviour theorist in the Hull/Spence tradition, distinguishes between sensory adaptation, which he does not allow to be learning, and habituation, which he does. Sensory adaptation (e.g. one becomes visually adapted to a darkened cinema upon entering it from a lit up foyer) is not lasting, nor does it depend upon a response being made. In habituation a response becomes progressively weaker consequent upon its being made a number of times under the same stimulus conditions. Some might have such an amorphous concept of learning that they would even allow sensory adaptation to be called learning, but that point is not of concern here. Champion states "the simplest, most precise definition of learning is as a change in behaviour which results from practice" (Champion, 1969, p. 2).

This definition is not without problems — e.g., it is doubtful that Champion would allow *any* change in behaviour resulting from practice, such as "anomalous" responses, to be called learning, but he is correct in seeing that from a behaviourist standpoint learning can be defined *only* in terms of overtly observable motor movements. Any definition which implies or pre-supposes some state of affairs akin to the acquisition of knowledge is cognitive, and is therefore inimical to behaviourism. E. L. Hartley, in a recent psychological encyclopaedia article on plant behaviour writes that "despite the lack of uniform success in the conditioning studies conducted so far, plants *do* learn. The evidence reported in studies examining photoperiodicity in plants makes this abundantly clear" (Hartley, 1984, p. 57). (It is difficult to decide, by the way, whether the inclusion of Hartley's article is a new sign of orthodox sanction or whether it is simply an expression of a most catholic editorial policy.)

Hartley then cites Farr's anecdote (mentioned in the previous chapter) of the effects of the reversal of light-darkness patterns of illumination on the sleeping behaviour of *oxalis bowei* as a photoperiodicity. Unlike Farr, Hartley uses the term "habituation". The change in the oxalis's sleeping habits shows it to have become habituated to new stimulus conditions. Farr wrote of plant "habits", which, as we have seen, were written of long before him by Erasmus Darwin. In this broad sense of habituation, i.e. akin to some usages of "adaptation" and "acclimatization", connoting systematic response changes as functions of changes in stimulus conditions, the concept is a very old one, even if it is not named as habituation. It was not new when Charles Darwin and other nineteenth century plant physiologists following him (e.g. Pfeffer in Germany) began to study it experimentally. Habituation is often used now in a narrower sense to mean the weakening of an unlearned response through repeated exposure to a stimulus which elicits that response. As was recorded in section 8.2, Francis Darwin noted that type of habituation in his account of the mimosa which ceased to respond to the pull of a metronome to which it was attached. In this century many more studies of plant habituation have taken place (e.g. see Warden, Jenkins and Warner, Vol. II, 1940; Applewhite, 1975). Some important ones were conducted by J.C. Bose, who has been discussed in section 9.7, and whose researches deserve to be remembered for their masterly ingenuity.

Plant movements may not be conditionable but they are modifiable in a significant sense. Accordingly from a behavioural standpoint plants learn, for what could learning be, above *modifiability*, to the behaviourist? The conclusion follows that within the behaviourist approach to psychology the notion of plant psychology must be a legitimate one. Whatever the reason may be for the relative neglect of the vegetable kingdom by behaviourist psychologists — habitual ("psychology is concerned with animals"), practical ("plants are too difficult and expensive to work with"), sociological ("it's not fashionable, grant-giving bodies would sneer") and so on, it cannot be conceptual.

CHAPTER 11

Contemporary plant psychology

11.1 Introduction

The *Psychological Abstracts* has not needed to revive the practice of having a separate plant behaviour heading, and Harry Fuller's invitation to psychologists to explore plant behaviour resulted in no Departments of Psychology setting up their own gardens or plant laboratories. Nonetheless there were attempts to condition plant responses in the 1960's and today we find plant psychology continuing. This chapter will consider two psychologists, Jean Piaget and Richard L. Gregory, and a botanist, Malcolm Wilkins. Although Piaget died in 1980 his psychology still lives, so it is not stretching the point too far to regard him as a contemporary. In reading Piaget and Gregory we see that the teleological concepts of purpose and design are taken seriously by some contemporary psychologists. Accordingly I think it is pertinent here to stray a little from the path of simply chronicling views to raise some critical problems of the concept of teleology in psychology. These criticisms will have application to teleologists generally.

11.2 *Jean Piaget* (1896-1980)

Adaptation is a central concept in Piaget's psychology. An organism
which has successfully adapted by means of the processes of assimilation of, and accommodation to, the environment is in a state of
equilibrium with it. The striving for equilibrium and the processes
involved in it are universal biological phenomena. Adaptation is
not confined to intellectual functioning; although most psychologists quite properly concentrate their attention on its intellectual or
cognitive aspects, it is a basic character of biological functioning. It
distinguishes animate organisms from inanimate objects. The sen-
sorimotor and conceptual knowledge which humans develop grow
out of innate behavioural capacities acquired through evolution. To
Piaget there is, as Pulaski (1980) puts it, "continuity between biological intelligence, as shown even by plants and lower animals, and
human knowledge as it develops from infancy onward" (p. 9). The
"biological intelligence" of lower organisms does not have a cognitive
component; it is, so to speak, the "intelligence of evolved instincts".
It is what makes behaviour *behaviour* rather than inert mechanically produced movement. In looking at the behavioural capacities
underlying the adaptation of lower organisms one then is concerned
primarily with inherited ones.

   In his later years, Piaget returned to his early interest in evolution
and in particular to the relation between behaviour and evolution.
His central thesis is that behaviour as an active force is itself an
agent of evolutionary change, and he sees this as opposed to the neo-
Darwinian idea that evolutionary changes occur as a result of natural
selection through chance mutations. Behaviour is not just a product

of evolution, but a cause of it as well. "Genetic recombinations succeed," says Piaget, in *Biology and Knowledge*, "by means of feedbacks
of progressive regulations, in molding themselves into the framework
or phenotypic model built up by interactions between the genotype
and its environment" (1967/1971, p. 298). Generally one is used
to thinking of behaviour as a dependent variable consequent upon
evolutionary factors as independent variables, but Piaget is revers-
ing this, emphasising behavioural factors as independent variables
bringing about evolutionary changes as dependent ones. There is
nothing novel about this idea, as Piaget notes, when, for example, he
discusses its similarity to James Mark Baldwin's principle of "organic
selection". At first it might seem that Piaget is advancing a Lamarckian doctrine of inheritance of acquired characters, especially when
one reads his hostile comments on the neo-Darwinian proponents
of evolution by means of "blind chance" —that is, random muta-
tion. It is not, however, a neo-Lamarckian doctrine. Piaget argued
as such in *Adaptation and Intelligence* (1974/80); Margaret Boden
(1979) observed in her critique of Piaget's evolutionary views that a
neo-Darwinist could readily account for the phenomena to which
Piaget draws attention.

As specific examples of Piaget's evolutionary claim, the two
empirical studies of his own which he uses as evidence may be
cited. Neither is very systematic nor tightly controlled, so they
should be regarded as suggestive demonstrations. The first concerns the plant *sedum*. The sedums (or stonecrops) are low-growing,
annual or perennial fleshy herbs of diverse habits. They are found
throughout temperate and colder regions of the Northern hemi-
sphere. There are about 300 species.

"He transplanted one lush Mediterranean variety to a site over a mile high in the Savoy Alps to see how it adapted to the extreme cold. The plants reacted by putting out much smaller, thicker leaves, to reduce their area of exposure while increasing chlorophyll production and photosynthetic power. While many of these plants reverted to type when transplanted back to Piaget's garden in Geneva, some retained their small size over thousands of descendants" (Pulaski, 1980, p. 8).

The second concerns a common pond-snail *Limnaea stagnalis*, "which in tranquil waters has an elongated shell. But when moved to the shores of the large Swiss lakes where the waves beat upon the rocks, Piaget reported that the young snail changes in shape. Clamping its sticky foot solidly to the supporting rock, the snail tightens the muscle that attaches it to its shell each time a wave dashes over it. This constant contracting tends to shorten the growing shell until it becomes globular in shape, rather than elongated. In time, the snail's adaptation to the turbulent water tends to be hereditary in these specimens. Piaget has moved some of them back to his aquarium and to a small, quiet pond, and has watched their descendants for many generations, during which they have retained their globular shape" (Pulaski, 1980, pp. 7-8).

Evolutionary change, then, is not a random matter. Organisms change their evolutionary course by their behaviour. Plants are organisms, they evolve, hence if Piaget's account of evolutionary change is correct he must be able to show that plants "behave" in the same sense that animals do, and it is here that Piaget becomes a plant psychologist.

271

The Behaviour of Plants

Piaget's views on plant behaviour are set out in *Behaviour and Evolution* (1976/79). Behaviour is conceived as teleological, as being goal-directed. Behaviour has an aim: to modify in some way the environment or the relation between the organism and its environment. In Piaget's words: "By "behaviour" I refer to all action directed by organisms toward the outside world in order to change conditions therein or to change their own situation in relation to these surroundings" (1976/79, p. ix). Searching for food, building a nest, using a tool, are all examples. What are *not* examples of behaviour are physiological processes such as muscular contractions and blood flow, although they do condition behaviour. Nor is the action of respiration on the atmosphere. Although respiration may affect the environment — for example, when plants produce oxygen —it is not intended to do so: the environmental effect is an artefact, it is not an object of the behaviour. The reflexes of animals, however, and the phototropic movements of some flowers (e.g., those of the *ornithogalum*, a family of small lilies, including the star-of-Bethlehem) do qualify as behaviour because "they are intended, no matter how locally or occasionally, to modify the relationship between organism and environment" (p. x). Perceptions in animals also count as behaviour. (Piaget does not attribute cognitive faculties to vegetables).

The range and amount of plant behaviour are less than those of animal behaviour because plants lack locomotion, they have no nervous system and they do not act upon, modify the environment. On this last limitation, Piaget (1976/79) says

"they act only upon themselves, seeking thereby to strengthen or establish vital links with the environment. Turning toward the light,

272

adapting flowers to the behaviour of insects, ensuring the dispersal
of seeds by a host of mechanisms —these all exemplify behaviour
limited in this way. It is genuine behaviour in that it is directed at
the environment. At the same time, it is limited in that movements
of external objects are not determined, each separately, by a direct
causality originating in the organism (with a few rare exceptions, e.g.,
the carnivorous *Drosera*). Instead, these movements are, so to speak,
solicited and then utilised by the plant's design, which is generated
and genetically programmed according to an overall plan" (pp. 126-7).

In addition, plants are not as highly evolved as are animals, for example, there is no plant equivalent of the primates. (This claim poses the
question of what could be meant by evolutionary "equivalence" between
the plant and animal kingdoms, but that issue will not be taken up here.)
There is less evolutionary range within the plant kingdom: one important gap is that between cryptogams (such as the mosses, ferns, and
algae which reproduce by spores) and phanerogams (which reproduce by
seeds), for it is in the area of the latter's flowering, fertilisation, and seed
propagation that most plant behaviour is found, such activities being
"based on an interaction with the environment, the dynamics of which
is largely extrasomatic and clearly distinct from the physico-chemical
metabolism" (p. 128). For example, orchids generally are not capable
of self-pollination. Fertilisation is done by insects, the structure of the
flowers' organs being such that insects cannot feed from flower to flower
without at the same time spreading pollen.

Some animal behaviour and all plant behaviour is instinctive.
Piaget recognises the difficulty of distinguishing between matura-
tional and experiential components of behaviour, and so limits his

273

definition of instinct to innate activities which are species-peculiar, without making any a prior assumptions about the nature of the innateness. Instinctive behaviour is of course teleological and Piaget describes as the "chief mystery of the instincts" the

> "anticipation of future situations which is intimately dependent on the environment and on possible changes in it. What we find here, in fact, is a differentiated and detailed *savoir-faire* which, if accounted for in terms of representational intelligence, presupposes a kind of inferential capacity and of systematic co-ordination far higher —and often far more wide scale —than that of the animal's abilities as displayed when it is confronted experimentally with tasks alien to its specific instinctual programming. How, in such cases, is concert achieved between the organism's behaviour and external objects or occurrences?" (pp. 85-86).

Piaget suggests that the processes indicative of instincts, the mechanisms found in all types of instinctive behaviour, are seven in number. (The magic number 7 held an attraction for another notable twentieth-century opponent of mechanism, William McDougall, who claimed that there were seven objective external marks of purpose in behaviour (McDougall, 1923)). The seven aspects of instinct are not involved in an invariable form in any given organization and are themselves subject to mechanisms of evolution. All seven are seen in plant behaviour and the following list accompanies them with Piaget's examples from the plant world:

(i) Anticipation. Here there is a shift from a simple regular succession (A,B,C) to a goal-directed anticipation (C) where the attainment of the goal implies a prior search for the effectuation of A and B. For example, sleep at first restores one after fatigue, but then becomes an anticipatory precaution against excessive fatigue. In some species of sedum there are sterile branches which fall to the ground and put down roots. This shedding is prepared for by an anticipatory mechanism observable at the beginning of the branch's growth; there is shrinking and splitting in it and at some point the slightest disturbance (e.g. rain) will cause the branch to fall.

(ii) Generalisation. A form of specific behaviour is used for a new purpose in a new situation. For example, sleep may become part of the "hibernation instincts" protecting the animal from undernourishment and thus no longer is associated merely with fatigue. In some plants the separation process listed above in branches transfers (generalises) below ground to some rhizomes or roots.

(iii) and (iv) Combinatorial systems (extrinsic or intrinsic). Several factors or elements may be coordinated in combinations giving rise to apparently fortuitous (i.e., not required by selection or by the environment) variations in structure or behaviour between closely related species. Extrinsic combination processes are seen in the differences between one species and its closest relative in the complex flowers or orchids. Intrinsic ones are seen in the formation of seeds when, for example, with wind-dispersed ones their lightness has to be reconciled with a form suited to the exploitation of the air's action, such as in having wing-like appendages.

(v) Compensatory mechanisms. These arise to annul or compensate for an endogenous disturbance. One such is the crawling in snakes and slow worms after their ancestors' loss of legs. Some sedum species show an increase in chlorophyll and in photosynthetic capacity when in the shade or in unfavourable conditions.

(vi) Complementary reinforcements. These are seen in phylogenetically progressive formation of certain organs intimately bound up with behaviour, for example legs.

(vii) Constructive coordinations. These are seen when the development of complementary reinforcements needs detailed information on the environment, as in the production of stinging organs and of toxic substances, in some animals and plants. Marks (vi) and (vii) together, complementary constructions generating new structures, have plenty of plant examples. One such is the different modes of fertilisation of the flowering plants.

All of these modes of operation of instinct have what Piaget calls a *function convergence* with the mechanisms of intelligence. They correspond with the basic procedures of human intelligence but, even though intelligence is rooted in biology, they are not to be conflated with intelligence.

We may now turn to the assessment of Piaget's plant psychology.

To begin with a minor objection, Piaget's list of the seven formative processes of instinct is idiosyncratic and obscure. It is not clear what basis dictates that they be seven in number, nor is it clear how they may be observed in actual plant movements, or, for that matter, animal ones. It is possible, however, that with training one could come to recognise both the rational basis for them and their separate manifestations. One suspects, however, that their teleological nature would impose a permanent difficulty with these, that is, the difficulty of identifying teleology in action anywhere.

On the general concept of instincts it may be said that Piaget does not see them in the way that some crude instinct theorists have done, namely, as hypostatised causes lying behind observed behaviour. In this familiar fallacy a phenomenon is named (here an item of behaviour is named "instinctive") and then the name is taken to be the explanation of the phenomenon (here "instinct" is then regarded as the *cause* of the behavioural item).

However, Piaget, rather than regarding instincts as forces lying behind behaviour, sees them presented in the *form* of behaviour itself, namely, behaviour which is some way related to innateness and is peculiar to a species. One could cavil at this: "*some* relationship with innateness" (Piaget, 1977/79, p. 81; italics added) is not informative because everything is related in some way to everything else, and "peculiar to a species" (p. 81) would seem to suggest that not more than one species could exhibit a particular instinct; perhaps "universal to a species" would be a better rendition.

However, the main problem with Piaget's account of instinct is the problem of his account of behaviour in general, that is, the problem of its purposive character.

The notion that what distinguishes behaviour from mere movement is that it is directed to a goal —it has a purpose, an end, it exhibits intention or plan —is incoherent. Remember that for Piaget the goal of behaviour is to modify the external environment or to alter the organism's relation with the environment.

Piaget, as do most psychologists and biologists who embrace teleology, does not run into the problem of *extrinsic* teleology, namely, the problem of saying intelligibly how a *future* goal could bring about a present occurrence of the phenomenon accounted for by reference to its goal. Instead for them the teleology is *intrinsic*, that is, the goal or end of the item of behaviour exists in the present as an *intention* or *purpose* to achieve the future goal. Accordingly, there is no temporal paradox involved in the notion of a present purpose bringing about a later piece of behaviour. Now if one describes behaviour, as Piaget does, as showing intention and purpose one has to ask what agent it is that does the planning, has the purpose, or forms the intention. If one is dealing with human beings the obvious answer is that it is the human being who envisages the end of his behaviour. This has its own problems, which are not of direct concern now, because Piaget does not want to say, when dealing with vegetables and brutes, that *they* themselves are the agents of their purposes. Who then is the planner of the behaviour of these lower beings?

The religious might say it is God, the Nature-Philosophers might say it is Nature, and the Marxists might say it is the Dialectic, but to seek such external agents of purposive behaviour would be to misunderstand Piaget's position, for his position is that behaviour carries *within itself* the marks of purpose, the intention does not reside in the mind of an agent above the behaviour but is *of* the behaviour; behaviour is *immanent* with purpose.

There are at least two important problems with this formulation of behaviour as intentional, both of them are fatal to it:

1.   It is impossible to specify objectively the underlying goal or end explaining any piece of behaviour. It should be pointed out first here that this is not an objection to the description or classification of behavioural acts in terms of their actual or desired outcomes (e.g., the rat pushing the bar, the mother repelling a predator, the tendril climbing a stake, the sundew catching an insect). Indeed one is often much more interested in the outcome of a behavioural act rather than in the means by which it is achieved (e.g., the precise motor movements or verbal utterances involved). With humans significant behavioural acts very often are described necessarily in purposive terms: intending to ...., believing that ...., seeking ...., and so on, with the appropriate object being specified. That is to say significant behaviour is cognitive (in a generic sense), and cognition cannot be other than cognition in action, that is, relating to an object. However, to recognise that the description of a particular act will be the description of intending to ...., believing that ...., as the case may be, is not to suppose that underlying it, standing apart from it, and *causing* it is a particular purpose. The objection to explanatory purposivism is relevant to all organismic behaviour, whether or not cognition is involved. The problem begins with specifying in a non-arbitrary way what the limits of any particular behavioural item are if behaviour is to be explained by reference to a goal. For example, take the sundew (*Drosera*) mentioned by Piaget. When one sees a fly land on one of its leaves, and the sticky glandular hairs of the leaf fold over the fly, one has first to decide whether the item of behaviour to be accounted for is just the movement through certain spatial dimensions in a certain time of the sundew's "tentacles", whether it is the movement of trapping the fly, or the beginning of the process of ingesting the fly, etc. Say it

was asked "What is the purpose of catching the fly?". "Why did the plant catch the fly?" There is a whole host of "in-order-to" answers: in order to cease the stimulation resulting from the fly's landing on the leaf; in order to prepare for propagation of the species; in order to participate in the evolutionary struggle; or in order to die. There are no objective marks, qualities, or properties of intention or plan in behaviour, what constitutes design in behaviour is relative to the standpoint of the observer: to one person the sundew's fly-catching behaviour might show the design of achieving a nutritive supplement, to another it might show a breakdown of the design by which the non-carnivorous majority of plants achieve effective nutrition. Consider the phenomenon of pseudocopulation in orchids. Flowers of the *ophrys* species resemble certain female wasps in form, colour, surface texture and in the emission of a pheremone-like odour. They are cross-pollinated by male wasps which land on them and attempt to copulate with them. Is the design here the mimicry of a female wasp (the pseudocopulation being an incidental after-event) or is it the ensuring of fertilization? There is no answer to this question.

2.   The second fatal objection is that no intelligible account can be given of the occurrence of behaviour. This kind of teleological account of behaviour appeals to the behavioural effect itself to account for its occurrence, it regards the behaviour as self-explanatory. But such a notion is inconceivable because the claim that something is to be understood as self-determining can only mean that it brings itself into existence. For anything to bring itself into existence it must have existed before the act of bringing itself into existence could occur. This is an inevitable problem for all accounts of self-maintaining,

self-regulating systems if the notion of "self" maintaining is taken literally, that is, if it is denied that determinism (causality) operates in them. Proponents of self-regulating purposive systems of course would say "we do not for one minute suppose that they cause themselves, there are conditions of their coming into existence." Piaget, for instance, notes that muscular contractions and blood flow "condition" animal behaviour. But if behaviour has conditions, that is, if the occurrence of certain events is efficient for bringing about a piece of behaviour, then has not the magic of "self-explanation" been exploded? Given the efficient conditions of a piece of behaviour the behaviour has to occur because by definition they are its conditions. There can be no point in saying it occurred "in order to ....". It is argued that all apparently teleological self-directing systems turn out to be classical, old-fashioned cause-and-effect machines and that the only way they could be supposed to be otherwise would be either to maintain the unspeakable claim of self-determinism or to retreat to metaphysics and find the explanation of the system's behaviour in some such occult entity as a vital force or a "self". As proof of the pudding is offered the fact that one can build machines, inanimate machines, which show behaviour as defined by Piaget, and considered by him to belong only to animate beings. One can build machines which show all of McDougall's marks of purposive behaviour, or, at least, all that are objectively specifiable.

If Rotman's (1977) assessment of Piaget is correct, then this criticism of Piaget is largely beside the point because according to Rotman, Piaget is really a "thorough-going mechanist". In *Jean Piaget: The Psychologist of the Real* Rotman says that the concept of self-maintaining equilibrium or self-regulation is "the only way to describe purposive behaviour —intelligence —in organisms, without crediting them with "intentions" or "will" or introducing what he considers the unhelpful metaphysics of final causes, life forces and the like" (1977, p. 34). The organism, seen as a structured system of self-regulating cycles in dynamic equilibrium with the environment, is in reality subject to determinism because the feedback mechanisms which are the core of self-regulation serve anti-vitalistically as a "mechanical equivalent of finality" (p. 34).

If Rotman is right the upshot is that the notion of behaviour as designed self-regulatory interaction with the environment is not meant to be taken literally; it is, in the end, a figure of speech. This is hard to believe, one wonders whether Rotman is not engaged in special pleading. The whole tenor of Piaget's treatment of "behaviour" and "instinct" is anti-mechanistic: the insistence on the distinction between inanimate movement and designed, purposeful, animate behaviour, and the hostility to neo-Darwinist views of evolution are prominent aspects of a theoretical approach which is shot through with the flavour of eighteenth- and nineteenth-century purposivism. How could anyone who objects to a mechanistic analysis of evolutionary change not take teleology seriously as a basic biological category?

Against Rotman's assessment of Piaget is Atkinson's in her *Making Sense of Piaget* (1983). She notes that Piaget's view of human behaviour

"sets him against empiricist theories such as behaviourism which sees man as a passive mechanism responding in predictable ways to the environment or rationalist theories such as Chomsky's linguistic theory which views man as a kind of computer with inbuilt patterns of processing.

Piaget is favouring a biological orientation as opposed to, say, a mechanistic orientation. Organisms are not simply passive recipients of input from the environment but nor are they, even at the purely biological level of functioning entirely pre-programmed .... Organisms spontaneously initiate their own actions and so play an active role in their own development" (p. 16).

If Atkinson is right (and it would seem that she is), so much the worse for Piaget: one can point out the incoherence of supposing that anything can initiate spontaneously its own actions, and the fact that any "biological" orientation opposed to a mechanistic one has to be some version of vitalism or teleology with its attendant confusions. To attack teleology, however, is not necessarily to commit oneself to the crude mechanism of American behaviourism or to a rationalist predeterminism.

11.3 *Richard L. Gregory*

If one is asked to associate names with the phrase "vegetable intelligence and its evolutionary basis" then Samuel Butler is a likely first association. Now there is another appropriate association: Richard Gregory. R. L. Gregory (b. 1923) is one of the best known contemporary British psychologists. His 1981 book *Mind in Science* is a survey of scientific and philosophical approaches to the nature of mind; it covers a wide range of topics, including the chapter which is of direct concern to us, *The Nature and Nurture of Intelligence*.

In this chapter Gregory speaks of vegetable intelligence. His treatment of it is different to Butler's in some important respects, but in others it is anticipated by Butler. Gregory is writing as a scientist, Butler wrote in an age the notion of science as a distinct profession was only coming into its own. Whereas Gregory has access to a tradition of formally articulated theories of intelligence, Butler had no such access. Both, however, work with an eye to evolution, but Gregory has the fruits of the victory of natural selection over Lamarckianism. It is not known whether Gregory knew of Butler's evolutionary writings when he wrote *Mind in Science*, but a later publication has a mention of Butler and his "prescient" views on intelligence in animals, plants and machines (Gregory, 1986, pp. 95-97). Like Piaget he regards plants as showing true behaviour, but his notion of plant behaviour has a much narrower denotative range than does Piaget's. Unlike Piaget Gregory does not see the dichotomy between the animate and inanimate (with its opposition between the teleological and mechanical modes of explanation) as being of central importance, for what Gregory seeks to do is to advance a theory of intelligence which embraces both organic nature and inorganic machines.

Perhaps it would not be too forced to say that in outline Gregory's treatment of intelligence is Kirkpatrick's concept of "organosis" extended to include (inanimate) machines. Whereas Kirkpatrick saw the behaviour of all living organisms as intelligent (being adapted to the goal of survival), Gregory allows that machines as well as living organisms may be intelligent. He shares with Kirkpatrick the desire to avoid any connotations of "consciousness" in intelligence.

A parallel also exists between Gregory and Bose. Like Bose he marvels at the details of the physiological processes of the plant kingdom, the achievements of plants, and like Bose he sees the inanimate world to be continuous with the animate.

Gregory notes that prevailing conceptions of intelligence view it as appropriate only to some kinds of activity —e.g. basic metabolic processes are not regarded as intelligent, nor are plants. "Plant activity is mainly restricted to metabolic processes, and it might be only just acceptable to ascribe intelligence to plant behaviour, such as climbing or fly-catching" (Gregory, 1981, p. 310). This is because intelligence seems to be restricted to notions of processes of problem-solving or appreciating problems.

> "In plants, the problems of metabolism, photosynthesis and so on are so great that they largely defeat human chemists, but they have already been solved in earlier generations of plants —though not exactly *by* plants. So they do not present problems that are solved by plants now. It is, I think, for this reason that we do not call plants (or our red corpuscles and so on) intelligent, though what they do is exceedingly clever —or at least it is exceedingly hard for us to understand how they do it. Plants have, it would seem, too much inbuilt skill to be judged intelligent!" (p. 310).

One is reminded here of Butler's comments on the astonishing skill of the "alchemical rose".

Here we have a paradox, but it is one which is open to resolution by broadening the usual concept of intelligence. This is done by distinguishing between the processes of problem solving and solutions to problems which have already been solved. This is a key distinction Gregory is making. He has already defined intelligence tentatively as "more or less: *creation and understanding of successful novelty*" (p. 300). This definition deliberately makes no reference to consciousness because this would disqualify machines, and we must "be allowed to talk about intelligent machines even if we doubt the possibility that machines can be intelligent" (p. 299). He wants also to keep the traditional distinction between intelligence as "possessing knowledge" and intelligence as "creating knowledge". Possessing knowledge covers the concept of solutions to problems which have already been solved, and creating knowledge covers the concept of processes of problem solving.

Gregory names the distinction:

" .... it is important to include in our notion of intelligence available knowledge, which can be called upon to solve current problems and give understanding; as well as the generation of current novelty, to solve problems for which adequate solutions are not available in memory store, or derivable purely by following available heuristic rules. I shall call the first "Potential Intelligence", and the second "Kinetic intelligence" "(p. 300).

Kinetic Intelligence, argues Gregory, is what I.Q. tests *try* to measure, it is by and large the intelligence that interests psychologists, but they cannot assess it without knowing the contributions made previously by intelligence and held in storage, i.e. Potential Intelligence.

Thus the distinction between Potential Intelligence and Kinetic Intelligence is the distinction between solutions (or part solutions) already available, and solutions which have to be discovered. The first resides in the "design" of the organism (which may include external artefacts such as tools) and the second is the "processing" required to solve the problem. The two forms of intelligence therefore might be called Design and Processing intelligence respectively, but Gregory prefers by partial analogy with potential and kinetic energy the terms

Potential and Kinetic Intelligence respectively. He emphasizes that the two concepts are mutually necessary for each other.

He makes a number of points about intelligence in this chapter, but we are concerned only with those relevant to plants. The topic of plant intelligence arises through consideration of the extreme cases of ratios between Potential Intelligence and Kinetic Intelligence. Perhaps the extreme cases are bizarre, but taking them up helps to clarify pertinent issues. At one extreme a relatively high Potential Intelligence: low Kinetic Intelligence ratio is seen in plants; at the other extreme a relatively low Potential Intelligence: high Kinetic Intelligence ratio is seen in intelligent machines (robots).

"Plants do have intelligence —if only Potential Intelligence" (p. 317). It is in their structure, not in the form of external artefacts. Their Kinetic Intelligence may be zero. Even the humblest plants, Gregory points out, have photochemical processes which are not yet fully understood. "Their structures for giving strength, accepting light, moisture and so on, are brilliantly clever designs adapted to the problems that the plants have to face" (p. 318).

We find in Butler, it could argued, a clear anticipation of Gregory's distinction between Potential and Kinetic Intelligence. Gregory's "Potential Intelligence" is what Butler saw as the inherited ancestral wisdom or memory possessed by organisms, which appears in humans as common sense and in plants as an innate efficiency in serving their own interests. The Erewhonian philosophers, it will be recalled, connected "both animal and vegetable development, either spent and now unconscious, or still upset and conscious," (Butler, 1901, p.264). Again, Butler says that memory in plants is shown by their ability to perform "an ineffably difficult and intricate action, time after time, with invariable success, and yet not knowing how to do it, and never having done it before." (1901, p. 266-267). Surely this is Gregory's "Potential Intelligence".

At this point we might be permitted to raise the kinds of questions which we have raised in connection with Piaget —eg. Has Gregory an implicitly teleological framework for his notion of Potential Intelligence? Are there a objective marks of design in plants which exist in them independently of the predilections of observers? What constitutes a "problem", for a plant? Would Gregory permit us to say that boulders have solved the "problem" of how to move along the ground when dislodged by having curved surfaces rather than angular ones? Or that lava solves the problem of how to get out of a volcano in upheaval by becoming liquid, or that the sun solves the "problem" of luminescence by being composed of burning gasses? Underlying this notion of intrinsic design is there an ancient rationalism which believes in the existence of an innate metaphysical wisdom? Gregory does not raise such questions, so let us continue with the description of plant intelligence.

Compared with humans plants have relatively little ability in dealing with novel situations, "but some plants do have genuine behaviour" (p.318). The stalks of some climbers twist in long one direction, left handed or right handed; some twist either way and can change direction. Runner bean stalks do their running counter-clockwise and being sensitive to gravity, but not to touch, climb vertical supports but, "ignore" horizontal ones.

"Climbing plants show some animal-like behavioural capabilities. The Venus fly-trap .... has logic circuits, activated by six hairs inside its death-trap, which distinguish the walking of a fly from raindrops.

The hairs must be touched in a fly-walking sequence for the trap door to close (p. 318).

Both the Passion flower and the white bryony (*bryonia diocia*), reach out to seek support. The passion flower's young tendrils first grow out straight and then curve in a helix of geometrical elegance. Upon finding support the tendrils again grow out straight at first but then form tight cylindrical spring-like coils which reverse their direction of turning after five or so turns, and may make several such reversals. Gregory makes a great deal of this reversibility of direction of tendril spirals, and compares it with that found in the spiral coils of modern telephone cords. After noting that the reversals in the plant spirals may prevent the tendrils twisting up he speculates:

"Did Post-Office engineers learn this trick from the plant, or is this a separate invention? Was it first invented millions of years ago in the evolution of climbing plants, or a few years ago by someone in the Post Office? If the former, man took over the Potential Intelligence of the plant (and needed but little inertia Intelligence to do so); if the latter, he created this invention by his own Kinetic Intelligence. Note that, although this is far beyond the ability of individual plants, it is clearly not beyond the Kinetic Intelligence of Evolution, which invented many structures and processes that we still do no understand and cannot reproduce" (p. 319).

For the moment let us pass over the personification of evolution in the passage above, but its presence indicates a profound difficulty for Gregory's general thesis.

Gregory states that the plant world is not entirely devoid of Kinetic Intelligence:

"Their repertoire of solutions to select from, and their individual novelty, are, however, extremely limited, so we should say that their Kinetic Intelligence is low by comparison with animals and far lower than ours .... As we have seen, plants have remarkably "intelligent" processes of photosynthesis and so on, though these are not "behaviour" because they are not controlled in at all the way animals deal with the world by their behaviour. Yet some plants do sense environmental situations and respond appropriately so we may be tempted to call this Kinetic Intelligence in plants. This is, however, vanishingly small by comparison with the enormous contribution of their inherited Potential Intelligence" (p. 319). The "behavioural capabilities" of climbers and the Venus fly-trap, for example, manifest Kinetic Intelligence".

In artificial intelligence machines, as has been noted, there is a ratio of low Potential Intelligence to high Kinetic Intelligence. The Potential Intelligence in the machines is imparted to them by their designers and programmes, but they require Kinetic Intelligence to bridge the gap between problem solving and their store of Potential Intelligence.

The imparting of the designer's Potential Intelligence to the machine calls upon the designer's Kinetic Intelligence. His "inbuilt Potential Intelligence was created "blindly" by Natural Selection" (p. 321). Machine Kinetic intelligence may be different to human Kinetic Intelligence.

The discussion of of plant intelligence is only a part of Gregory's chapter, there is no attempt here to list all the points he has to make , but we have covered enough material to raise two related critical issues. They are general questions, not related peculiarly to plant intelligence, but they underpin the coherence of Gregory's particular thesis about it.

The first questions to be raised is whether the distinction between Potential Intelligence and Kinetic Intelligence help elucidate the nature of intelligence. It is doubtful that it does.: it merely serves to postpone the problem of defining intelligence and it presents no conceptual advance on our understanding of the term. This is not to deny that the distinction may have other uses —eg if it is valid then it does have important implications for intelligent assessment. However, it would seem that it is not a distinction between *kinds* of intelligence, it is a distinction between *sources* of intelligenceKinetic Intelligence is sometimes located in terms of the exclusion of Potential Intelligence. When a problem has to be solved, and the solution is available at hand, the Potential Intelligence is called upon, but if the solution is not at hand, then Kinetic Intelligence is called upon, ("Kinetic Intelligence is on this account mainly gap-filling, necessary where solutions are not adequate as stored Potential Intelligence" (p. 312)). Potential Intelligence is sometimes located in terms of Kinetic Intelligence (Potential Intelligence is thus Kinetic Intelligence frozen form the past (p. 314). The one performance may be at the same time the product of Potential Intelligence from one viewpoint, but of Kinetic Intelligence, from another. For example the tendril-twining behaviour of the passion flower vine reflects Potential Intelligence on the vine's part and Kinetic on Evolution's part.

Thus Gregory is not talking a out qualitatively different kinds of intelligence, the difference between them is a purely relative one, i.e. relative to their temporal sources. Potential Intelligence comes from the past, Kinetic Intelligence from the present. But this leaves unaddressed the question of what intelligence is, and this is the question which should be raised.

Admittedly Gregory is concerned in this chapter to offer only a tentative definition of intelligence ("creation and understanding of successful novelty"), and therefore only a tentative point of criticism is raised. We are not concerned here to take up the definition of terms such as "creation", "successful", and "novelty", as important as those terms are, but to ask just this one questions,: novelty and success are both predicated of solutions, and the concept of "solution" depends upon the concept of "problem". Now to repeat again the question asked earlier: what in Gregory's psychology constitutes a problem? In terms of human beings, it may not be too much of a job to define a problem in cognitive terms: one has a gap in one's knowledge which one wishes to fill. Clearly a conception of "problem" in terms of individual cognitive states is not sufficient for Gregory because he wants to speak also of planets, and artificial intelligence machines as facing problems to solve. In the case of machines a possible reply would be that although the machine do not have cognitive states themselves they embody (eg in programming) the cognitive states of their users. This cognitive definition of problem is no good for plants unless one adopts, say, a Maeterlinck approach to vegetable intelligence and predicates cognition of plants. This Gregory does not do. It might be aesthetically pleasing but it is no conceptual advance to remove the "problem" of tendril twisting-up from individual passion flower vines to the mind of Evolution personified.

Consider these telling sentences:

"As I have said, it would require superhuman intelligence to design a plant. The problem beats any human and the whole of science. So if "Design a plant" was set as an intelligence test problem no human (or the whole of science) would pass the test. Yet plants are answers to this problem" (pp. 319-320).

Clearly what Butler has in mind as the "interests" of plants is of a kind with Gregory's concept of "problems" for plants: the plant's job is to adapt successfully to the environment. Recall how Butler anticipates Gregory's claim that no human would pass the test of designing a plant when he wrote that no chemist could ever duplicate the nutritional system of the rose.

Herein lies the core of the conception of "problem" underlying Gregory's notion of intelligence. If, upon being told that "plants are answers to this problem" we were to ask "whose problem —Evolution's (Nature's, God's, which superhuman intelligence, and so on)?" we would be at the same time both showing our own naiveté and exposing the hidden content of the notion of "problem". For it is not any mind, superhuman or other, which entertains the problem, the "problem" is such only in the context of a prior conception of "design" in nature. The idea that there is intrinsic design (and hence "problems" of designing) in nature hearkens back to a rationalist world-outlook, one which follows a Neo-platonist metaphysics if it sees the world as the temporary product of an external transcendental Mind or Reason, a product in which Reason and the hall-marks of its design appear. Gregory, however, wants to divorce intelligence from minds. Thus it is more likely that his path is an Aristotelian one, which sees design not as the legacy of an external designer, but as immanent in the *form* of things. By what means we could detect design is still to be answered.

Gregory's suggestion that "Potential Intelligence" could be called "Design Intelligence" is a good one, for that is what it is, but the design is a metaphysical conceit. Just as it has been argued in connection with Piaget that there are no objective marks of purpose in behaviour so it can be argued that there are no objective marks of design, or of problems, intrinsic to nature. Furthermore of course, to refer to Butler, no plant has objective "interests" of its own: what we call plant interests are relative to our own psychological predilections about plant destinies.

This does not mean, of course, that we cannot find aspects of nature which are problems to our own understanding or our own ends —we may well wonder why the tendrils of the passion flower do not twist up together —but the answers to such questions will be historical cause-and-effect ones, answers which require only natural-istic explanations to be given.

Those who would read into natural phenomena "problems" and "intelligence" should realize that the "problems" and "intelligence" are not objectively discoverable aspects of the world, but are merely vehicles of pre-conceived expectations that they have. For example, if it is said that the passion flower's possession of tendrils shows its Potential Intelligence in solving the problem of its getting to light, it could equally be said that it shows its lacking of Potential Intelligence in imposing a barrier to its transportation to cold climates (frosts nip off its tendrils). If the mode of twisting of the tendrils solves the problem of them not getting twisted-up together it also creates the problem of making it vulnerable to those insect and animal predators which love succulent young tendrils.

It may be that upon a fuller exposition of his views Gregory will show that there is an empirical component to his notion of intelli-gence, including plant intelligence, but for the time being he must be placed with other rationalist theorists such as Lord Herbert of Cher-bury (the Neoplatonic doctrine of Natural Instinct), the Reverend John Shute Duncan (Paley's natural theology vindicated by botany), various nature-philosophers and poets of the Romantic movement, Gustav Fechner, Maurice Maeterlinck, and Jean Piaget.

11.4   A Sign of the Future?

Knowing of no way in which the course of science generally or of particular disciplines such as psychology can be forecast accurately, I shall limit myself to a simple guess about the future of plant psychology. On purely inductive grounds it would seem that because there have been plant psychologists since the earliest era of western scientific thought we should expect that they will continue to exist. This guess may be wrong, and it has nothing to do with one's attitude to the concept.

Perhaps a sign of a future trend is given in Malcolm Wilkins's book *Plantwatching* (1988). Subtitled "how plants live, feel and work", the book is intended to communicate some aspects of modern plant science to the intelligent lay reader. Wilkins is Regius Professor of Botany at the University of Glasgow. There is some material relevant to our interests, viz. passages arguing that the Venus fly-trap has not only the ability to count, but a memory as well. What should be noted here is that the argument is couched in terms of information theory (the information processing approach to cognition is now received orthodoxy in modern experimental psychology).

Some plants, says Wilkins, can be said to have nervous systems because they can transmit information from one part of the plant to another by means of electrical potentials. The hairs in the trap-lobes of the Venus fly-trap are transducers in that they convert a mechanical (physical) stimulus into an electrical one. With this "nervous system" (functionally defined) counting and memory are possible. Admittedly the plant can only "distinguish" between zero, one and two, but the sophisticated computer can only distinguish between zero and one. Their memory is short, "retaining information for only 30 to 40 seconds, yet it is a genuine memory storing very specific information" (Wilkins, 1988, p. 136).

In a passage which calls to mind Clifford Farr on plant mathematical abilities, Wilkins says

"Using a fine glass filament held in a mechanical manipulator, it is possible to give one of the trigger hairs a single touch. Rather surprisingly, nothing happens, even though the hair may be bent right over. However, if the hair is touched a second time, the trap shuts instantly. It is clear, then, that the plant can distinguish between one touch or two; that is, it can count. In order to do this it must have a memory. The first assumption might be that information about the first touch is stored in the hair itself, but this is not so. The second touch can be given to any of the other five hairs and the trap will respond just as promptly. The memory of the first touch may be stored in the motor cells themselves, so that arrival of a certain action potential, from whatever source, will trigger the collapse of the cells. This part of the story has yet to be fully unravelled" (p. 139). The second touch must be within 40 seconds of the first for the trap to close.

If we were to pursue the matter we should find that Wilkins's use of psychological terms such as "distinguishing", "counting" and "memory" depends upon analogy, just as does the use of similar psychological terms in connection with computers. The psychological terms are only metaphors in this context. An ordinary balancing set of scales can be shown to have "memory": if one end of the beam has a 20 gm weight on it, and a 5 gm weight is attached to the previously unweighted other end, then nothing will happen. Nor will it if a 15 gm weight is attached to the unweighted end. But if the 5 gm weight is attached to the unweighted end and then a 15 gm weight is attached, the scale will "remember" that it already has a 5 gm weight there, and "adding" the 5 and 15 gms, will "see" that they equal the 20 gms at the other end, whereupon the beam will move into horizontal equilibrium.

Analogy may have been extravagant in eighteenth century biology, as Ritterbush pointed out, but it is something we "do naturally". It does not matter what the formal theoretical context is, e.g. the information processing model of cognition, there are always likely to be some individuals, usually unorthodox, who will want to bring the vegetable kingdom into the purview of psychology.

APPENDIX

PLANT PARAPSYCHOLOGY

1. Introduction

That the vegetable kingdom is of great service to practitioners of supernatural arts such as priests, witches and shamans, and that plants themselves are possessed of magical properties, are propositions of ancient belief. The history of those beliefs belongs to areas such as folklore and ethnology and is thus outside our present scope. The scope of this chapter is the contention that plants are possessed of parapsychological capacities, "parapsychological" being understood in the modern usage of the term.

Most modern parapsychologists seek to provide some objective basis for a belief in paranormal phenomena, rather than to appeal only to subjective conviction, hence we have seen attempts over the past hundred years to place the subject on a scientific footing. Accordingly we shall review now putative scientific arguments for the existence of paranormal capacities in plants. It is convenient to distinguish between the earlier arguments, which are based on anecdotal "field observations" and the later ones, which are based on controlled experiments yielding quantitative data.

Three major preliminary points should be made:

(i) It has been, and still is, a matter of controversy within parapsychological circles as to what the meaning of terms such as "parapsychological" and "paranormal" is. Not wishing to take up that controversy, it shall be understood that "parapsychological" and "paranormal" phenomena are phenomena which appear to be impossible to understand within a materialist scientific framework, they are definable further by simple denotation: telepathy, extra-sensory perception, clairvoyance, precognition, psychokinesis and so on.

(ii)   Such phenomena generically will be referred to as "psi phenomena". This has the sanction of orthodox usage (Thouless and Wiener, 1964-9), but more importantly means that one does not have to use the terms "psychic" and "psychical" unless one is quoting from a source which does use them. Throughout this monograph "psychic" and "psychical" have been used in their historical contexts as meaning just "mental", without occult overtones. To change this usage now might be to create confusion.

(iii)   We shall be concerned only with claims that plants possess psi capacities (e.g. are capable of extra-sensory perception) and not with claims that their growth and behaviour may be influenced by the psi capacities of humans (or other non-vegetable agents). There is an increasing body of literature, going back well into the last century, which professes that plants can be influenced by human psychokinetic or "mental forces" generally and by prayer, but to suppose this is not to suppose necessarily that plants themselves have any psi capacities. Also, we shall not be concerned with claims of novel or unusual material stimuli affecting plants — for example, it is now well known that plants can respond to mechanical stimuli, and it is accordingly a straightforward empirical question as to whether different kinds of music might have differential effects on plant growth. The vibrations of the music create patterns of mechanical stimuli in the plants.

2. Earlier studies

"With *THE HUMAN SIDE OF PLANTS*" wrote Royal Dixon in 1914, "I am blazing a trail. In many of the plant acts described I am declaring heretofore unpublished truths, truths which must unquestionably meet the censure of the book-taught botanists of the old schools, but which will quite as unquestionably meet the entire approval of those naturalist-botanists of the more modern type" (Dixon, 1914, p. xii). Dixon (1885-1962), a naturalist, author, lecturer and founder of Wildflower Day in America in 1929, belongs in the ranks of the romantics with Taylor, Francé, Gentry, Fechner and Farr, and would have been included in their chapter had not his attribution of a "psychic" sense ("psychic" in the paranormal usage of the term) to plants meant the holding over of his name to this chapter.

In *The Human Side of Plants* Dixon makes copious use of analogy to argue that plants can do everything humans do; he believes plants have both instincts and highly developed minds and that they also have spiritual lives. "Plants" he writes in the introduction,

"no longer are lifeless things labelled and grouped under ponderous Latin titles; they are highly developed organisms, which see, hear, taste, feel, walk, swim, run, fly, jump, skip, hop, roll, tumble, set traps and catch fish; decorate themselves that they may attract attention; powder their faces; imitate birds, animals, serpents, stones; play hide and seek; blossom underground; protect their children, and send them forth into the world prepared to care for themselves — indeed, do all those things which we ourselves do! We know that plants have even minds and souls, with which to think and to worship", (Dixon, 1914, pp. ix-x).

These claims are illustrated in a series of chapters drawing parallels between plant and human behaviour. For example, the fishing plant is the aquatic bladderwort, *utricularia*:

> "The bladders or sacs of the plant are apparently devised especially to entrap animal life. Little fish swim into a mouth or opening at one end of the oval bladders and the doors swing in before them allowing the fish to enter; but when they would depart, the doors will not accommodatingly open out, and the minnows find themselves prisoners. There they die and their decaying bodies are slowly fed upon by the voracious plant" (p. 22).

Plants such as sweet potatoes and strawberries walk by sending out lateral shoots which themselves take root. Dandelions launch airships; a large list of flowers which open or shut at various hours around the clock shows that plants can tell the time, for example,

> "At five, usually with the striking of the hour, open the naked-stalked poppy, the copper-coloured day-lily, the smooth sow-thistle, and the blue-flowered sow-thistle; while within the following minutes, until six, the morning-glory and the common nipplewort unfold" (pp. 105-106).

There are both new and old analogies in Dixon's list, but so far there is nothing substantially new in his ideas, nor is there in his treatment of plant spirituality. He appeals to folk lore and to the authority of writers including Bonnet, Fechner and Gentry for licence to grant plants "souls". The source of the spiritual inspiration which flowers give to man "must be from the spirituality of the flower, from the degree of universal spirit in the flower" (p. 200).

Dixon's originality lies in his discussion of the mental life of plants.

There are seven senses in plants, six of them comprise "passive" mentality and the seventh comprises "active" mentality.

Active mentality involves the power of reason, an intelligence which can direct voluntary motion and which is above the level of sensation. Its sense is the "physical" sense, the "sense of the fitness of things". A number of phenomena show active mentality in action, a reasoning capacity to detect the fitness of things. For example the oxalis whose sleeping habits have been changed by the artificial reversal of day and night illumination will change them back upon restoration of natural patterns of illumination; the sundew and the Venus fly trap can distinguish between nutritive and non-nutritive particles, retaining the former and rejecting the latter; some climbers seem to know just where appropriate holds for their tendrils may be, even when those holds are at a distance. The most striking example of the physical sense's origin in intellect "not in instinct" (p. 195) is cited

"by an American woman, Mrs Treat, who proved conclusively that the leaves of the plant actually were conscious of the nearness of insects, even when there was no contact between the plant and the body of the insect. This was demonstrated by pinning a live fly half an inch from a leaf of sundew, whereupon the leaf moved itself with the succeeding two hours near enough to fasten its tentacles about the insect. Perhaps this realization of the insect's proximity was a matter of "passive" mentality, of hearing, or seeing, or smelling, or a psychic sense; but the voluntary motion toward it cannot fairly be attributed to any source than to a degree of reasoning power and a definite understanding of the circumstances, on the part of the plant" (p. 195).

Mrs Treat's 1873 article made no claims about plant sentience, consciousness, or reason, but Dixon's interpretation appears to be based on Gentry's account of the study.

As the above quotation shows, the "psychic" sense of plants is not part of their active mentality. It is part of their passive mentality, the mentality which is "natural", being explicable in terms of instinct rather than reason or intelligence and requiring no volition. The six senses comprising passive mentality are touch or feeling, smell, taste (plants prefer certain chemicals over others), sight, hearing (the sensitive plant is susceptible to vibrations, and sound is the effect of vibrations) and the psychic sense. Dixon's evidence for the "psychic" sense is based on anecdote. If a plant grows

"between two mounds or ridges, and behind one ridge stands a wall, which will afford good climbing, but is invisible from the position of the plant, while behind the other ridge is no form of support, the plant invariably will bend its course over the ridge behind which is the wall. Examples of this may be found wherever climbing or creeping plants grow. The support is invisible from the plant's starting point; and there is no odour which, as is possible in the location of water, might give the plant some clue to the direction in which its support may be found. The only explanation seems to be the existence in the plant of a psychic sense" (p. 190).

The "psychic sense" then exists by default. When the other senses have been ruled out it is invoked to render the inexplicable explicable. A mere verbal solution, the critic would say, but the fact that Dixon appeals to it is a sign of the times: the occult is becoming increasingly influential as an alternative source to materialist science of hypotheses about the explanation of natural phenomena. Nothing more is said about the "psychic sense" by Dixon, it is a minor aspect of his theory of plant mentality.

Mention should be made here of another 1914 publication, *Have Plants an Unknown Sense?* by S. Leonard Bastin in the *Scientific American*. A science journalist, Bastin wrote many papers, mostly on botany, in popular magazines. He was sympathetic to the idea of plant mentality, mentioning, for example, Francis Darwin's theories of plant consciousness and memory in a 1913 article on the perception of pain by plants.

A Bose-type demonstration that a chloroformed sensitive plant will no longer respond to heat stimulation is accompanied by the comment that " .... the word pain, when used in connection with a plant, can scarcely involve suffering in the sense in which the term is generally employed. Nevertheless, there is small doubt that plants do feel pain to the extent of making them show real signs of discomfort" (Bastin, 1913, p. 186). In his book *Wonders of Plant Life* (Bastin, 1912) he defines plant feelings in terms of what the older writers would have called irritability, i.e. sensitivity to stimuli, e.g. light and touch. In the 1914 paper the "unknown sense" of plants is hinted to have occult properties — it is called a "mysterious power", belongs to "the realm of events which are difficult, if not impossible" for science to account for, and the possibility of an empirical explanation of it is not raised, but there is no direct claim that it really is occult in nature. In fact "it is too early to hint at an explanation of the happenings" (Bastin, 1914, p. 417) which point to the "sensational" fact of the special sense of plants.

What is this sense? It is, not surprisingly to us, the ability "to feel objects at a distance. That is to say, they act as if they were aware of the presence of a certain thing, even though they may not be in contact at all" (p. 417). The special sense, which contemporary parapsychologists might call apparent extra-sensory perception, is seen at work in a number of anecdotes — for example, the newly germinated parasitic dodder sends out thread-like growths which, upon coming within range of a host plant, grow towards it at a rapid rate; once again we read of the tendrils of climbers "sensing" supports at a distance ("one could not very well get away from the idea that the tendril knew, if the word is permissible, that a support was within reach" (p. 417)); Charles Darwin's metaphor about plant roots duly is mentioned, and one of the illustrations of its aptness reads:

> " .... a little fern sought out some water with an intelligence that seems to be almost uncanny. The plant was growing in a pot, which was kept standing in a saucer; the latter was always well filled with water. Now one may suppose that the fern did not have a sufficient supply of water to meet its needs in the ordinary way, and it determined to get into touch with that in which the pot was standing. Accordingly, the plant sent down a special root, on the *outside* of the pot to the water in the saucer" (p. 417).

Bastin's leading example of the mysterious sense is Mrs Treat's sundew experiment (without acknowledgement to Mrs Treat), in which, as we have seen, Dixon had perceived volition guided by reason at work, but not the "psychic sense".

3.   Later Studies

Most modern parapsychologists have adopted the standard

experimental model for their researches. They use controlled conditions of observation, employing experimental and control groups of subjects; quantitative data are yielded which are then analysed according to principles derived from the calculus of probability. There is an increasing body of research on psi-phenomena in non-human biological organisms, especially other animals (Randall, 1976; Morris, 1977), but there is very little on plants as active psi agents.

The most important experimental work in this area is that of Cleve Backster, who claimed that he had demonstrated experimentally the existence of a "primary perception" in plant life (Backster, 1968). His general notion was that plants, at the level of individual cells, can detect noxious events happening to other organisms at a distance from them in their vicinity. The detection is accompanied by a change in electrical resistance in their leaves, which can be monitored by standard PGR (psychogalvanic reflex) methods (Backster was an expert in the use of polygraphic "lie-detectors"). The "primary perception" hypothesis was generated when, having attached a polygraph to a leaf of a common indoor pot-plant, *dracaena fragrans*, (Messangeana form), Backster observed that at the precise moment of his thinking of injuring the leaf by burning it, it generated a polygraph reading of a contour similar to those obtained under conditions of human emotional arousal. It was as if the plant had detected his fancied threat and had reacted emotionally to it. His next step was to test the hypothesis by means of a formal experiment.

In outline this is what Backster did: electrodes were attached to the leaves of three *philodendron cordatum* plants. These plants have stiff, broad and thick leaves. Variations in electrical resistances in the leaves were continuously recorded on a chart. Several rooms away were living brine shrimp, held in a dump dish which could precipitate them to their deaths into boiling water. The fatal precipitation was to occur on one out of six possible occasions, on the other five occasions nothing untoward happened to them. Each of the six periods lasted thirty five seconds. The deadly one of the six possibilities was selected randomly by the use of a random number generator (RNG). To eliminate unwanted possible confounding effects of human involvement the whole experimental procedure was automated except for the activation of the RNG, after which the experimenter left the premises until the experiment had finished. It was possible then to compare changes (if any) in the leaves' electrical resistance on occasions of shrimp killing with changes (if any) on occasions of no shrimp killing. Such comparisons were done by "blind" judges who were ignorant of what events any given period on the chart might correspond to, and they found overall that there was a statistically significantly greater amount of electrical activity in the plants' leaves on the shrimp-killing trials than on the non-killing ones. When control runs were done later in which water containing no shrimps was dumped into the boiling water there were no significant differences between dump and non-dump trials.

Backster interpreted the "primary perception" as a capacity of the individual living cell, a capacity showing a "similarity to that which has been called "extrasensory" perception when related to animal life" (Backster, 1968, p. 345). He claimed that other observations of plant leaf PGR-type records supported the hypothesis of "primary perception" (see, for example, Tompkins and Bird, 1973).

Backster's research received enormous publicity, especially when written up in several popular books (e.g. Tompkins and Bird, 1973;

Watson, 1973; Huxley, 1974), not to mention a number of magazine articles. Of these Tompkins and Bird's *The Secret Life of Plants* was a highly successful best-seller which inspired several imitators and received international attention in the media of mass entertainment. If there is to be a Bible of pseudo-science then *The Secret Life of Plants* assuredly must be one of its books for it contains a wealth of portents about the plant world. Its contents are sensationalistic, the style smooth and seductive, but the scholarship and criticism are lacking. It was part of the huge revival of the vulgar concern with the occult and super-natural which developed in the 1960's. There must have been many a credulous reader persuaded by Tompkins and Bird that mankind was on the threshold of penetrating the material curtains with which orthodox science shrouded the vegetable kingdom, and that within a few short years new cosmic forces would be harnessed to usher in a new age.

The years come to pass but not so the prognostications of Tomp-kins, Bird and their like. Unfortunately for them Cleve Backster's research findings have not been able to be repeated under care-fully controlled conditions in any of three quite separate replication attempts (Johnson, 1972; Horowitz, Lewis and Gasteiger, 1975; Kmetz, 1975). According to Galston and Slayman (1979) Backster's "significant" plant recordings may be artefacts of extraneous uncon-trolled variables in the experimental apparatus. They say

" .... the initial records were rather noisy .... There was also a seg-ment (of the single record that Backster published) that superficially resembled the slow rise-and-fall of resistance that occurs in human polygraph records during verified lying ....

At this point there took place a totally unscientific discontinuity of logic. Without investigating the recording conditions to identify the sources of unexpected noise and drift Backster jumped to the conclusion that because the plant record resembled in a single respect human records obtained during emotional reaction, the plant must have been experiencing something like human emotion" (Galston and Slayman, 1979, pp. 339-340).

Galston and Slayman's paper is worth reading also for its taking to task Tompkin and Bird's interpretation of Bose's work:

"Bose", Galston and Slayman conclude, "quite properly pointed out functional similarities between the electrical/mechanical responsiveness, or irritability, of plant and animal tissues, but his data do not in any way support Tompkins and Bird's conclusion that plants perceive their environment in the manner of human beings and other higher animals" (p. 338).

No experimenter after Backster has argued from well-controlled experiments that good evidence of extra-sensory perception in plants exists, but there is a study by the prominent American parapsychologist Hoyt L. Edge which he feels produces some data on plant psychokinesis which are worth following up. The general aim of the experiment (Edge, 1978) was to see whether corn plants deprived of light could "make" a light switch on (presumably by psychokinesis) more often than it would by chance.

Edge grew corn plants in a dark closet. When they were two to three inches high they were placed about twelve inches away from a light source in an otherwise darkened experimental room. The light source was connected to a RNG. On a given trial the RNG could either switch the light on for 17 seconds, or not (i.e. the probability of the light coming on was .5). It was expected that the plants, being light-starved, would increase the number of RNG "hits". The plants were removed from the light source for about two hours during the experiment at a time not known by the experimenter, while the RNG continued to run. The plant moving was done by a "blind" assistant who also read the trials and hits counter.

Hoyt could then ask whether the number of hits significantly deviated from chance when the plants were present to the light source, and also when they were absent. After his initial study he ran a further four "confirmatory" ones which included variations on the nature of the lighting and period of light starvation.

On none of the five studies when the plants were absent from the light source was there a significantly above chance hit rate, but on three of the five when the plants were present there was. Edge admits that he has not eliminated the human element or a possible source of experimental influence, but says that he has some "significant results" in what is only an exploratory study.

If, however, we look at the three "significant" results we must call them into question. Of the three two are described as being "marginally" significant. This is a meaningless notion. According to the logic of statistical decision making a result must be either significant or insignificant according to a pre-ordained criterion of significance. Either a given result meets that criterion or it does not, there cannot be "marginal" significance any more than there can be, say, "marginal" uniqueness. Only one of Edge's three results would be accepted unquestioningly as significant according to any conventionally rigourous criterion.

When we look at that one particular hit rate which all scientists would accept as "significant" in statistical terms we discover in fact that it is a "negative hit rate", i.e. that there are significantly *less* occasions of "light-on" in the presence of the plant than would be expected by chance. This is also true of one of the other two "marginally" significant results. What Edge does to convert what is clearly a falsification of his hypothesis into a positive result is to explain it tentatively as "psi-missing", an ingenious but logically indefensible manoeuvre which is all too frequent in parapsychology. It is absurd in an experiment which is aimed at establishing the very existence of a phenomenon to invoke the *selective* non-appearance of that phenomenon under the experimental conditions in order to save a falsified hypothesis.

Thus we still await evidence of psi phenomena in plants. We may be waiting for some time.

REFERENCES

A Botanical Society at Lichfield (1787). *The families of plants, with their natural characters, according to the number, figure, situation, and proportion of all their parts of fructification.* Lichfield: printed by John Jackson.

A.G.   (1874) Do plants eat insects? *The Gardeners' Chronicle,* 1 (N.S.), 565-566 and 597-598.

ACOSTA, C.(1578) *Tractado delas drogas, y medicinas de las Indias Orientales.* Burgos: por Martin de Victoria impressor de su magestad.

ANON.   (1883). Plant Instinct. *Chambers's Journal of Popular Literature, Science and Arts.* New Series 20, 500-502.

APPLEWHITE, P.B. (1975) Learning in bacteria, fungi and plants. In W.C. Corning, J.A. Dyal and A.O.D. Willows (Editors), *Invertebrate learning.* Vol III. New York and London: Plenum Press.

ARBER, A.   (1986) *Herbals: Their origin and evolution.* Third edition, reissue of second edition 1938, with introduction and annotation by W.T. Stearn. Cambridge: Cambridge University Press.

ARISTOTLE.   (1931) *On the soul* (Tran's. title: *De anima*). In J.A. Smith (Trans.) *The works of Aristotle,* Vol. III. Oxford: Clarendon Press.

[ARISTOTLE]   (1936) *On plants.* In W.S. Hett (Trans.) *Minor works.* London: William Heinemann.

ARMUS, H.L.   (1970) Conditioning of the sensitive plant, *mimosa pudica.* In M.R. Denny and S.C. Ratner (Editors), *Comparative psychology, research in animal behaviour.* Pp. 597-600. Revised edition. Homewood, Ill.: Dorsey Press.

ATKINSON, C.   (1983) *Making sense of Piaget.* London: Routledge and Kegan Paul.

BACKSTER, C.   (1968) Evidence of a primary perception in plant life. *International Journal of Parapsychology, 10*, 329-348.

BALL, N.G.   (1963) Plant tropisms. In W.B. Turrill, (Ed.), *Vistas in botany*, Vol. III, pp. 228-254. Oxford: Pergamon.

BARRET, H.M.   (1940). *Boethius: some aspects of his time and work*. Cambridge: Cambridge University Press.

BARTHOLOMEW THE ENGLISHMAN. (1975) *On the properties of things* (originally written c. 1240). John Trevisa's translation of Bartholomaeus Anglicus, *De proprietatibus rerum*, M.C. Seymour (General ed.) Vol. II. Oxford: Clarendon Press.

BARTRAM, W.   (1791) *Travels Through North & South Carolina, Georgia, East & West Florida* .... etc. Philadelphia: James and Johnson.

BASTIN, S.L.   (1912) *Wonders of plant life*. London: Cassell and Co.

BASTIN, S.L.   (1913) Can a plant feel pain? *Scientific American, 109,* 186.

BASTIN, S.L.   (1914) Have plants an unknown sense? *Scientific American, 110,* 417.

BAUHIN, C.   (1623) *Pinax theatri botanici*. Basileae: Sumptibus et typis Ludovici Regis.

BECHTEREV, V.M.   (Originally 1928, fourth Russian edition). *General principles of human reflexology*. E. & W. Murphy (Trans. 1932). New York: Arno Press Reprint, 1973.

BELL, G.   (1785) De physiologia plantarum. J. Currie (Trans.) *Memoirs of the Literary and Philosophical Society of Manchester, 2*, 394-419.

BENTLEY, I.M.   (1902) President Minot on "The problem of consciousness in its biological aspects". *Science* (new Series), *16*, 386-391.

BINET, A.   (1889)(a)*The psychic life of micro-organisms*. T. McCormack (Trans.) London: Longmans, Green & Co.

BINET, A.   (1889)(b) The psychic life of micro-organisms. A rejoiner to Mr George John Romanes. *The Open Court,3*, 1931-1935. (b).

BINET, A.   (1890) Remarks by M. Binet. *The Open Court, 3*, 2065-2066.

313

BLAU, G.L. and WALTHALL, W.J., Jr. (1976) Conditioning in *Mimosa pudica. Journal of Biological Psychology,* 18 (2), 32-35.

BODEN, M.A. (1979) *Piaget.* Brighton, Sussex: The Harvester Press.

BONNET, C. (1766) *The contemplation of nature.* Vol. II. Originally 1764. London: Longman and Becket and de Hondt.

BOSE, J.C. (1902) *Response in the living and non-living.* London: Longmans, Green and Co.

BOSE, J.C. (1906) *Plant response as a means of physiological investigation.* London: Longmans, Green and Co.

BOSE, J.C. (1927) *Plant autographs and their revelations.* London: Longmans, Green and Co.

BOSE, J.C. (1929) Is the plant a sentient being. *The Century Magazine,* 117, 385-393.

BRADLEY, R. (1721) *A philosophical account of the works of nature.* London: W. Mears.

BRETT, G.S. (1912) *A history of psychology.* London: George Allen & Co.

BREUER, H.-P. and HOWARD, D.F. (Eds.). (1981) S. Butler, *Erewhon or Over the Range.* Newark: University of Delaware Press.

BROWNE, J. (1989). Botany for gentleman: Erasmus Darwin and *The loves of the plants. Isis,* 80, 593-621.

BUFFON, G. -L. (Georges-Louis Leclerc, Count de Buffon). (1775) *The natural history of animals, vegetables and minerals; with a theory of the earth in general.* W. Kenrick (Trans.) London: T. Bell.

BUTLER, S. (1878). *Life and habit.* London: Trübner and Co.

BUTLER, S. (1882) *Alps and sanctuaries of Piedmont and the Canton Ticino.* Second edition. London: David Bogue.

BUTLER, S. (1887) *Luck, or cunning, as the main means of organic modification?* London: Trübner and Co.

CADDEN, J. (1980). Albertus Magnus' Universal physiology: The example of nutrition. In J.A. Weisheipl (Ed.) *Albertus Magnus and the sciences:*

Commemorative essays 1980,. Pp. 320-339. Toronto: Pontifical Institute of Mediaeval Studies.

CALKINS, M.W. (1905) The limits of genetic and of comparative psychology. *British Journal of Psychology,* 1, 261-285.

CHAMPION, R.A. (1969) *Learning and activation.* Sydney: John Wiley and Sons Australasia.

CLARK, M. (1915) *Maurice Maeterlinck.* London: George Allen and Unwin.

CLEVE, F.M. (1973). The philosophy of Anaxagoras. The Hague: Martinus Nijhoff.

COLE, G.D.H. (1952, revised 1961) *Samuel Butler.* London: British Council and Longmans, Green and co.

COLEMAN, B. (1974). Samuel Butler, Darwin and Darwinism. *Journal of the Society for the Bibliography of Natural History,* 7, 93-105.

COLIN, A. (1619) (Trans.). *Traicté de Christophe de la Coste.* Lyon: Aux despense de Jean Pillehotte, à l'enseigne du nom de JESUS.

COPLESTON, F. (1953). *A history of philosophy,* Vol. III. London: Burns Oates and Washbourne Ltd.

CORNFORD, F.M. (1937). Plato's cosmology: The *Timaeus* of Plato translated with a running commentary. Reprinted 1977. London and Henley: Routledge & Kegan Paul.

dal COVOLO, G. (1767) *A discourse concerning the irritability of some flowers.* B. Stillingfleet (Trans.) London: J. Dodsley; S. Baker & G. Leigh; T. Payne.

COWLES, T. (1933). Dr. Henry Power, disciple of Sir Thomas Browne. *Isis, XX,* 344-366.

DARWIN, C. (1875)(a) *Insectivorous plants.* London: John Murray, Albemarle St.

DARWIN, C. (1875)(b) *The movements and habits of climbing plants.* Second edition, revised. London: John Murray, Albemarle St.

DARWIN, C. (1880) *The power of movement in plants.* London: John Murray.

DARWIN, E. (1791) *The botanic garden.* London: J. Johnson..

DARWIN, E.   (1794) *Zoonomia; or, the laws of organic life.* Vol. I. London: J. Johnson.

DARWIN, E.   (1800) *Phytologia; or the philosophy of agriculture and gardening.* London: J. Johnson.

DARWIN, F.   (1878)(a) Insectivorous plants. *Nature, 17,* 222-223. (a).

DARWIN, F.   (1878)(b) The analogies of plant and animal life. *Nature, 17,* 388-390 and 411-414.

DARWIN, F.   (1901) The movements of plants. *Nature, 65,* 40-44.

DARWIN, F.   (1906) Lectures on the physiology of movement in plants. 1. Associated stimuli. *The New Phytologist, 5,* 199-207.

DARWIN, F.   (1909) President's address. *British Association for the Advancement of Science, report of the seventy-eighth meeting, Dublin, September 1908.* London: Murray.

DE BEER, E.S. (Ed.). (1955) *The diary of John Evelyn.* Vol. III. Oxford: Clarendon Press.

DELAPORTE, F.   (1982). Nature's second kingdom: Explorations of vegetality in the eighteenth century. A. Goldhammer (Trans.)(Originally 1979). Cambridge, Massachusetts: MIT Press.

DESMOND, R.   (1977) *Dictionary of British and Irish botanists and horticulturalists.* London: Taylor & Francis.

DIXON, R.   (1914) *The human side of plants.* New York: Frederick A. Stokes Co.

DUNCAN, J.S.   (1826) *Botanical theology; or evidences of the existence and attributes of the deity, collected from the appearances of nature.* Second edition. Oxford: J. Vincent.

EDGE, H.L.   (1978) Plant PK on an RNG and the experimenter effect. In W. G. Roll (Editor), *Research in parapsychology 1977.* Metuchen, New Jersey and London: The Scarecrow Press.

EDITOR, PORT FOLIO.   (1815) Vegetable life. *The Port Folio.* Third series, 6, 237-241.

EDITORIAL NOTE. (1937) *Psychological Abstracts, 11,* 1.

ELLIS. J. (1770) *A botanical description of the Dionaea Muscipula, or Venus's Fly-Trap.* Attached to *Directions for bringing over seeds and plants from the East-Indies and other distant countries in a state of vegetation ....* " etc. London, L. Davis.

EMPEDOCLES. (1898) *Fragments,* Book I. In A. Fairbanks, (Ed. & trans.) *The first philosophers of Greece.* London: Kegan Paul, Trench, Trübner.

EXELL, A.W. (1932). Barometz: the Vegetable Lamb of Scythia. *Natural History Magazine,* 3, 194-200.

FARR, C.H. (1922) The psychology of plants. *The Atlantic Monthly, 130,* 775-783.

FECHNER, G.T. (1848) *Nanna, oder über das Seelenleben der Pflanzen.* Leipzig: L. Voss.

FRANCE, R. H. (1926) *The love-life of plants..* London: Simpkin, Marshall and Co., Limited.

FULLER, H.J. (1934) Plant behaviour. *Journal of General Psychology, 11,* 379-393.

GALSTON, A.W. and SLAYMAN, C.L. (1979) The not-so-secret life of plants. *American Scientist, 67,* 337-34.

GENTRY, T.G. (1900) *Intelligence in plants and animals.* New York: Doubleday, Page and Co.

GOMPERZ, T. (1912) *Greek thinkers.* Vol. IV. G.G. Berry (Trans.), London: John Murray.

GREEN, J.R. (1914) *A history of botany in the United Kingdom from the earliest times to the end of the nineteenth century.* London: J.M. Dent and Sons.

GREGORY, R.L. (1981) *Mind in science.* London: Weidenfeld and Nicolson.

GREGORY, R.L. (1986). *Odd perceptions.* London and New York: Methuen.

GRIGSON, G. (1974) *A dictionary of English plant names.* London: Allen Lane.

GRUBER, H.E. (1974) *Darwin on man.* New York: E.P. Dutton and Co.

GUSSIN, A.E.S. (1963). Jacques Loeb: The man and his tropism theory of animal conduct. *Journal of the History of Medicine and Applied Sciences, 18,* 321-336.

GUTHRIE, W.K.C. (1965). *A history of Greek philosophy.* Vol. II. Cambridge: Cambridge University Press.

HABERLANDT, G. (1914) *Physiological plant anatomy.* First edition 1884. M. Drummond (Trans.). London: Macmillan.

HAECKEL, E.H.P.A. (1929) *The riddle of the universe.* Originally published 1899. J. McCabe (Trans.). London: Watts.

HALE, M. (1677) *The primitive origination of mankind, considered and examined according to the light of nature.* London: printed by William Godbid for William Shrowsbery.

HALL, G.S. (1908) A glance at the phyletic background of genetic psychology. *American Journal of Psychology, 9,* 149-212.

von HALLER, A. (1936) *A dissertation on the sensible and irritable parts of animals.* 1755. O. Temkin (Ed.). Baltimore: Johns Hopkins Press.

HALLS, W.D. (1960) *Maurice Maeterlinck.* Oxford: Clarendon Press.

HAMILTON, W. (Ed.) (1849) *The works of Thomas Reid, D.D.* Second edition. Edinburgh: Maclachlan and Stewart.

HANCOCK, T. (1824) *Essay on instinct, and its physical and moral relations.* London: William Phillips.

HANEY, R.E. (1969) Classical conditioning of a plant: *mimosa pudica. Journal of Biological Psychology, 11*(1), 5-12.

HARPER, F. (Ed.). (1958) *The travels of William Bartram.* New Haven: Yale University Press.

HARRIS, Sir C. Alexander (1928) (Ed.). *A relation of a voyage to Guiana by Robert Harcourt.* London: Hakluyt Society.

HARTLEY, E.L. (1984) Plant behaviour. In R.J. Corsini (Ed.). *Encyclopaedia of Psychology,* Vol. 3, pp. 56-57. New York: John Wiley and Sons.

HARVEY, W. (1847) *On animal generation.* (Originally 1651). R. Willis (Trans.). London: The Sydenham Society.

HERBERT, E. (Lord Herbert of Cherbury) (1937) *De veritate.* (Originally 1624). M.H. Carré (Trans.). Bristol: J.W. Arrowsmith Ltd. for the University of Bristol.

HERING, E.   (1920) *On memory.* (Originally 1870). S. Butler (Trans.). In S. Butler, *Unconscious memory.* Third edition. London: A.C. Fifield.

HILL, J.   (1757) *The sleep of plants, and cause of motion in the sensitive plant, explain'd.* London: R. Baldwin.

HOLMES, E. and GRUENBERG, G. (1965) Learning in plants? *Worm Runner's Digest,* 7 (1), 9-12.

HOLMES, E. and YOST, M. (1966) "Behavioural" studies in the sensitive plant. *Worm Runner's Digest,* 8 (2), 38-40.

HOLT, N.R.   (1971). Ernst Haeckel's monistic religion. *Journal of the History of Ideas,* 32, 265-280.

HOOKE, R.   (1665) *Micrographia: or some physiological descriptions of minute bodies made by magnifying glasses.* London: printed by J. Martin and J. Allestry, Printers to the Royal Society.

HOROWITZ, K.A., LEWIS, D.C. and GASTEIGER, E.L. (1975) Plant "primary perception": electrophysiological unresponsiveness to brine shrimp. *Science,* 189, 478-480.

HUNTER, A.   (1770) *On vegetation, and the analogy between plants and animals.* In *Georgical essays.* Pp. 79-98. London: T. Durham.

HUXLEY, A.   (1974) *Plant and planet.* London: Allen Lane.

HUXLEY, T.H.   (1894) On the border territory between the animal and vegetable kingdoms. (Originally 1876). In *Discourses: Biological and Geological.* Pp. 162-195. London: Macmillan and Co.

J.R.W.   (1815) (a) Reply to T.C.'s essay on vegetable life. *The Port Folio.* Third series, 5, 19-37. .

J.R.W.   (1815) (b) Untitled letter to editor. *The Port Folio.* Third series, 6, 241-254..

JACKSON, M.E.   (1811) *Sketches of the physiology of vegetable life.* London: John Hatchard.

JAMES, W. (1977) *A pluralistic universe*. Lectures first delivered 1908. Cambridge, Massachusetts, and London: Harvard University Press.

JENNINGS, H.S. (1906) *Behaviour of the lower organisms*. New York: Columbia University Press.

JOHNSON. R.V. II. (1972) Letter to the editor. *Journal of Parapsychology*, 36, 71-72.

JOHNSON, T. (1633) *The herball, or generall historie of plants. Gathered by John Gerarde of London Master in Chirurgerie. Very much enlarged and amended*. London: printed by Adam Islip, Joice Norton and Richard Whitakers.

JONES, J. (1657) *Ovid's Invective or Curse against Ibis, faithfully and familiarly translated into English verse*. Oxford: Richard Davis.

JORDAN, D.S. (1898) The evolution of the mind. *Popular Science Monthly*, 52, 433-445.

KAEMPFFERT, W. (1915) What plants feel. *McClure's Magazine*, 44, 66-76 and 122-124.

KEITH, P. (1816) *A system of physiological botany*. Vol. 2. London: Baldwin, Craddock, and Joy.

KERNER VON MARILAUN, A. (1894) *The natural history of plants*. Vol. 1. F.W. Oliver (Trans.). London: Blackie and Son.

KEYNES, G.(Ed.) (1931). *The works of Sir Thomas Browne*, Vol VI. London: Faber & Faber Ltd.

KING-HELE, D.(Ed.) (1968). *The essential writings of Erasmus Darwin*. London: MacGibbon & Kee.

KING-HELE, D. (1977) *Doctor of revolution, the life and genius of Erasmus Darwin*. London: Faber and Faber.

KING-HELE, D. (Ed.) (1981). *The letters of Erasmus Darwin*. Cambridge: Cambridge University Press.

KIRBY, W. (1835) *On the power wisdom and goodness of God as manifested in the creation of animals and in their history habits and instincts*. Vol. II. London: William Pickering.

KIRK, G.S., RAVEN, J.E. & SCHOFIELD, M. (1983). *The presocratic philosophers: A critical history with a selection of texts.* Second ed. Cambridge: Cambridge University Press.

KIRKPATRICK, E.A.   (1907) A broader basis for psychology necessary. *The Journal of Philosophy, Psychology and Scientific Methods,* 4, 542-546.

KMETZ, J.M.   (1975) An examination of primary perception in plants. *Parapsychology Review,* 6, 21.

KNIGHT, T.A.   (1811) *On the causes which influence the direction of the growth of roots.* Read to the Royal Society. In T.A. Knight (1841), *A selection of the physiological and horticultural papers.* London: Longman, Orme, Brown, Green and Longmans. .

LADD, G.T.   (1896) Consciousness and evolution. *Psychological Review,* 3, 296-300.

LAIRD, J.   (1920) *A study in realism.* Cambridge: Cambridge University Press.

LAMARCK, J.B.   (1914) *Zoological philosophy.* (Originally 1809). H. Elliot (Trans.). London: Macmillan and Co.

LAYCOCK, T.   (1860) *Mind and brain: or, the correlations of consciousness and organisation.* Edinburgh: Sutherland and Knox.

LEE, H.D.P.   (1969). Plato: *Timaeus and Critias,* reprint of 1965 edition. Harmondsworth: Penguin.

LEVY, E., ALLEN, A., CATON, W. and HOLMES, E.   (1970) An attempt to condition the sensitive plant: *Mimosa pudica. Journal of Biological Psychology,* 12 (1), 86-87.

LEWES, G.H.   (1879) *The study of psychology.* London: Trübner and Co.

LINDZEY, G. (Ed.). (1954) *Handbook of social psychology.* Reading, Massachusetts: Addison-Wesley.

LISTER, M.   (1673) A further account concerning the existence of veins in all kinds of plants; together with a discovery of the membranous substance of those veins, and of some acts in plants resembling those of sense; as also of the agreement of the venal juice in vegetables with the *blood* of animals, etc. *Philosophical Transactions ,* 7 (90), 5132-5137.

LLOYD MORGAN, C.   (1894) *An introduction to comparative psychology.* London: Walter Scott, Ltd.

LLOYD MORGAN, C.   (1902-3) The beginnings of mind. *The International Quarterly, 6,* 330-352.

LOCKE, J.   (1975) *An essay concerning human understanding.* Book I. (Originally 1690). Oxford: Clarendon Press.

LOEB, J.   (1901) *Comparative physiology of the brain and comparative psychology.* London: John Murray.

LONG, R.J.   (1985). Alfred of Sareshel's commentary on the Pseudo-Aristotelian *De Plantis*: A critical edition. *Mediaeval Studies, 47,* 125-167.

LOWRIE, W.   (1946) *Religion of a scientist.* New York: Pantheon Books.

MACDOUGAL, D.T.   (1895) Irritability and movement in plants. *The Popular Science Monthly, 47,* 225-234.

MAETERLINCK, M.   (1907) The intelligence of the flowers. In *Life and flowers.* A. Teixeira de Mattos (Trans.). London George Allen.

McDOUGALL, W.   (1923) *An outline of psychology.* London:Methuen and Co.

McNEIL, M.   (1987). *Under the banner of science: Erasmus Darwin and his age.* Manchester: Manchester University Press.

MERTON, E.S.   (1949). *Science and imagination in Sir Thomas Browne.* Columbia University, New York: King's Crown Press.

MEYER, E.H.F.   (1965). *Geschichte der Botanik.* Vol. IV. (Originally 1857). Amsterdam: A. Asher & Co.

MORRIS, R.L.   (1977) Parapsychology, biology and ANPSI. In B.B. Wolman (Ed.), *Handbook of parapsychology.* Pp. 687-715. New York: Van Nostrand Reinhold Co.

MORTON, A.G.   (1981) *History of botanical science.* London: Academic Press.

MORTON, A.G.   (1986). *John Hope 1725-1786: Scottish botanist.* Edinburgh: Edinburgh Botanic Garden (Sibbald) Trust.

MURCHISON, C. (Ed.) (1935) *A handbook of social psychology*. Worcester, Massachusetts: Clark University.

MUSES, C. and YOUNG, A.M. (Editors). (1972) *Consciousness and reality*. New York: Outerbridge and Lazard.

NICANDER (1953) *The poems and poetical fragments*. A.S.F. Gow & A.F. Scholfield (Eds. & trans.). Cambridge: Cambridge University Press.

NICOLAUS OF DAMASCUS See [ARISTOTLE].

OKEN, L. (1847) *Elements of physiophilosophy*. (Originally 1810). A. Tulk (Trans.). London: Ray Society.

OWEN, G.E.L. (1970) *Aristotle*. In N.G.L. Hammond, & H.H. Scullard, (Eds). *The Oxford classical dictionary*, Second edition. Oxford: Clarendon.

PAGEL, W. (1967) Harvey and Glisson on irritability with a note on van Helmont. *Bulletin of the History of Medicine*, 61, 497-514.

PAGEL, W. (1969). William Harvey revisited. *History of Science*, 8, 1-31.

PERCIVAL, E. (1807) *Memoirs of the life and writings of Thomas Percival, M.D.* London: J. Johnson.

PERCIVAL, T. (1785)(a) *Speculations on the perceptive power of vegetables: addressed to the Literary and Philosophical Society of Manchester*. Warrington, W. Eyres.

PERCIVAL, T. (1785)(b) Speculations on the perceptive power of vegetables. *Memoirs of the Literary and Philosophical Society of Manchester*, 2, 114-130.

PIAGET, J. (1971) *Biology and knowledge*. (Originally 1967). B. Walsh (Trans). Chicago and London: University of Chicago Press.

PIAGET, J. (1980) *Adaptation and intelligence: organic selection and phenocopy*. (Originally 1974). S. Eames (Trans.). Chicago and London: University of Chicago Press.

PIAGET, J. (1979) *Behaviour and evolution*. (Originally 1976). D. Nicholson-Smith (Trans.). London and Henley: Routledge and Kegan Paul.

PLATO. (1953) *Timaeus*. In B. Jowett (Trans.). *The dialogues of Plato*. Vol. III. Fourth edition. Oxford: Clarendon Press.

PLINY (1956) *Natural history.* Book XXIV. W.H.S. Jones (Trans.). London: William Heinemann.

PLUTARCH. (1965) Causes of natural phenomena. In *Plutarch's Moralia,* vol. XI, L Pearson & F.H. Sandbach (Trans.). London: W. Heinemann Ltd.; Cambridge, Massachusetts: Harvard University Press.

POWER, H. (1656). Unpublished letter to Dr. R. Robinson. British Library Sloane MS 1326, f. 30.

POWER, H. (1663) *Experimental philosophy.* London: John Martin and James Allestry.

PRIESTLEY, J. (1775) *Hartley's theory of the human mind, on the principle of the association of ideas; with essays relating to the subject of it.* London: J. Johnson.

PRIESTLEY, J. (1806). *Memoirs of Dr Joseph Priestley, to the year 1795, written by himself: with a continuation, to the time of his decease, by his son, Joseph Priestley: and observations on his writings, by Thomas Cooper, President Judge of the 4th District of Pennsylvania: and the Rev. William Christie.* Printed for J. Johnson, London.

PULASKI, M.A.S. (1980) *Understanding Piaget.* Revised and expanded edition. New York: Harper and Row.

PULTENEY, R. (1790) *Historical and biographical sketches of the progress of botany in England from its origin to the introduction of the Linnaean system.* Vol. I. London: T. Cadell.

PURCHAS, S. (1906, originally published 1625). *Hakluytus Posthumus or Purchas his pilgrimes,* Vol. XVI. (Hakluyt Society, extra series XXIX, ch. III. pp. 44-106). Glasgow: James MacLehose and sons).

RANDALL, J.H., Jr. (1962). *The career of philosophy.* Vol. I. New York: Columbia University Press.

RANDALL, J.L. (1976) Psi phenomena and biological theory. In R.A. White (Ed.), *Surveys in parapsychology.* Metuchan, New Jersey: The Scarecrow Press.

REEDS, K.   (1980). Albert on the natural philosophy of plant life. In J.A. Weisheipl (Ed.), *Albertus Magnus and the sciences: Commemorative essays 1980*, pp. 341-354. Toronto: Pontifical Institute of Mediaeval Studies.

RITTERBUSH, P.C. (1962). Lohn Lindsay and the sensitive plant. *Annals of Science*, 18, 233-254.

RITTERBUSH, P.C. (1964) *Overtures to biology*. New Haven and London: Yale University Press.

ROBINSON, E.   (1953) The Derby Philosophical Society. *Annals of Science*, 9, 359-367.

ROMANES, G.J.   (1882) *Animal intelligence*. London: Kegan Paul, Trench and Co.

ROMANES, G.J.   (1883) *Mental evolution in animals*. London: Kegan Paul, Trench and Co.

ROMANES, G.J.   (1889) The psychic life of micro-organisms. *The Open Court*, 3, 1715-1719.

ROMANES, G.J.   (1890) The psychic life of micro-organisms. *The Open Court*, 3, 2063-2065.

ROTMAN, B.   (1977) *Jean Piaget: psychologist of the real*. Hassocks, Sussex: Harvester Press.

von SACHS, J.   (1890) *History of botany* (1530-1860). H.E.F. Garnsey (Trans.) Oxford: Clarendon Press.

SCHILLER, J.   (1974). Queries, answers and unsolved problems in eighteenth century biology. *History of Science*, 12, 184-199.

SEMON, R.   (1921) *The mneme*. L. Simon (Trans.) London: George Allen and Unwin.

SEWARD, A.   (1804) *Memoirs of the life of Dr. Darwin*. London: J. Johnson.

SEXTUS EMPIRICUS.   (1935) *Against the logicians*, Book II. R.G. Bury (Trans.) London: William Heinemann Ltd.

SEYMOUR, M.C. (1975).   See   BARTHOLOMEW   THE ENGLISHMAN.

SHARROCK, R. (1660) *The history of the propogation and improvement of vegetables by the concurrence of Art and Nature*. Oxford: Thomas Robinson.

SIEGEL, R.E. (1968). Galen's system of physiology and medicine. Basel: S. Karger.

SIMON, A. (1978) A theoretical approach to the classical conditioning of botanical subjects. *Journal of Biological Psychology, 20* (1), 35-43.

SMELLIE, W. (1790) *The philosophy of natural history*. Vol. I. Edinburgh: Heirs of Charles Elliot; and C. Elliot & T. Kay, T. Cadell; & G.G. and J. Robinsons, London.

SMITH, E. (1855) *Structural and systematic botany*. London: Houlston and Stoneman; Orr and Co.

SMITH, J.E. (1788) Some observations on the irritability of vegetables. *Philosophical Transactions of the Royal Society of London, 78,* 158-165.

SORLEY, W.R. (1894). The philosophy of Lord Herbert of Cherbury. *Mind, III*. N.S. 491-508.

SPENCER, H. (1855) *The principles of psychology*. London: Longman, Brown, Green and Longmans.

STRATTON, G.M. (1917). Theophrastus and the Greek physiological psychology before Aristotle. London: George Allen & Unwin.

T.C. (Thomas Cooper). (1814) On vegetable life. *The Port Folio*. Third series, 4, 59-74; 176-191.

T.C. (1815)(a) For the Port Folio — on vegetable life. *The Port Folio,* Third series. 5, 428-438.

T.C. (1815) (b) On the analogy between animal and vegetable physiology. *The Port Folio*. Third series, 6, 27-32.

TAYLOR, J.E. (1884) *The sagacity and morality of plants*. London: Chatto and Windus.

TEMKIN, O. (1936) *Introduction to von Haller, Albrecht: A dissertation on the sensible and irritable parts of animals*. Baltimore: Johns Hopkins Press.

TEMKIN, O. (1964) The classical roots of Glisson's doctrine of irritation. *Bulletin of the History of Medicine, 38,* 297-328.

TEMKIN, O.   (1972) *Francis Glisson*. In C.C. Gillispie (Ed. in chief), *Dictionary of scientific biography*. Vol. 5. New York: Charles Scribner's Sons.

THE GENTLEMAN'S MAGAZINE.   (1739) 9, 477.

THEOPHRASTUS   (1976) *Causes of plants* (Eds'. title: *De causis plantarum*). B. Einarson & G.K.K. Link (Eds. & trans.) London: William Heinemann.

THEOPHRASTUS   (1916) *Enquiry into plants* . A. Hort (Trans.). London: Heinemann.

THORNE, J.O. & COLLOCOTT, T.C. (Eds.) (1983). *Chambers biographical dictionary*. Revised edition. Edinburgh: W. & R. Chambers.

THOULESS, R.H. and WIESNER, B.P. (1946-1949) The psi processes in normal and „paranormal" psychology. *Proceedings of the Society for Psychical Research, 48*, 177-196).

TITCHENER, E.B.   (1898) *A primer of psychology*. New York: The Macmillan Co.

TITCHENER, E.B.   (1909) *A text-book of psychology*. Part I. New York: The Macmillan Co.

TOMPKINS, P. and BIRD, C.   (1973) *The secret life of plants*. London: Allen Lane.

TOWNSON, R.   (1799) *Objections against the perceptivity of plants, so far as is evinced by their external motions*. In *tracts and observations in natural history and physiology*, 137-146. The author: London.

TREAT, M.   (1873) Observations on the sundew. *The American Naturalist, 7*, 705-708.

TUPPER, J.P.   (1811) *An essay on the probability of sensation in vegetables*. London: White, Cochrane and Co.

TYLOR, A.   (1886) *On the growth of trees and protoplasmic continuity*. London: Edward Stanford.

VAUGHAN, T.   ("Eugenius Philalethes") (1650). *Anthroposophia theomagica; or A discourse of the nature of man and his state after death; Grounded on his creator's proto-chimistry, and verifi'd by a practicall examination of principles in the Great World*. London: T.W. For H. Blunden at the Castle in Corn-hill.

VERWORN, M.   (1893-4) Modern physiology. *The Monist*, 4, 355-374.

VERWORN, M.   (1889) *Psycho-physiologische Protisten-Studien.* Jena: Gustav Fischer.

W.D.   (1815) Remarks on J.R.W.'s reply to T.C. on vegetable life. *The Port Folio*. Third series. 5, 359-362.

WARD, J.   (1899) *Naturalism and agnosticism.* London: Adam and Charles Black.

WARD, J.   (1913) *Heredity and memory.* (The Henry Sidgwick Memorial Lecture, at Newnham College, 9 November, 1912). Cambridge: University Press.

WARDEN, C.J., JENKINS, T.N. and WARNER, L.H. (1934) *Introduction to comparative psychology.* New York: Ronald Press.

WARDEN, C.J., JENKINS, T.N. and WARNER, L.H. (1935-40) *Comparative psychology.* (Vol. I, 1935; Vol. II, 1940; Vol. III, 1936). New York: Ronald Press

WASHBURN, M.F. (1908) *The animal mind.* New York: Macmillan.

WATKINS, G.P.   (1900) Psychical life in protozoa. *American Journal of Psychology*, 11, 166-180.

WATSON, J.B.   (1913) Psychology as the behaviourist views it. *Psychological Review*, 20, 158-177.

WATSON, L.   (1973) *Supernature.* Garden City, New York: Anchor Press/ Doubleday.

WATSON, R.   (1787) *On the subjects of chemistry and their general division.* In *Chemical essays*, vol. V. London: T. Evans.

WEBSTER, C.   (1966). The recognition of plant sensitivity by English botanists in the seventeenth century. *Isis*, 57, 5-23.

WEBSTER, C.   (1967). Henry Power's experimental philosophy. *Ambix*, 14, 150-178.

WHEATLEY, H.B. (Ed.) (1904) *The diary of Samuel Pepys.* Vol. I. London: George Bell and Sons.

WILKES, K.V.   (1988). — yìshì, duh, um, and consciousness. In A.J. Marcel & E. Bisiach (Eds.). *Consciousness in contemporary science.* Pp. 16-41. Oxford: Clarendon Press.

WILKINS, M.   (1988). *Plantwatching. How plants live, feel and work.* London: Macmillan.

WOLMAN, B.B.   (1960). *Contemporary theories and systems in psychology.* New York: Harper and Row.

WUNDT, W.   (1894) *Lectures on human and animal psychology.* J.E. Creighton and E.B. Titchener (Trans.). London: Swan Sonnenschein.

"X" (Dr. Hawkesworth). (1771) Review of R. Watson, *On the subjects of chemistry and their general division. The Gentleman's Magazine, 41,* 410-411 & 464-466.

YERKES, A.W.   (1914) Mind in plants. *The Atlantic Monthly, 114,* 634-643.

YERKES, R.M.   (1905) Animal psychology and criteria of the psychic. *Journal of Philosophy, Psychology and Scientific Methods, 2,* 141-149.

INDEX

(Photographs are referred to in **bold** Roman numerals. Publications are in *Italics* and under author's name.)

his studies of plant growth and movement, 227

Theory of Evolution, 18

Darwin, Charles - publications

Insectivorous Plants, 153, 156

The Origin of the Species by Means of Natural Selection, 153

The Power of Movement in Plants, 157

Darwin, Erasmus (physician), 84, 131, 165, 188, 214, 242, 266

a compulsive inventor, 115

followed the Lockian heritage, 126

founded the Lunar Society of Birmingham, 115

his deep sciemtific insight, 115

his evolutionary speculations, 158

his plant psychology, 18, 107, 130

member of the Lunar Society of Birmingham, 107

a vast knowledge of natural philosophy, 117

and vegetable mentalism, 130

Darwin, Erasmus (physician) - publications

The Botanic Garden (poem), 5

The Movement and Habits of Climbing Plants, 153

The Power of Movement in Plants, 153

Darwin, Francis (botanist), 153, 214

awarded a Fellowship of the Royal Society, 188

a great grandson of Erasmus Darwin, 188

impressed with Samuel Butler, 196

as a pioneer vegetable psychologist, 188

son of Charles Darwin, 188

Darwin's 1908 Presidential address to the British Association for the Advancement of Science, 194

De La Mettrie, 79

de l'Ecluse, Charles (French botanist), 48

de Puertorico, John, as Earle of Cumberland, 51

Delaporte, François, *Nature's Second Kingdom: Exporations of Vegetality in the Eighteenth Century*, 83

Democritus (philosopher), 31, 54

credited that the universe was made out of atoms, 26

as an originator of plant psychology, 40

views on plant mentality, 44

Denny, H R, 263

Derby Philosophical Society, 117

Descartes (philosopher), 12, 25

Diogenes of Apollenia, 39

Dobbs, Arthur, 95

doctrines

of the chain of being, 106

of inheritance, 185, 270

of irratability, 69, 76

of plant instincts, 143–144

of rritability, 18

of vegetable perception, 141

dualism, 25

Duncan, John Shute, 190, 294

Duncan, John Shute - publications, *Botanical Theology*, 144

Dutrochet, R J H, 68

an opponent of vitalism, 140

E

eclipses, 25

Economy of Vegetatiion, 119, 123

ecphorisis, 194

Ecphory, 209

Egerton, Francies, 145

Elder (*Sambucus Nigra*), 225

Ellis, John, Liannaeus's description of him, 95

Empedocles (philosopher), 31, 41

conceptions of evolution, 86

father of evolutionary thought, 26

his account *On Plants*, 33

as an originator of plant psychology, 40

saw plants as wholly or partly animal, 28

views on plant mentality, 44

views on plants, 26

Empiricus, Sextus (Greek doctor of medicine), 41

Enquiry into Plants, 53

epi-phenomenalism, 236

epistemology, vii

ethnographic data, 4

Euphrates lily, 37, 47, 62, 67

Evelyn, John, 52

evolution

and natural selection, 152, 181, 184

in plants, 158

extra-sensory perception, 19

F

F R S, 136

Farr, Clifford H

focussed on abilities of plants, 235

a Professor of Botany, 235

Farr, Clifford H - publications, *The Psychology of Plants*, 235

Fechner, Gustav Theodor, 44, 295

eulogy, 221

his thesis of the sensate plant soul, 218

influences, 216

www.ingramcontent.com/pod-product-compliance
Lightning Source LLC
Chambersburg PA
CBHW050803270326
41926CB00025B/4515